POETRY OF THE SPANISH CIVIL WAR

"Say that we saw Spain die."
Edna St. Vincent Millay

"Viva Franco! Arriba Espana!"
Roy Campbell

MARILYN ROSENTHAL

NEW YORK · NEW YORK UNIVERSITY PRESS

Library of Congress Cataloging in Publication Data

Rosenthal, Marilyn
    Poetry of the Spanish Civil War.
    Bibliography: p.

    1. Spain—History—Civil War, 1936-1939—Literature
and the war. 2. Poetry, Modern—20th century—History
and criticism. I. Title.
PN1080.R65   809.1   74-18952
ISBN 0-8147-7356-7
ISBN: 0-8147-7376-1 (paper)

PERMISSIONS

Johannes Robert Becher:
"General Mola"—*Ausgewählte Dichtung der Zeit der Verbannung, 1933-1945*
(Berlin: Aufbau-Verlag, 1945).
"Barcelona" } *Gedichte 1936-1941* (Berlin: Aufbau-
"Fliehende Mutter" } Verlag, 1966).

Giorgio Braccialarghe:
"Terra di Spagna . . ." } *Romancero de los voluntarios de la*
"Ai fratelli lontani . . ." } *libertad* (Madrid: Ediciones del
"Fratelli dell'Internazionale" } Comisariado de las Brigadas Interna-
"Notti di Spagna" } cionales, 1937).

Bertolt Brecht:
"Mein Bruder war ein Flieger"—*Gedichte 1934-1941* (Frankfurt: Suhrkamp Verlag,
1961). Translation © by Stefan S. Brecht.

Excerpts from Roy Campbell: *Flowering Rifle* (London: Curtis Brown Ltd., 1937).

Paul Eluard:
"Novembre 1936" }
"La Victoire de Guernica" } *Cours naturel* (Paris: Gallimard, 1938).
"Espagne" and "En Espagne"—*Poèmes politiques* (Paris: Gallimard, 1948).

León Felipe:
"La insignia"—*Obras completas* (Buenos Aires: Editorial Lasada, 1963).

Miguel Hernández:
"Vientos del pueblo me llevan" } *Obras completas* (Buenos Aires:
"Recoged esta voz" } Editorial Losada, 1960).

Excerpts from Hugh MacDiarmid:
The Battle Continues (Edinburgh: Castle Wynd Printers Limited, 1957).

Pablo Neruda:
"Explico algunas cosas" }
"Llegada a Madrid de la Brigada } *Poesía política, Vol. I* (Santiago de
Internacional" } Chile: Editora Austral, 1953).
"Almería" }

Muriel Rukeyser:
"Mediterranean," copyright © Muriel Rukeyser, 1938, 1966.
"Third Elegy," copyright © Muriel Rukeyser, 1939, 1967.
"Nuns in the Wind," copyright © Muriel Rukeyser, 1938, 1963.
All by permission of Monica McCall, ICM.

Stephen Spender:
"Ultima Ratio Regum" }
"Two Armies" } *Collected Poems 1928-1953* (London:
"To a Spanish Poet" } Faber and Faber, 1965).

Nikoláy Semyónovich Tíkhonov:
"Ispantsi otstupili za Pirenyiei" } *Izbránnye proizvédenija v dvuch tómach*
"Govorit fashist" } (Moscow: State Publishing Co. of
"Govorit antifashist" } Literature of Art, 1955).

César Vallejo:
"Pequeño responso a un héroe
de la República" } *España, aparta de mí este cáliz* (Mexico:
"Masa" } Editorial Séneca, 1940).
"España, aparta de mí este cáliz" }

For my mother and father

Preface

The Spanish Civil War deeply engaged the feelings and loyalties of poets of many countries—chiefly, of course, the poets of Spain and Latin America. I shall briefly survey here poets of six languages, undertaking a selective consideration of the involvement of, mainly, thirteen poets: two Spanish, one Peruvian, one Chilean, two English, one South African, one Scottish, one North American, one German, one French, one Russian, and one Italian. I have isolated a few poems by each as representative in order to make a close study of poems rather than survey, with less depth, many poems of the war. My purpose is to analyze and—to a certain extent—to compare poetic and political reactions to the war. The reason is, simply, that such research can throw light on the interplay between the poet's art and contemporary history.

The premise is that there is value to be derived from juxtaposing a historical event of considerable importance and of serious implications and the poetry of recognized poets. In undertaking this study of poems by significant poets on the same subject, I have tried to determine their differences, similarities, and relative importance. I have considered the war in all of its contexts to see what could be made of selected poems resulting from it. Poems, when studied comparatively, illuminate one another. Perhaps, too, human and historical truth is better understood through art than through politics. If we are to understand what happens in the world, not merely intellectually, but also emotionally, poetry can help us reach a higher sense of reality. As the Mexican poet Octavio Paz has said: there is no voice more faithful to a people than the voice of its poets.

My purpose is not to write a history of Spanish Civil War poetry, subdivided into styles and movements. It is to present a limited selection of poets, and also (in Appendix I) to look at the broad spectrum of contributors and their contributions. Because of the character of the conflict and reactions to it, the war extends a unique opportunity to study a number of poets whose artistic response might be considered representative of their varied nationality, background, temperament, talent, values.

An initial biographical sketch will be followed by the poems and individual analyses. My method has been to analyze, in depth and comparatively, one to three poems (rarely four) by each of these writers, drawing comparative conclusions. The works I have chosen are the following:

Spain: "La insignia" (1937) by León Felipe and "Vientos del pueblo me llevan" and "Recoged esta voz" (two parts), both included in *Viento del pueblo* (1937) by Miguel Hernández.

Peru: "Pequeño responso a un héroe de la República," "Masa," and "España, aparta de mí este cáliz," from *España, aparta de mí este cáliz* (1937) by César Vallejo.

Chile: "Explico algunas cosas," "Llegada a Madrid de la Brigada Internacional," and "Almería," collected in *España en el corazón* (1936-1937) by Pablo Neruda.

South Africa: Roy Campbell's *Flowering Rifle* (1939).

Scotland: Hugh MacDiarmid's *The Battle Continues* (1957).

England: W. H. Auden's *Spain* (1937) and Stephen Spender's "Ultima Ratio Regum," "Two Armies," and "To a Spanish Poet," included among his "Poems about the Spanish Civil War, 1936-1939."

North America: Muriel Rukeyser's "Mediterranean" (1937), published in *New Masses,* and "Third Elegy: Fear of Form" and "Nuns in the Wind," included in *A Turning Wind* (1939).

Germany: Johannes R. Becher's "General Mola: Aus dem spanischen Bürgerkrief," located in *Ausgewählte Dichtung aus der Zeit der Verbannung, 1933-1945,* and "Barcelona" and "Fliehende Mutter," from his *Gedichte 1936-1941.*

France: Paul Eluard's "Novembre 1936" and "La Victoire de Guernica," from *Cours naturel* (1938), and two short poems from *Poèmes politiques* (1948): "Espagne" and "En Espagne."

Russia: Níkolay Semyónovich Tíkhonov's "Ispantsi otstupili za Pirenyiei" (from the section "Gorï") and "Govorit fashist" and "Govorit antifashist" (from the section "Numancia"), located in his collection *Izbránnye proizvédenija v dvuch tómach* (1955).

Italy: Giorgio Braccialarghe's "Notti di Spagna," "Ai fratelli lontani . . . ," "Fratelli dell'Internazionale," and "Terra di Spagna . . . ," all four poems published by the Commissariat of the International Brigades in *Romancero de los voluntarios de la libertad* (1937).

I have translated all non-English poems into their English equivalents, which are found in Appendix II. I have included all the poems within the text except for W. H. Auden's *Spain,* for which permission is not available, and the very long poems by Roy Campbell (*Flowering Rifle*) and Hugh MacDiarmid (*The Battle Continues*), from which, instead, I have selected illustrative quotations of sufficient length.

The sequence of the poets and of the poems by each poet is roughly chronological within each grouping. Precision in this matter is impossible because some of the older poets outlived the younger ones, and some of the poets are contemporaneous. Besides, the dates of the individual poems are not always known. There are occasional gaps in biographical material, depending upon the sources, or lack thereof, available.

Auden wrote only one poem on the Spanish War. I have also included one poem each by Campbell, MacDiarmid, and Felipe, but only because of the length of their poems.

I have surveyed the corpus of each poet's work and alluded to additional poems to see what effect the war may have had on the poet's development. Biographical considerations are included to increase understanding of the poet and his poems.

Why have I chosen these particular poets and poems? They represent a varied selection of countries, backgrounds, politics, ages, and interests. These are major poets in their respective countries or, if not (as in the case of Braccialarghe), they offer something representative of war poetry and, specifically, of that war's poetry. The poems combine psychic, philosophical, and verbal elements. They reveal varying degrees of technical skill, intellectual achievement, and emotional quality. Some are more valid than others, whether poetically or politically. For the most part, these poems will survive the passage of time. Where the poems are not intrinsically valuable, they are, at least, of historical interest. Roy Campbell is the only Franco advocate among them because he was almost the only poet who supported Franco, and surely the most important poet on the Nationalist side. Among the thirteen poets, Auden, Becher, Eluard, MacDiarmid, Neruda, Spender, Tíkhonov, and Vallejo may be numbered among the communists, or their supporters, at least during the war.

I have made three main groupings: Chapter II combines Spanish and Latin poets because of the intimate connection between them; Chapter III isolates English-language poets, not only because of their cultural and linguistic affinity, but also because their reactions to the Spanish Civil War have elements in common. There are interesting distinctions and similarities to be derived from dividing the chapters in this way. Chapter IV focuses on four poets with a few poems by each in German, French, Russian, and Italian. Chapter V deals with more general conclusions concerning the poetry of the Spanish Civil War. This final chapter summarizes their approach, theme, language, tone, imagery, and general "experience" of the war. It also includes a consideration of war poetry in general. Appendix I includes a listing of many poets (other than my poets of concentration) who wrote in Spanish, English, German, French, Russian, and Italian. Appendix II offers my translations into English of all foreign poems that have been analyzed.

I do not value equally all of the poems included here, but each time I made a selection I had a particular reason. For the most part I find the poems in Spanish superior in quality to the others. Vallejo was my first choice, and the rest evolved from him.

I take this opportunity to thank Professor Gabriel H. Lovett, of the Spanish Department at Wellesley College, who introduced me to the Spanish Civil War. I am deeply indebted to Professor M. L. Rosenthal, of the English Department of New York University, who inspired, supported, and criticized this study. Professor Helene Anderson of New York University generously shared her understanding of the Hispanic poets with me through discussion and criticism. I also thank Professor Robert J. Clements, Chairman of the Comparative Literature Department at New York University, for encouragement and support from the very beginning. Among my translating assistants have been Professor Kenneth Negus of Rutgers University and Professors Segundo Cardona, Luis MacFie, Angie Noriega, and Michael Reck of the University of Puerto Rico, to all of whom I am grateful.

M.R.

Blacksburg, Virginia

Foreword

In the late Thirties poets were even busier than novelists converting the throes of the Spanish Republic into urgent words and
reminders. The novelists' concern for the human condition,
heightened by the Spanish Civil War, has been ably chronicled
in Frederick Benson's volume *Writers in Arms: The Literary
Impact of the Spanish Civil War* (N. Y. U. Press), the companion
volume to the present one. As Salvador de Madariaga wrote in his
introduction to Benson's book: "Those cities in ruins, those
trenches soaked in human blood, those cemeteries for not quite
dead human beings, which were the concentration camps, were to
act on the Western soul like a spiritual bombardment, and to
reduce it to shambles." Of the present book, whose contents page
was sent him, Madariaga found it most interesting, but wondered
why only the polarized poets of Left and Right were included,
leaving out such middle-of-the-road poets as himself. While it is
true that the great scholar Madariaga, spokesman for Spain in the
League of Nations during the Thirties, wrote a few poems less

directly concerned with the war, it is even more true that there
were almost no poetic chroniclers of the war who were not driven
to the Left or Right, as was every individual living within embattled Spain itself. Having been in Spain during the early phase
of the war, I had an opportunity to see how there was no option
for neutralism or washing of hands. Brothers within the same
family had to take sides, sometimes opposing sides, and the same
held true of poets. What is interesting and clearly demonstrated
by Marilyn Rosenthal in the following pages is that poets loyal to
the Republic—the majority—wrote the best poetry.

The poet in Spain has for centuries taken up his pen against
wars and oppression, ever since Cervantes in *Numancia* showed
how the will of the people could be pitted against that of the
legions of ancient Rome. Byron later joined the ranks of Spanish
poets decrying the one-sided struggles of the Spanish people, "without freedom's stranger-tree growing native of the soil." In a country which has enjoyed only six years of parliamentary government
during a two-thousand year history, poetry was always on the defensive. Larra, the poet who died one century before the Spanish
Civil War, predicted its outcome in the prophetic words: "here
lies half Spain, done to death by the other half." A young painter
told me one night in Madrid's Café Gijón that the history of
Spanish painting was the history of hunger. Reflecting on his
meaning, I eventually concluded that this comment applied as
well to poetry. Spanish poets in the Thirties were not like their
mesmerized counterparts in Italy, who believed like the Demokos
of Giraudoux that "la guerre exige un chant de guerre." Sadly
turning to the theme of war, they embraced rather the theme not
of fighting, but of fighting back. As if aware of their millennial
duty, the Spanish poets felt obliged to speak out with clarity. In
"La insignia," León Felipe observes that everyone has had his say
about the war except the one most likely to speak truth—the poet:

> Entonces falto yo solo.
> Porque el poeta no ha hablado todavía.

In "España, aparta de mí este cáliz" César Vallejo explains the
secular tragedy of Spain and instructs Spaniards how to cope with

the future in case of defeat. The same epic sweep of history is recalled by the "impassioned" voice of Miguel Hernández, even as he slips into the language of Vergilian heroic poetry:

Naciones, hombres, mundos, esto escribo.

The Hispanic poet, even if he witnessed only fleetingly the kaleidoscope of the war, wrote with posterity in mind. Neruda reveals his sense of duty to record what his eyes have seen: "Comrades, I have seen you, then, and my eyes are full of pride."

Just as the poets outside Spain—French, Chilean, Russian, or other—wish to remind the peninsular Spaniards that the outside world is empathizing with them, these same poets felt a great need to tell the outside world what was really going on in Spain. One of the most unreliable in his interpretations, as Marilyn Rosenthal documents, was Roy Campbell, whose single voice did damage to the forces in the Anglo-Saxon world who were trying to enlist more help for the Republic. Playing on racial and religious prejudices, he made of poetry, even more than the committed Marxists, an outright form of propaganda. If one must concede that his sentiments were sincerely felt, then one can only be gratified that the war bred few such poets. Campbell was clever enough to show that the Falangist side, too, had its moments of heroic courage to be commemorated, such as the defense of Toledo's Alcázar.

The insularity of Spain, the little real knowledge outside of the issues in conflict, the dual forces of propaganda sustained in Europe and America—these left much misunderstanding outside the peninsula. One side said nuns were raped; the other said peasants were being shot down. It is small wonder that poets inside and outside Spain felt it their mission to "explain." Thus, Neruda entitles one of his most cogent poems "Explico algunas cosas." From an explainer of Chile and Peru he has become that of Spain.

I am going to tell you all that happens to me . . .
You will ask why my poetry
Does not speak to you of the soil, of the leaves,
Of the great volcanoes of my native country.
Come see the blood in the streets.

Presenting the suitation in Spain to his Slavic comrades, Níkolaij Tíkhonov mocks the attitude of poet as teacher and explainer when this role is assumed by a Fascist poet: "Now let me explain to you why . . ."

The Spanish Civil War was not only a battle for survival of political institutions, but of prose and poetry as well. Stephen Spender makes this point in the following pages. And Auden hoped that the war would generate a land of great and prolific poetry: "Tomorrow for the young, the poets exploding like bombs." Their concern for the future was well-founded. Even if the pro-Communist group among the Republicans had wrested power after the war, the concern would have been justified. The exodus of writers from Spain, analogous to that of authors from Soviet Russia, was probably the greatest drain of talent that Spain ever experienced. Many tasted what Dante called the salty bread of exile. I have broken bread with many of them and enjoyed their friendship: Amado Alonso, Francisco Ayala, Arturo Barea, Ernesto DaCal, Jorge Guillën, Pedro Salinas, Ramón Sender, to mention a few. These writers were not middle-of-the-road. As I have suggested, the war polarized the writers to the extent that there were not enough middle-of-the-road poets to become a third element in Dr. Rosenthal's study. The greatest fluctuator toward the center of the road was Auden, who, as we learn below, after writing a splendid *légende des siècles* on Spain, denied his poem and claimed to have sacrificed doctrine to rhetoric. Auden made the same fastidious repudiation of his moving poem on the outbreak of the second World War, "September 1, 1939."

Middle-road poets would need a middle course to espouse. There was none. Even the novelists like Hemingway were rare who could assert that there were heroes and villains on both sides. The disunity of the free world was all too clear from the poets represented here. The weakness of the League of Nations left Republican Spain vulnerable. The Tory appeasement of Germany and Italy left the Falangists a free rein, and one indignant poet below will voice greater respect for the villains of Germany and Italy than for the weakling Britain. It became easy for the Communist Russians to appear as heroes in this tragic war, even though, as McDiarmid admits, he will be a Bolshevik only *before* the Revolution (here, war), for real literature cannot be written when communism "comes to rule the roost." Many poets, like Paul Eluard, saw Spain as a curtain-raiser for the polarization of the entire European continent. Its role as an experimental area for armaments and technology has no better poetic articulation than in Sender's poem on the dead child:

> Ask. Was so much expenditure justified
> On the death of one so young and so silly
> Lying under the olive trees, O world, o death?

The question has remained valid for all wars, a lament also for the little brown children of Viet Nam, napalmed and carpet-bombed so diligently.

Echoing the phrase of Malraux and Sender, the poets inside and outside Spain referred to the crisis of the human condition. It was an endemic crisis, threatening all times and all places. The struggle between Juan and Pedro was that of Hector and Achilles, Cain and Abel, Satan and Christ. Compare Maurice English's lines:

> Cain, Cain, Cain! Where is your brother Abel?
> Abel your brother—where is Abel, Cain?
> In bombed Guernica and Badajoz
> Calling among the ruin of the stones.

It occurs to me that the Spanish War was probably the first one which liberated poetry entirely from traditional Western forms of verse. Elegy loses metre, sonnets burst their bonds, odes defy syllable-counts. The forms of lyric poetry are cast aside as though the poet had discovered that there is no longer anything lyrical about war. Rhyme is more and more rejected, as though the poet no longer found rhyme or reason in war. Giorgio Braccialarghe, from a country which invented and codified many a lyrical form over the centuries, begins his poem to his Spanish brothers:

> Tonight I wish to sing for you
> without rhyme or meter.
> Poor palpitant words

as when after crying very much
one searches for one who is gone forever.

The best example of the explosion of metric rhythm and poetic
structure is Paul Eluard's threnody on the bombing of Guernica
(below). In total union with his friend Picasso's painting *Guernica,*
Eluard not only expresses his thoughts in brief patches of words
in Cubist fashion, but arranges these patches on the page as though
they had been fractured by the detonation of a bomb from a dis-
appearing Stuka.

The question of whether a poet writes best about what he has
actually seen and experienced is probably an academic one. Or
more likely, the disparate proofs on one side and the other make it
impossible to draw a conclusion. We know that Muriel Rukeyser
saw little but the first hours of the Civil War—and that from a de-
parting ship—because she tells us so. Yet her poetry seems authentic
and moving. In any case, there are certain dim indications from
the poetry below that most poets lived through the agony of
Spain, and not all these indications deal with cadavers and bursting shells. Let me choose just one evidence familiar to me.

The outbreak of the Civil War found me in Madrid as a vaca-
tioning student. During the months of July and August my brother
and I traversed the peninsula from Irún to Algeciras, eyewitnesses
to heightening hatreds and war. Barbarities and madnesses pre-
vailed in this war, as Goya preached in his *Disasters of War* and his
The Sleep of Reason. Or more simply, perhaps, Goya's *Saturn,* as
Spain cannibalized its children. Yet there were long lulls and
periods when daily life went on uneventfully and one wondered
whether the country was really at war. These long interregna of
calm and silence surprised us, even late in July, when we were
jailed for two weeks in the little anarchical village of La Campana,
in Andalucía Province. From the court of the jail we could enjoy
the lovely moonlit skies over the *plaza mayor,* hear distant music,
and see cranes listlessly flapping around their nest under the
church steeple. Every afternoon the population observed the siesta
hour, and later fell silently into bed around midnight. All this
despite the fact that the Falangists took in turn Lora del Río,
Carmona, and Ecija, all within an hour's drive from La Campana.

It was like the epic poetry of a Virgil or a Ronsard where the fighting is interrupted for long intervals of pastoral peace. Or more exactly, long periods of peace were interrupted only occasionally by war.

This curious sensation, this illusory armistice, is noted by Spender's lines:

> Clean silence drops at night, when a little walk
> Divides the sleeping armies . . .

An even clearer approximation to what I mean is found in Braccialarghe's "Nights of Spain," which must be read in full.

> Nights of Spain,
> the toads singing
> along the long ditches
> in the meadows . . .
> Nights of Spain,
> capes of peace thrown
> over tortured days
> returns of calm
> indefinite whispers
> quiet murmurs . . .

Then comes the finale to the poem, the gunshot in the starry night. This finale occurred during our stay in La Campana when army tanks raced through the sleepy Sunday siesta hour, shot and burned everything in sight, stacked the bodies like cordwood in the square, destroyed the water supply, ignited the late summer wheat, and raced out with us and the other prisoners. Spender visited wartime Spain on three occasions. Braccialarghe, having fought with the Garibaldi Battalion, also knew from experience these unreal periods of détente between assaults and air raids. Perhaps we may conclude that one does write most authentically about what one has lived through. Another generalization which may be permitted after a reading of this volume is that those poets who have not lived through an actual battle tend to paint more graphic, naturalistic scenes than those who have experienced these moments of truth.

A final word on Marilyn Rosenthal and her fine book. The author was hardly born when the Spanish Civil War began. Youth, as Burke put it, needs no apology, certainly not in this case, any more than for Hugh Thomas, author of one of the most used histories of the war, whose youth made his view of that event totally retrospective. Miss Rosenthal, whose doctorate is in Comparative Literature, found herself at an early age deeply preoccupied with this war. Her depth of feeling is as solid as her scholarship. It was remarkable that when she was ready for her book on this important theme, no one had yet worked this literary vein. The results, you will see, are useful and important. Not only does she supply the reader with ample biographical and historical material to understand the total meaning of the poetry (Spanish poems are translated totally and accurately, as are those from other languages), but as a literary scholar Marilyn Rosenthal has not neglected her function as literary critic and textual commentator, presenting the poems not only as historical documents, but as literary masterworks as well.

Robert J. Clements

Contents

CHAPTER I

Introduction

The Spanish Civil War, which ravaged Spain and reverberated around the world, had among its side effects a decisive impact upon literature and culture. It aroused the emotions of writers, artists, and intellectuals, affecting not just what they created as artists, but often how they behaved as human beings. It inspired much poetry of many kinds. In fact, seldom has a single socio-political event provoked so many poets to write so many poems.

The war, which erupted in 1936 and lasted thirty-three months, not only cost Spain "un millon de muertos" but also struck poets all over the world as a test of Western civilization. To many, the struggle threatened the very structure of society and the requisites of civilized life. Defending the role poets played in the war, Stephen Spender wrote:

> the struggle of the Republic . . . seemed a struggle for the conditions without which the writing and reading of poetry are almost impossible in modern society.[1]

1

Miguel Hernández also warned of the danger:

> Un porvenir de polvo se avecina,
> se avecina un suceso
> en que no quedará ninguna cosa:
> ni piedra sobre piedra ni hueso sobre hueso.[2]

> (A future of dust advances,
> a fate advances
> in which nothing will remain,
> neither stone on stone nor bone on bone.)

Since all the literature about the war was political (to a greater or lesser degree) and since it is impossible to comprehend the literary motivations and provocations without, at least, being acquainted with the major outlines of the conflict, I shall briefly survey the war, emphasizing its literary implications.

The Great Depression, the feeling that capitalism in its existing form was doomed, and the rise of the totalitarian dictators, reaching a climax in Hitler's assumption of power in January 1933, preceded and accompanied the Spanish Civil War. A long history of economic, social, and political problems within Spain precipitated it.[3] But the fighting actually began on July 17, 1936, when a group of generals led by Emilio Mola, Sanjurjo, Francisco Franco, and others started revolts in various cities in Spain and in Spanish Morocco against the weak but representative and liberal Spanish Republic (with Manuel Azaña as President). From the beginning, the rebels were supported by large elements of the clergy, nobility, and army. In addition, they quickly received supplies of materials and men from Germany and Italy, suggesting that they had received promises of foreign support in advance of the uprising.

The war brought devastation to many areas of Spain. It assumed an international character as men from twenty-odd nations came to Spain to take part. However, because of the efforts of Western democracies to prevent the Spanish conflict from extending beyond the Spanish borders, in a sense these great powers permitted the fascists to defeat Republican Spain. As many as 40,000 foreigners fought in the International Brigades on the Republican side, contrary to the policies of their individual countries and at great personal sacrifice. Of these, perhaps a third died in action in Spain. Many more later suffered political or professional ostracism because of their Spanish experiences. Many were executed in the purges of Eastern Europe of 1949 simply because they had been to Spain. So, most outside aid for the government of the Republic was shut off by the nonintervention policy of the big democratic powers; and, despite the support of most of the Spanish population, as well as of the moderate and Left-wing political parties— and despite the aid of Russian communists and International Brigades—the Republic fought a losing battle against the better-organized, better-supplied troops on Franco's side. By the spring of 1939, the organized Popular Front resistance had practically ceased, and General Franco became the dictator of a totalitarian state, while Hitler and Mussolini turned their attention, manpower, and matériel to World War II.

The Republic was unequivocally defeated by April of 1939. This result was predictable. There was intervention for Franco by Hitler's and Mussolini's forces. There was the tragically short-sighted aloofness of the Western democracies. There was the foreshortened intervention of Russia, supporting only what it approved, and only as long as it was useful to communism. Russia's duplicity, fascist support, democratic neutrality, and International Brigades made the war a tremendously complicated struggle.

On both sides the war was marked, especially in its early stages, by a ruthlessness which astounded the civilized world. Churches were burned or desecrated, and public religious observances forbidden throughout Republican Spain; ten bishops, many thousands of priests, and religious members of the laity were murdered in cold blood, for no political activity or crime. The Nationalists shot nonpolitical Federico García Lorca. They organized mass executions (e.g., in Badajoz) and subjected the Basque town of Guernica to terrorist air bombardment, while German ships vengefully attacked the town of Almería.

Participants and even survivors of a civil war, with its contingent postwar reprisals,[4] pay dearly. As André Malraux has Garcia muse: "Whichever way this war ends, what sort of peace can possibly prevail after such bitter hatred?"[5] Poor and limited supplies, sketchy training, inefficiency, betrayals, and atrocities increased despair and death. For the Loyalists to continue an increasingly hopeless struggle demanded extreme bravery. Even spectators—those who saw Spanish Loyalists as betrayed in a just cause—were outraged. Such a combination of circumstances offered abundant raw material as well as inspiration to writers. Faith in the Republican cause encouraged Hemingway to write:

> You felt, in spite of all bureaucracy and inefficiency and party strife something that was like the feeling you expected to have and did not have when you made your first communion. It was a feeling of consecration to a duty toward all the oppressed of the world which would be difficult and embarrassing to speak about as religious experience and yet it was authentic . . . It gave you a part in something that you could believe in wholly and completely and in which you felt an absolute brotherhood with the others who were engaged in it.[6]

The fact that the Insurgents were supported by Hitler's Germany and Mussolini's Italy, and that the military superiority was clearly on their side, helps account for the challenge to humanitarian values felt by many authors and for the note of despair common in their works. The war attracted writers of many nations and elicited varied reactions. Viewpoints differed but, for the most part, the literature reflects the idealism as well as the disillusionment of those who had seen it as a holy war. Albert Camus looked back at the defeat of the Republic as a debacle:

> It is now nine years that men of my generation have had Spain within their hearts. Nine years that they have carried it with them like an evil wound. It was in Spain that men learned that one can be right and yet be beaten, that force can vanquish spirit, that there are times when courage is not its own recompense. It is this, doubtless, which explains why so many men, the world over, feel the Spanish drama as a personal tragedy.[7]

The fate of the Spaniards, combined with his high opinion of them, influenced Arturo Barea's choice of the following epigraph for the final section of his autobiography:

. . . honour eternal is due to the brave and noble people of Spain, worthy of better rulers and a better future! And now that the jobs and intrigues of their juntas, the misconduct and incapacity of their generals, are sinking into the deserved obscurity of oblivion, the national resistance rises nobly out of the ridiculous details . . . That resistance was indeed wild, disorganized, undisciplined and Algerine, but it held out to Europe an example which was not shown by the civilized Italian or intellectual German.[8]

Notes

1. Introduction to *Poems for Spain* (London: Hogarth Press, 1939), p. 7.

2. "Recoged esta voz," *Imagen de tu huella, el silbo vulnerado, el rayo que no cesa, otros poemas, viento del pueblo* (Buenos Aires: Editorial Losada, S. A., 1963), p. 110. (See pp. 49-52 for complete text.)

3. Sources for historical facts throughout this study are: Gabriel Jackson, *The Spanish Republic and the Civil War, 1931-1939* (Princeton: Princeton University Press, 1965); and Hugh Thomas, *The Spanish Civil War* (New York: Eyre, 1961).

4. Franco had 200,000 men executed after the war, according to an estimate from Jackson's *The Spanish Republic and the Civil War, 1931-1939,* pp. 538-39.

5. André Malraux, *Man's Hope* (New York: Random House, 1938), p. 252.

6. Ernest Hemingway, *For Whom the Bell Tolls* (New York: Scribner, 1940), p. 235.

7. Quoted as epigraph to Allen Guttmann's *The Wound in the Heart* (New York: Free Press of Glencoe, 1962).

8. The quotation from Richard Ford's *Handbook for Travellers in Spain and Readers at Home* appears as an epigraph to the third part of Arturo Barea's *The Forging of a Rebel* (New York: Reynal & Hitchcock, 1946), p. 420.

CHAPTER II

Civil War Poets of Spain and Latin America

The Spanish Civil War, fought on Spanish soil, affecting every level of Spanish society, culture, economy, and politics, complicated by strong international elements, had an enduring effect upon its population and sympathizers. For the Spaniards the war was an immediate and harrowing experience, resulting in radical changes. It had an effect still at the root of Spanish being and thinking. Spain and its people will never again be the same as before the war. This accounts for the fact that many literary works (prose as well as poetry) were published long after the war had ended, and that many of the writers went into exile. For Spanish poets, the war had ethnic as well as cosmic significance. They were caught up in it politically, poetically, personally, and emotionally. There is an intimate connection felt by Latin Americans for the Spanish people and a close affinity between their cultures. Even though Latin American-Spanish history has been characterized by love-hate ambivalence between an offspring and its mother country, there has always been a deep awareness of common Hispanic origins and ties. The Spanish and Latin American poets shared an identification and involvement unavailable to non-Spaniards. There are noticeable differences between the Spanish/Latin view of Spain and the war and that of non-Spaniards.

For Spanish and Latin American poets, conception of the war had a distinctive quality—an added dimension. Their differences and similarities manifest themselves in their perspectives, poetic images, and tones. As an example, some deduction can surely be drawn from the frequent inclusion of blood imagery in their poetry.

Their common Roman Catholic background, even if later formally rejected, left an impact which frequent referral to God and religious symbols confirms. They had also been made aware, through Catholicism, of a resigned and fatalistic attitude about death. The nature of the Spanish language and culture influenced their poems. For example, Hernández, knowing his people, divided them by provinces and characteristics in his poem "Vientos del pueblo me llevan." Stephen Spender could characterize Spain by olive trees in his war poems; but Neruda went deeper in sensing the Spanish concept of death in "Llegada a Madrid de la Brigada Internacional." And Felipe clarified the nature of Spanish factiousness in "La insignia." The holocaust of Madrid and Neruda's personal world were inextricably connected in "Explico algunas cosas." Hernández could identify totally with the Spanish soldiers, having been one. The close association of these poets to what they wrote showed itself also in their preference for first-person narration of their poems. Their emotionality stems both from their relation to the subject matter and from the lack of reserve characteristically Latin (and not Anglo-Saxon). With the exception of Felipe, they had all written emotional, sometimes passionate, love poems prior to the Spanish Civil War. Felipe's "La insignia" is very Spanish, with its allusions to Don Quijote, patriotism, real understanding of the complexities of the situation, and deep feeling. The poems of all four poets offer authentic expressions of feeling.

Spain became a tormenting preoccupation for Vallejo, Neruda, Hernández, and Felipe. Felipe was deeply troubled by the divisions which rent his country. His view is cosmopolitan and transcends the national to an extent that one would not expect of a Spaniard. Hernández was both appalled and inspired by the situation. His idealism is attributable, in part, to his youth (twenty-six years) in 1936. Neruda found hope in the International Brigades but was poignantly discouraged by much else. He expressed the most bitterness (of the four) in his poem "Almería." Vallejo, with his "tragic sense of life," [1] apparent in all of his poetry ("Esta tarde llueve como nunca; y no/tengo ganas de vivir, corazón" [2]) felt a common suffering.

These four poets are representative of Spain and South America, and have written some of the finest poems on the subject of the Spanish Civil War. Vallejo and Neruda are major figures of twentieth-century Latin American poetry. Despite their affinities, they also had different preparations and preoccupations. They all had provincial backgrounds, although they were later attracted to urban centers of culture and literature. But Felipe had the least humble origin. Their rural backgrounds put them close to the land and nature, affecting their feeling for the land, their choice of images and sense of values. Vallejo and Neruda later turned to communism as a solution to the poverty and other inequities they had witnessed as children; penury was a state Vallejo endured as an adult as well. The Civil War and, hopefully, possible revolution were tied together. But while Neruda put his poetry at the service of his ideology, such ideology was not directly present in Vallejo's poems. Felipe was the most objective; he was also the oldest (fifty-two) at the time of the war. Hernández and Felipe were concerned with moral issues—in which politics seemed suddenly to deal with choices between life and death, civilization and barbarism. Felipe's background was the most academic. Any intellectual analysis of his poem "La insignia" testifies to this. Hernández had done the least traveling, and had the weakest international perspective. His poetry was the least academic and most idealistic, and his audience was the simplest. Also, he was the only one of the four who had actually fought in the war, although they had all been in wartime Spain and had firsthand experience of the war.

At the outbreak of the war in 1936 Felipe was fifty-two; Hernández was twenty-six; Vallejo, forty-four; and Neruda, thirty-two.

Felipe's life had been very much a part of everything that led up to the war. His exposure to the patterns of Spanish politics gave him a focus. Also, his presence in Mexico after its 1910 Revolution as well as during the political and cultural ferment of the 1920s molded his perspective. He had witnessed there the factions of the mid-1920s and the falling out among the groups that had overthrown the former dictatorship. The similar weakness of the Spanish Republican side was the main thrust of "La insignia." His background enabled him to be an objective commentator on the immediate circumstances and the entire period of the Spanish Civil War. Hernández was just emerging to consciousness as a man at the time he was catapulted into the war. His maturity and his death coincided. His youth helps account for his inflamed sense of injustice, his idealism, and the importance to him of the moment—of the here and now. His was a youthful idealism not solidified by formal ideological channeling. In the case of Vallejo, there are overtones of tiredness. He was weary of inequities, suffering, and injustice. Neruda, on the other hand, was more militant and accusing.

Biographical and literary sketches should provide further insight into their positions. After we have examined in detail the forces that shaped both the poets and their works, we shall be able to see in depth the nature of their individuality and collectivism, only touched upon in this introductory chapter. Beginning with the Spaniards, in the order of their birthdates, and then the South Americans, I am presenting brief histories of the four poets' lives and careers, followed by analyses of chosen poems.

León Felipe Camino y Galicia (1884-1963) used the pseudonym León Felipe so extensively that almost nobody remembers his real name.[3] He was born in Tabara, in the province of Zamora, Spain, on April 11, 1884. His father was a notary. From the age of two to nine years he lived in Sequeros, a village in the province of Salamanca. In 1893 his family moved to Santander, where León began his studies nearby at a school in Vallacarriedo; he later finished high school in Santander. Drawn to the theater, he directed a group of student actors in Santander at the age of eighteen. He also experienced the theater of Madrid, where he became acquainted with Shakespeare's plays. His interest in the theater helps account for the dramatic and rhetorical nature of his poetry. When his father died, Felipe finished his study of pharmacy, but from practical rather than deeply felt motivation. He practiced pharmacy in Santander and later in Balmaceda (Vizcaya), but a few years later left to join a theatrical troupe traveling around Spain and Portugal. During this time his interest in writing poetry increased. To facilitate his writing, he divided his year: winters in Madrid; and the other part practicing pharmacy in various Castilian towns, all the while composing his *Versos y oraciones de caminante.* This first work was published in 1920, when Felipe was nearly forty.

In Madrid he frequented the Universal Café in the Puerta del Sol, where literary people gathered. In 1920 he left for Africa, where he lived two years in Fernando Poo as an administrator of the hospitals of the Gulf of Guinea. Next he went to Mexico, where he met such intellectuals as Antonio Caso, the philosopher; Rivera, the painter; Pedro Henriquez Ureña; and Daniel Cosio Villegas. He worked for a time as a librarian. After meeting his wife-to-be in Mexico, he returned with her to Brooklyn, New York, where they were married. For a short period he taught Spanish at the Berlitz School. He studied for one year at Columbia University under Federico de Onis, then went to Cornell University to study Spanish language and literature. He stayed there from 1925 to 1929, his wife having joined its faculty. In collaboration, he and his wife translated Waldo Frank's *España virgen,* and Felipe composed the poems of the second volume of *Versos y oraciones de caminante,* which was published in 1929 by the Instituto de las Españas in New York.

Drop a Star was published in 1930 in Mexico. Felipe's nostalgia for his native country increased, and he returned for a few months. In 1933 he reinstated himself in North America, this time going to Las Vegas University in New Mexico. From there he proceeded to Mexico City, giving a course on Quijote to North American students at the Universidad Nacional and, at the same time, working for the Secretary of Education. He returned to Spain in 1934, occupying himself with translations. *Antología,* edited by friends in homage, appeared the following year in Madrid. He again crossed the Atlantic, this time going to Panama as professor at its university and, also, as Cultural Attaché at the Spanish Embassy.

It was in Panama in July of 1936 that he first received news of the rebellion in Spain. He quickly sided with what he saw as the justice of the Republican cause and embarked for Spain. In Madrid he suffered the cruel bombings of October and November. Afterward, in January of 1937, he went to Valencia, along with the intellectuals of the Casa de la Cultura.

From the tragic events of the Spanish Civil War, Felipe was able to write deeply motivated poetry. In 1937 he wrote "La insignia"; and in March of 1938, when the bombings of Barcelona worsened, he wrote "Oferta," which was combined in a book with "El payaso de las bofetadas y el pescador de caña." Both are tragic poems about the war. The latter work cynically considers the fate of Christ-like figures as this world goes:

> —Pero . . . Don Quijote . . . ¿está loco y vencido?
> ¿No es un héroe?
> ¿No es un poeta prometeico?
> ¿No es un redentor?
> —¡Silencio! ¿Quién ha dicho que sea un redentor?
> Está loco y vencido y por ahora no es más que un
>   clown . . .
> un payaso . . .
> Claro que todos los redentores del mundo han sido
>   locos y derratados.
> . . . Y payasos antes de convertirse en dioses.
> También Cristo fue un payaso.
>
> (—But . . . Don Quijote . . . is he crazy and
>   defeated?
> Is he not a hero?
> Is he not a Promethean poet?
> Is he not a redeemer?
> —Silence! Who has said that he is a redeemer?
> He is crazy and conquered and now is only a
>   clown . . .
> a payaso . . .

Surely all the redeemers of the world have been crazy
   and defeated.
. . . And clowns before turning into gods.
Christ was also a clown.)

Restless and disillusioned over the outcome of the war, Felipe left
Spain and returned to Mexico City, joining other Spanish exiles
in the Casa de España set up by President Cardenas.

He stayed seven years in Mexico, during which he wrote and
read publicly a series of sad and critical poems: "El hacha: Elegía
española" (1939), "El español del éxodo y del llanto" (1939), "El
gran responsable" (1940), and "Ganarás la luz . . ." (1943). "El
hacha" expressed his hopeless view of Spain's massacre by a metaphorical axe:

> ¡Oh, este llanto de España,
> que ya no es más que arruga y sequedad . . . !
> ¿Por qué habéis dicho todos
> que en España hay dos bandos,
> si aquí no hay mas que polvo? . . .
> No hay más que un hacha amarilla
> que ha afilado el rencor.
> Un hacha que cae siempre,
> siempre,
> implacable y sin descanso . . .
> Y el hacha es la que triunfa.

> (Oh, this weeping of Spain,
> that now is only frown and dryness! . . .
> Why have you all said
> that in Spain there are two bands (factions),
> if here there is only dust? . . .
> There is only a yellow axe
> sharpened by animosity,
> an axe that falls always,
> always,
> always,
> implacable and without rest . . .
> And it is the axe that triumphs.)

In 1945, he traveled throughout South America, reciting poetry and lecturing. In his later years he produced further works, including *Antología rota* in 1947 and *Llamadme publicano* in 1950. His 1947 poem "Variante" expressed disgust with the injustice of contemporary Spain: "La España de la tierra ya no me importa más que para sacar de allí a los que buscan la justicia." He died in Mexico in 1963 at the age of seventy-nine.

Felipe's poetry was strongly influenced by Walt Whitman, whose works he had translated, and by Antonio Machado, Cervantes, and the Bible. His religiosity was apparent as early as 1920 in *Versos y oraciones de caminante*, when he wrote about his verses with humility before God:

> ¡Oh pobres versos míos,
> hijos de mi corazón,
> que os vais ahora solos y a la ventura por el mundo . . .
> que os guíe Dios!

> (Oh my poor verses,
> children of my heart,
> that go through the world alone and at a risk . . .
> May God guide you!)

On February 11, 1937, after the fall of Málaga, Felipe wrote the first version of his first poem of the Spanish Civil War, "La insignia." He revised it a number of times, and read this poetic speech, as he called it, first in Valencia and, afterwards, in the Coliseum of Barcelona on March 28. Published in 1938, it is included for analysis here.

LA INSIGNIA [4]
Alocución Poemática (1937)

Este poema de guerra se inició a raíz de la
caída de Málaga y adquirió esta expresión después
de la caída de Bilbao. Así como va aquí es la
última variante, la más estructurada, la que

prefiere y suscribe el autor. Y anula todas las
otras anteriores que ha publicado la Prensa. No
se dice esto por razones ni intereses editoriales.
Aquí no hay Copyright. Se han impreso quinientos
ejemplares para tirarlos en el aire de Valencia y
que los multiplique el viento.

—León Felipe

¿Habéis hablado ya todos?
¿Habéis hablado ya todos los españoles?
Ha hablado el gran responsable revolucionario,
y los pequeños responsables;
ha hablado el alto comisario,
y los comisarios subalternos;
han hablado los partidos políticos,
han hablado los gremios,
los Comités
y los Sindicatos;
han hablado los obreros y los campesinos;
han hablado los menestrales;
ha hablado el peluquero,
el mozo de café
y el limpiabotas.
Y han hablado los eternos demagogos también.
Han hablado todos.
Creo que han hablado todos.
¿Falta alguno?
¿Hay algún español que no haya pronunciado su
    palabra? . . .
¿Nadie responde? . . . (Silencio).
Entonces falto yo sólo.
Porque el poeta no ha hablado todavía.

¿Quién ha dicho que ya no hay poetas en el mundo?
¿Quién ha dicho que ya no hay profetas?

Un día los reyes y los pueblos,
para olvidar su destino fatal y dramático

y para poder suplantar el sacrificio con el cinismo y con la
   pirueta,
sustituyeron al profeta por el bufón.
Pero el profeta no es más que la voz vernácula de un pueblo,
la voz legítima de su Historia,
el grito de la tierra primera que se levanta en el barullo del
   mercado, sobre el vocerío de los traficantes.
Nada de orgullos:
ni jerarquías divinas ni genealogías eclesiásticas.
La voz de los profetas—recordadla—
es la que tiene más sabor de barro.
De barro,
del barro que ha hecho al árbol—al naranjo y al pino—
del barro que ha formado
nuestro cuerpo también.
Yo no soy más que una voz—la tuya, la de todos—
la más genuina,
la más general,
la más aborigen ahora,
la más antigua de esta tierra.
La voz de España que hoy se articula en mi garganta como
   pudo articularse en otra cualquiera.
Mi voz no es más que la onda de la tierra,
de nuestra tierra,
que me coge a mí hoy como una antena propicia.
Escuchad,
escuchad, españoles revolucionarios,
escuchad de rodillas.
No os arrodilláis ante nadie.
Os arrodilláis ante vosotros mismos,
ante vuestra misma voz,
ante vuestra misma voz que casi habíais olvidado.
De rodillas. Escuchad.

Españoles,
españoles revolucionarios,
españoles de la España legítima,
que lleva en sus manos el mensaje genuino de la raza para

colocarle humildemente en el cuadros armonioso de la
Historia Universal de mañana, y junto al esfuerzo generoso
de todos los pueblos del mundo . . .
escuchad:
Ahí están—miradlos—
ahí están, los conocéis bien.
Andan por toda Valencia,
están en la retaguardia de Madrid
y en la retaguardia de Barcelona también.
Están en todas las retaguardias.
Son los Comités,
los partidillos,
las banderías,
los Sindicatos,
los guerrilleros criminales de la retaguardia ciudadana.
Ahí los tenéis.
Abrazados a su botín reciente,
guardándole,
defendiéndole,
con una avaricia que no tuvo nunca el más degradado
    burgués.
¡A su botín!
¡Abrazados a su botín!
Porque no tenéis más que botín.
No le llaméis ni incautación siquiera.
El botín se hace derecho legítimo cuando está sellado por una
    victoria última y heroica.

Se va de lo doméstico a lo histórico,
y de lo histórico a lo épico.
Este ha sido siempre el orden que ha llevado la conducta del
    español en la Historia,
en el ágora
y hasta en sus transacciones,
que por eso se ha dicho siempre que el español no aprende
    nunca bien el oficio de marcader.
Pero ahora,
en esta revolución,

el orden se ha invertido.
Habéis empezado por lo épico,
habéis pasado por lo histórico
y ahora aquí,
en la retaguardia de Valencia,
frente a todas las derrotas,
os habéis parado en la domesticidad.
Y aquí estáis anclados,
Sindicalistas,
Comunistas,
Anarquistas,
Socialistas,
Troskistas,
Republicanos de Izquierda . . .
Aquí estáis anclados,
custodiando la rapiña
para que no se la lleve vuestro hermano.
La curva histórica del aristócrata, desde su origen popular y
    heroico, hasta su última degeneración actual, cubre en
    España más de tres siglos.
La del burgués, setenta años.
Y la vuestra, tres semanas.
¿Dónde está el hombre?
¿Dónde está el español?
Que no he de ir a buscarle al otro lado.
El otro lado es la tierra maldita, la España maldita de Caín
    aunque la haya bendecido el Papa.
Si el español está en algún sitio, he de ser aquí.
Pero, ¿dónde, dónde? . . .
Porque vosotros os habéis parado ya
y no hacéis más que enarbolar todos los días nuevas banderas
    con las camisas rotas y con los trapos sucios de la cocina.
Y si entrasen los fascistas en Valencia mañana, os encontrarían
    a todos haciendo guardia ante las cajas de caudales.
Esto no es derrotismo, como decís vosotros.
Yo sé que mi línea no se quiebra,
que no la quiebran los hombres,
y que tengo que llegar hasta Dios para darle cuenta de algo

que puso en mis manos cuando nació la primera substancia
española.

Eso es lógica inexorable.

Vencen y han vencido siempre en la Historia inmediata, el
pueblo y el ejército que han tenido un punto de conver-
gencia, aunque este punto sea tan endeble y tan absurdo
como una medalla de aluminio bendecida por un cura
sanguinario.

Es la insignia de los fascistas.

Esta medalla es la insignia de los fascistas.

Una medalla ensangrentada de la Virgen.

Muy poca cosa.

Pero, ¿qué tenéis vosotros ahora que os una más?

Pueblo español revolucionario,
¡estás solo!
¡Solo!

Sin un hombre y sin un símbolo.

Sin un emblema místico donde se condense el sacrificio y la
disciplina.

Sin un emblema solo donde se hagan bloque macizo y único
todos tus esfuerzos y todos tus sueños de redención.

Tus insignias,

tus insignias plurales y enemigas a veces, se las compras en el
mercado caprichosamente al primer chamarilero de la Plaza
de Castelar,

de la Puerta del Sol

o de las Ramblas de Barcelona.

Has agotado ya en mil combinaciones egoístas y heterodoxas
todas las letras del alfabeto.

Y has puesto de mil maneras diferentes, en la gorra y en la
zamarra

el rojo

y el negro,

la hoz,

el martillo

y la estrella.

Pero aún no tienes una estrella SOLA,

después de haber escupido y apagado la de Belén.

Españoles,
españoles que vivís el momento más trágico de toda nuestra
   Historia,
¡estáis solos!
¡Solos!
El mundo,
todo el mundo es nuestro enemigo, y la mitad de nuestra
   sangre—la sangre podrida y bastarda de Caín—se ha vuelto
   contra nosotros también.

¡Hay que encender una estrella!
¡Una sola, sí!
Hay que levantar una bandera.
¡Una sola, sí!
Y hay que quemar las naves.
De aquí no se va más que a la muerte o a la victoria.
Todo me hace pensar que a la muerte.
No porque nadie me defienda
sino porque nadie me entiende.
Nadie entiende en el mundo la palabra "justicia." Ni vosotros
   siquiera.
Y mi misión era estamparla en la frente del hombre
y clavarla después en la Tierra
como el estandarte de la última victoria.
Nadie me entiende.
Y habrá que irse a otro planeta
con esta mercancía inútil aquí,
con esta mercancía ibérica y quijotesca.
¡Vamos a la muerte!
Sin embargo,
aún no hemos perdido aquí la última batalla,
la que se gana siempre pensando que ya no hay más salida
   que la muerte.
¡Vamos a la muerte!
Este es nuestro lema.
¡A la muerte!
Este es nuestro lema.
Que se despierte Valencia y que se ponga la mortaja.

¡Gritad,
gritad todos!
Tú, el pregonero y el speaker
echad bandos,
encended las esquinas con letras rojas
que anuncien esta sola proclama:
¡Vamos a la muerte!
Vosotros, los Comisarios, los capitanes de la Censura,
envainad vuestra espada,
guardad vuestro lápiz rojo
y abrid a este grito las puertas del viento:
¡Vamos a la muerte!
Que lo oigan todos. Todos.
Los que trafican con el silencio
y los que trafican con las insignias.
Chamarileros de la Plaza de Castelar,
chamarileros de la Puerta del Sol,
chamarileros de las Ramblas de Barcelona,
destrozad,
quemad vuestra mercancía.
Ya no hay insignias domésticas,
ya no hay insignias de latón.
Ni para los gorros
ni para las zamarras.
Ya no hay cédulas de identificación.
Ya no hay más cartas legalizadas
ni por los Comités
ni por los Sindicatos.
¡Que les quiten a todos los carnets!
Ya no hay más que un emblema.
Ya no hay más que una estrella,
una sola, SOLA y ROJA, sí,
pero de sangre y en la frente,
que todo español revolucionario ha de hacérsela
hoy mismo,
ahora mismo
y con sus propias manos.
Preparad los cuchillos,

aguzad las navajas,
calentad al rojo vivo los hierros.
Id a las fraguas.
Que os pongan en la frente el sello de la justicia.
Madres,
madres revolucionarias,
estampad este grito indeleble de justicia
en la frente de vuestros hijos.
Allí donde habéis puesto siempre vuestros besos más limpios.
(Esto no es una imagen retórica.
Yo no soy el poeta de la retórica.
Ya no hay retórica.
La revolución ha quemado
todas las retóricas.)

Que nadie os engañe más.
Que no haya pasaportes falsos
ni de papel
ni de cartón
ni de hojadelata.
Que no haya más disfraces
ni para el tímido
ni para el frívolo
ni para el hipócrita
ni para el clown
ni para el comediante.
Que no haya más disfraces
ni para el espía que se sienta a vuestro lado en el café,
ni para el emboscado que no sale de su madriguera.
Que no se escondan más en un indumento proletario esos que
   aguardan a Franco con las últimas botellas de champán en
   la bodega.
Todo aquel que no lleve mañana este emblema español revolucionario, este grito de ¡Justicia!, sangrando en la frente,
   pertenece a la Quinta Columna.

Ninguna salida ya
a las posibles traiciones.
Que no piense ya nadie

en romper documentos comprometedores
ni en quemar ficheros
ni en tirar la gorra a la cuneta
en las huidas premeditadas.
Ya no hay huidas.
En España ya no hay más que dos posiciones fijas e incon-
    movibles.
Para hoy y para mañana.
La de los que alzan la mano para decir cínicamente: Yo soy
    un bastardo español,
y la de los que la cierran con ira para pedir justicia bajo los
    cielos implacables.
Pero ahora este juego de las manos ya no basta tampoco.
Hace falta más.
Hacen falta estrellas, sí, muchas estrellas
pero de sangre,
porque la retaguardia tiene que dar la suya también.

Una estrella de sangre roja,
de sangre roja española.
Que no haya ya quien diga:
esa estrella es de sangre extranjera.
Y que no sea obligatoria tampoco.
Que mañana no pueda hablar nadie de imposiciones,
que no pueda decir ninguno que se la puso una pistola en el
    pecho.
Es un tatuaje revolucionario, sí.
Yo soy revolucionario,
España es revolucionaria,
Don Quijote es revolucionario.
Lo somos todos. Todos.
Todos los que sienten este sabor de justicia que hay en nuestra
    sangre y que se nos hace hiel y ceniza cuando sopla el viento
    del Norte.
Es un tatuaje revolucionario,
pero español.
Y heroico también.
Y voluntario, además.

Es un tatuaje que buscamos sólo para definir nuestra fe.
No es más que una definición de fe.

Hay dos vientos hoy que sacuden furiosos a los hombres de
   España,
dos ráfagas que empujan a los hombres de Valencia.
El viento dramático de los grandes destinos, que arrastra a los
   héroes a la victoria o a la muerte,
y la ráfaga de pánicos incontrolables que se lleva la carne
   muerta y podrida de los naufragios a las playas de la cobardía y del silencio.
Hay dos vientos, ¿no lo oís?
Hay dos vientos, españoles de Valencia.
El uno va a la Historia.
El otro va al silencio.
el uno va a la épica,
el otro a la vergüenza.

Responsables:
El gran responsable y los pequeños responsables:
Abrid las puertas,
derribad las vallas de los Pirineos.
Dale camino franco
a la ráfaga amarilla de los que tiemblan.
Una vez más veré el rebaño de los cobardes huir hacia el
   ludibrio.
Una vez más veré en piara la cobardía.
Os veré otra vez,
asaltando, con los ojos desorbitados, los autobuses de la evacu-
   ación.
Os veré otra vez
robándole el asiento
a los niños y a las madres.
Os veré otra vez.
Pero vosotros os estaréis viendo siempre.
Un día moriréis fuera de vuestra patria. En la cama tal vez.
   En una cama de sábanas blancas, con los pies desnudos (No
   con los zapatos puestos, como ahora se muere en España),
   con los pies desnudos y ungidos, acaso, con los óleos santos.

Porque moriréis muy santamente, y de seguro con un cruci-
fijo y con una oración de arrepentimiento en los labios.
Estaréis ya casi con la muerte, que llega siempre. Y os
acordaréis—¡claro que os acordaréis!—de esta vez que la
huisteis y la burlasteis, usurpándole el asiento a un niño
en un autobús de evacuación. Será vuestro último pensami-
ento. Y allá, al otro lado, cuando ya no seáis más que una
conciencia suelta, en el tiempo y en el espacio, y caigáis
precipitados al fin en los tormentos dantescos—porque yo
creo en el infierno también—no os veréis más que así,
siempre, siempre, siempre,
robándole el asiento a un niño en un autobus de evacuación.
El castigo del cobarde ya sin paz y sin salvación por toda la
eternidad.

No importa que no tengas un fusil,
quédate aquí con tu fe.
No oigas a los que dicen: la huida puede ser una política.
No hay más política en la Historia que la sangre.
A mí no me asusta la sangre que se vierta,
a mí me alegra la sangre que se vierta.
Hay una flor en el mundo que sólo puede crecer si se la riega
con sangre.
La sangre del hombre
está hecha no sólo para mover su corazón
sino para llenar los ríos de la Tierra,
las venas de la Tierra
y mover el corazón del mundo.

¡Cobardes: hacia los Pirineos, al destierro!
¡Héroes: a los frentes, a la muerte!

Responsables:
el grande y los pequeños responsables:
organizad el heroísmo,
unificad el sacrificio.
Un mando único, sí.
Pero para el última martirio.
¡Vamos a la muerte!

Que lo oiga todo el mundo.
Que lo oigan los espías.
¿Qué importa ya que lo oigan los espías?
Que lo oigan ellos, los bastardos.
¿Qué importa ya que lo oigan los bastardos?
¿Qué importan ya todas esas voces de allá abajo,
si empezamos a cabalgar sobre la épica?
A estas alturas de la Historia ya no se oye nada.
Se va hacia la muerte . . .
y abajo queda el mundo de las raposas,
y de los que pactan con las raposas.

Abajo quedas tú, Inglaterra,
vieja raposa avarienta,
que tienes parada la Historia de Occidente hace más de tres
    siglos,
y encadenado a Don Quijote.
Cuando acabe tu vida
y vengas ante la Historia grande
donde te aguardo yo,
¿qué vas a decir?
¿Qué astucia nueva vas a inventar entonces para engañar a
    Dios?
¡Raposa!
¡Hija de raposos!
Italia es más noble que tú.
Y Alemania también.
En su rapiña y en sus crímenes
hay un turbio hálito nietzscheano de heroísmo en el que no
    pueden respirar los mercaderes,
un gesto impetuoso y confuso de jugárselo todo a la última
    carta, que no pueden comprender los hombres pragmáticos.
Si abriesen sus puertas a los vientos del mundo,
si las abriesen de par en par
y pasasen por ellas la Justicia
y la Democracia heroica del hombre,
yo pactaría con las dos para echar sobre tu cara de vieja raposa
    sin dignidad y sin amor,

toda la saliva y todo el excremento del mundo.
¡Viejo raposa avarienta:
has escondido,
soterrado en el corral,
la llave milagrosa que abre la puerta diamantina de la
    Historia . . .
No sabes nada.
No entiendes nada y te metes en todas las casas
a cerrar las ventanas
y a cegar la luz de las estrellas!
Y los hombres te ven y te dejan.
Te dejan porque creen que ya se le han acabado los rayos a
    Júpiter.
Pero las estrellas no duermen.

No sabes nada.
Has amontonado tu rapiña detrás de la puerta, y tus hijos,
    ahora, no pueden abrirla para que entren los primeros
    rayos de la nueva aurora del mundo.
Vieja raposa avarienta,
eres un gran mercader.
Sabes llevar muy bien
las cuentas de la cocina
y piensas que yo no sé contar.
Sí sé contar.
He contado mis muertos.
Los he contado todos,
los he contado uno por uno.
Los he contado en Madrid,
los he contado en Oviedo,
los he contado en Málaga,
los he contado en Guernica,
los he contado en Bilbao . . .
Los he contado en todas las trincheras,
en los hospitales,
en los depósitos de los cementerios,
en las cunetas de las carreteras,
en los escombros de las casas bombardeadas.

Contando muertos este otoño por el Paseo de El Prado, creí
   una noche que caminaba sobre barro, y eran sesos humanos
   que tuve por mucho tiempo pegados a las suelas de mis
   zapatos.
El 18 de noviembre, sólo en un sótano de cadáveres, conté
   trescientos niños muertos . . .
Los he contado en los carros de las ambulancias,
en los hoteles,
en los tranvías,
en el Metro . . . ,
en las mañanas lívidas,
en las noches negras sin alumbrado y sin estrellas . . .
y en tu conciencia todos . . .
Y todos te los he cargado a tu cuenta.
¡Ya ves si sé contar!
Eres la vieja portera del mundo de Occidente,
tienes desde hace mucho tiempo las llaves de todos los postigos
   de Europa,
y puedes dejar entrar y salir a quien se te antoje.
Y ahora por cobardía,
por cobardía nada más,
porque quieres guardar tu despensa hasta el último día de la
   Historia,
has dejado meterse en mi solar
a los raposos y a los lobos confabulados del mundo
para que se sacien en mi sangre
y no pidan en seguida la tuya.
Pero ya la pedirán,
ya la pedirán las estrellas . . .

Y aquí otra vez,
aquí
en estas alturas solitarias
aquí
donde se oye si descanso la voz milenaria
de los vientos,
del agua
y de la arcilla

que nos ha ido formando a todos los hombres.
Aquí,
donde no llega el desgañitado vocerío de la propaganda mer-
cenaria.
Aquí,
donde no tiene resuello ni vida el asma de los diplomáticos.
Aquí,
donde los comediantes de la Sociedad de Naciones no tienen
papel.
Aquí, aquí,
ante la Historia,
ante la Historia grande
(la otra
la que vuestro orgullo de gusanos enseña a los niños de las
escuelas
no es más que un registro de mentiras
y un índice de crímenes y vanidades).
Aquí, aquí,
bajo la luz de las estrellas,
sobre la tierra eterna y pristina del mundo
y en la presencia misma de Dios.
Aquí, aquí. Aquí
quiero decir ahora mi última palabra:

Españoles,
españoles revolucionarios:
¡El hombre se ha muerto!
Callad, callad.
Romped los altavoces
y las antenas,
arrancad de cuajo todos los carteles que anuncian vuestro
drama en las esquinas del mundo.
¿Denuncias? ¿Ante quién?
Romped el Libro Blanco,
no volváis más vuestra boca con llamadas y lamentos hacia la
tierra vacía.
¡El hombre se ha muerto!
Y sólo las estrellas pueden formar ya el coro de nuestro trágico
destino.

No gritéis ya más vuestro martirio.
El martirio no se pregona,
se soporta
y se echa en los hombros como un legado y como un orgullo.

La tragedia es mía,
mía,
que no me la robe nadie.
Fuera,
fuera todos.
Todos.
Yo aquí sola.
Sola
bajo las estrellas y los Dioses.
¿Quiénes sois vosotros?
¿Cuál es vuestro nombre?
¿De qué vientre venís?
Fuera . . . Fuera . . . ¡Raposos!
Aquí,
yo sola. Sola,
con la Justicia ahorcada.
Sola,
con el cadáver de la Justicia entre mis manos.
Aquí
yo sola,
sola
con la conciencia humana,
quieta,
parada,
asesinada para siempre
en esta hora de la Historia
y en esta tierra de España,
por todos los raposos del mundo.
Por todos,
por todos.
¡Raposos!
¡Raposos!
El mundo no es más que una madriguera de raposos
y la Justicia una flor que ya no prende en ninguna latitud.

Españoles,
españoles revolucionarios.
¡Vamos a la muerte!
Que lo oigan los espías.
¿Qué importa ya que lo oigan los espías?
Que lo oigan ellos, los bastardos.
¿Qué importa ya que lo oigan los bastardos?
A estas alturas de la Historia
ya no se oye nada.
Se va hacia la muerte
y abajo queda el mundo irrespirable de los raposos y de los
    que pactan con los raposos.
¡Vamos a la muerte!
¡Que se despierte Valencia
y que se ponga la mortaja! . . .

Epílogo

Escuchad todavía . . .
Refrescad antes mis labios y mi frente . . . tengo sed . . .
Y quiero hablar con palabras de amor y de esperanza.
Oíd ahora:
La justicia vale más que un imperio, aunque este imperio
    abarque toda la curva del Sol.
Y cuando la Justicia, herida de muerte, nos llama a todos en
    agonía desesperada nadie puede decir:
"yo aún no estoy preparado."
La Justicia se defiende con una lanza rota y con una visera de
    papel.
Esto está escrito en mi Biblia,
en mi Historia,
en mi Historia infantil y grotesca
y mientras los hombres no lo aprendan el mundo no se salva.

Yo soy el grito primero, cárdeno y bermejo de las grandes
    auroras de Occidente.
Ayer sobre mi sangre mañanera el mundo burgués edificó en
    América todas sus factorías y mercados,

sobre mis muertos de hoy el mundo de mañana levantará la
   Primera Casa del Hombre.
Y yo volveré,
volveré porque aún hay lanzas y hiel sobre la Tierra.
Volveré,
volveré con mi pecho y con la Aurora otra vez.

The title, "La insignia," names the poem's central subject. It is
essentially an exhortation to unify, to abandon plural insignias
which multiply rapidly, and to have only one insignia that would
sum up all insignias luminously: "¡Hay que encender una estrella!
—una sola, sí!" For Felipe there is only one insignia—that of Justice. The multiple insignias represent the many factions compris-
ing the Republican side: socialists, communists, working class,
antifascists, etc. Felipe points out their multiplicity ironically, by
listing them one to a line:

   Sindicalistas,
   Comunistas,
   Anarquistas,
   Socialistas,
   Troskistas,
   Republicanos de Izquierda . . .

Each organization or political group had its own letters and, as
Felipe put it, "Has agotado ya en mil combinaciones egoístas y
heterodoxas todas las letras del alfabeto." One thinks of such acro-
nyms as CNT (Anarcho-Syndicalist Trade Union), FAI (Anarchist
Secret Society), JSU (Socialist and Communist Youth group),
POUM (Trotskyites), PSUC (United Catalan Socialist-Communist
Party), UGT (Socialist Trade Union), and UMRA (Republican
Officers group).
   The poem begins by introducing the voice of its poet/prophet
dramatically and rhetorically. It is addressed to Spaniards of every
level of society as Felipe establishes that everyone has already had
his say on the subject of the war, except himself—not as an individual person, but rather as the generic poet. His voice represents
them all:

Yo no soy más que una voz—la tuya, la de todos—
la más genuina,
la más general,
la más aborigen ahora,
la más antigua de esta tierra.
La voz de España que hoy se articula en mi garganta como
    pudo articularse en otra cualquiera.

Despite his apparent diffidence, he sees himself as the poet-prophet
who towers above the crowd:

Pero el profeta no es más que la voz vernácula de un
    pueblo . . .
Nada de orgullos . . .
La voz de los profetas—recordadla—
es la que tiene más sabor de barro.
De barro,
del barro que ha hecho al árbol—al naranjo y al pino—
del barro que ha formado
nuestro cuerpo también.

Only he has the magnitude of vision, the insight, and the critical
evaluation to assume this role. Only he is capable of speaking for
them all. Detached from their pettiness, only he sees their predica-
ment objectively. The tone of the poem belies his claim to be
only the vernacular voice, made of the same clay as the trees.

In the fourth and fifth stanzas he singles out "españoles revolucionarios" as his audience. They belong to "la España legítima"
and carry in their hands "el mensaje genuino de la raza." Felipe
carefully distinguishes between the "pueblo español" and those
who are leading them. He is proud of the Spanish people. What
he objects to is the in-fighting and selfish materialism of those who
are supposed to be supporting the Republican side but who are
losing sight of the main goal and creating divisiveness. He criticizes
their preoccupation with selfish, superficial values:

Abrazados a su botín reciente,
guardándole,

defendiéndole,
con una avaricia que no tuvo nunca el más delgado burgués.

The connotations of *botín* are strictly materialistic, reminding us of theft and piracy, and *burgués* was undoubtedly a despicable term in his lexicon. They forfeit epic and historic importance for the sake of petty domesticity:

Habéis empezado por lo épico,
habéis pasado por lo histórico
y ahora aquí,
en la retaguardia de Valencia,
frente a todas las derrotas,
os habéis parado en la domesticidad.
Y aquí estáis anclados, . . .
custodiando la rapiña
para que no se la lleve vuestro hermano.

Instead of being suspicious and petty, they must combine forces against the real enemy. They are alone in their divisiveness, and final victory may allude them: "El botín se hace derecho legítimo cuando está sellado por una victoria última y heroica." They are struggling among themselves in the rearguard (as opposed to the front line) of Valencia because they have the mentality of businessmen.

On the other hand, "el español no aprende nunca bien el oficio de mercader." Felipe equates the revolutionary, fighting Spaniard and Don Quijote. He feels that Spaniards have an innate sense of justice: "este sabor de justicia que hay en nuestra sangre," and a willingness to sacrifice themselves. The true Spaniard, whom Felipe is searching for, is not to be found among the dissenting factions, with their pragmatic intrigues and politics. And he is certainly not to be found among the fascists, who have betrayed their fellow Spaniards and represent "la España maldita de Caín." The real Spaniard can only be on the Republican side, "Pero, ¿dónde, dónde? . . . ¿Dónde está el hombre?/¿Dónde está el español?"

Felipe recognizes the tragic circumstances in which "todo el mundo es nuestro enemigo, y la mitad de nuestra sangre—la sangre

podrida y bastarda de Caín—se ha vuelto contra nosotros también."
The Republican side is being weakened by internal strife while
enemy forces from inside and outside of Spain are attacking them.
They are being betrayed by the very forces who are supposed to be
helping them.

Felipe does not deal in the clichés of political propaganda. He
is critical of the Republican side because he wants them to overcome their dissension and win. At the same time he can give the
fascist side credit, at least, for having a single insignia and the
unification it implies. The fascist insignia is a religious one because
the enemy side, ironically, is like a Crusade united in Christ. Yet
Felipe is skeptical of their religious pretensions. His irony is unmistakable:

> El otro lado es la tierra maldita, la España maldita de Caín
> aunque la haya bendecido el Papa.

Justice is at stake and no one understands it. It is the single
insignia of value. According to Felipe, justice is a very Spanish
concept. The attitude of Spain ("inútil . . . ibérica y quijotesca")
is different from that of the rest of the world. Spain does not have
a marketable quantity. She can be truly revolutionary, being un-
encumbered by the established concerns of business. The ideology
of justice is not foreign: it is Spanish:

> Una estrella de sangre roja,
> de sangre roja española.
> Que no haya ya quien diga:
> esa estrella es de sangre extranjera.

Spain is the embodiment of the fight for an ideal, such as Don
Quijote. The Spanish Civil War is the last in a series of quixotic
battles. Thus, Felipe has an idealized vision of the Spanish revolutionary and Spain. In the present conflict, Felipe believes that
"justice" is misunderstood by both sides:

> Y habrá que irse a otro planeta
> con esta mercancía inútil aquí,
> con esta mercancía ibérica y quijotesca.

He ironically and bitterly refers to "justicia" as "inútil . . . ibérica y quijotesca," appending the materialistic term "mercancía," with its disparaging overtones. However, he is not completely pessimistic, and that is probably the reason he can write a poem urging reform: "aún no hemos perdido aquí la última batalla." The poem, after all, was written in 1937, two years before the end of the war.

Felipe suggests that the revolutionary insignia of justice in the form of a star replace all others and be tattooed onto each person's forehead. In this way, those in the rear guard would shed their blood, he snidely adds. Those who do not wear the voluntary insignia would, thus, according to Felipe, belong to the Fifth Column.[5] Wearing this tattoo, his motto would be: "¡Vamos a la muerte!" Málaga had already fallen (the poem was begun February 11, 1937, the day after the Nationalists took over Málaga), and Felipe suspects that Valencia will be next. The poet is well aware of the frustrating and fatal circumstances that had surrounded the Republican fall in Málaga:

The situation in Málaga epitomized all the worst conditions existing in the Republican zone. In the second week of June (1937), labor violence had cost three lives through assassination. In the weeks after July 18 the city's shops were looted and the best residential quarters burned . . . . The sailors' committees in the fleet and the city administration were divided in mortal rivalry between CNT and Communist adherents. Valencian and Almerian truck drivers' syndicates could not agree on the division of labor between them for the delivery of supplies to Málaga, and one of the bridges on the main coastal road remained unrepaired for five months preceding the city's fall. Like all the Republican cities, it lacked antiaircraft defense. Its militiamen, mostly anarchists, built no trenches or road blocks. In January, the government assigned a dependable professional officer, Colonel Villaba, to organize the defense; but without ammunition to give his soldiers, and without the slightest possibility of controlling the bitter political rivalries within the city, there was virtually nothing he could do. . . . On February 6 about 100,-000 persons began a disorganized mass exodus along the coastal road to Almería.[6]

"¡Vamos a la muerte!" because only if Valencia awakens from its disunity and prepares for a last-ditch stand, can Justice perhaps survive. Felipe further suggests that "hay que quèmar las naves." The analogy is with Hernando Cortéz, the Spanish conqueror who, upon arrival in Mexico with his troops, had burned his ships and marched on Mexico City. In other words, there would be no escape: "De aquí no se va más que a la muerte o a la victoria." This is like "Vientos del pueblo me llevan," in which Hernández writes "vais de la vida a la muerte" and proceeds to glorify the manner in which he would die were he to die in such a cause ("Si me muero, que me muera con la cabeza muy alta . . . cantando espero a la muerte . . .").

We have seen that Felipe distinguishes between the brave, noble Spanish revolutionary and the disappointing, destructive leadership. He also points out the dichotomy between those who will fight bravely and perhaps die and those who will panic out of cowardice and flee on evacuation buses:

¡Cobardes: hacia los Pirineos, al destierro!
¡Héroes: a los frentes, a la muerte!

He urges them all to "keep the faith." Felipe writes as if inspired: "No importa que no tengas un fusil,/quédate aquí con tu fe." This reminds us of the conclusion of "Recoged esta voz": "fusil de nardos . . . espada de cera." And, then, from the Epilogue: "La Justicia se defiende con una lanza rota y con una visera de papel." The image is directly from Don Quijote; it is inspirational, impractical, and hopeless. He also juxtaposes two sets of values in the poem: those of Justice, Don Quijote, and Spain versus those of Spain's enemies, pragmatism, and cowardice.

Two-thirds of the way through the poem, Felipe begins his attack against England, "vieja raposa avarienta"; England is a very responsible party to the tragedy. The fox is an astute, flesh-eating animal, pragmatic about its own survival. He singles out England for vituperation for a number of reasons. Traditionally England was mercantile and had been the cradle of the Industrial Revolution. Spain and England had a long history of conflict, one of their most famous battles involving the Spanish Armada. And England's

Prime Minister at the time, Neville Chamberlain, gained a reputation for appeasement and, in a sense, the selling out of Republican Spain. England's neutrality affected the Republican side unfavorably. Felipe sees more nobility in Italy and Germany than in England. They, at least, by their inflated postures, did not reflect the petty world of merchants. They were capable of "jugárselo todo a la última carta," a flamboyant gesture beyond the conception of a practical bourgeois.

Felipe keeps count of the dead, mimicking the business accounts of England, and the poet holds up the specter of the bloody body of Spain. England had the power to help the Republicans: "tienes . . . las llaves de todos los postigos de Europa," and it is their reluctance to help, out of practical and cowardly concerns, that he condemns. He blames England for indirectly allowing Spain to be overrun by fascists and Nazis. Thus, there is a contemporary, political point to Felipe's focusing on England as an object of his bitterest scorn as well as a historical one.

Felipe personally identifies with the terrible course of events. At the end (as well as at the beginning) he assumes his role of poet/prophet along with its responsibilities: "La tragedia es mía." The poet/prophet who believes he is the sole custodian of Justice feels that the tragedy is his. "El mundo no es más que una madriguera de raposas y la Justicia una flor que ya no prende en ninguna latitud." For Felipe "¡El hombre se ha muerto!," that is, men who understand Justice have died. In the last two lines, awakening and death are part of the same process: "¡Que se despierte Valencia/y que se ponga la mortaja! . . ."

In the Epilogue Felipe reasserts the high value of Justice versus the triviality of material gain ("un imperio"). Like Christ, he is ready to rise again, to expose himself, and to triumph: "Y yo volveré" to combat the "lanzas y hiel sobre la Tierra" . . . with "una lanza rota y con una visera de papel."

Felipe has a declamatory, rhetorical style. When he claims he is not rhetorical, he means in the sense of not being complicated or artificial. Felipe frequently employs an enumerative technique. There are, also, many repetitions that emphasize through cumulative effects.

Even the beginning of the poem is framed by the reiteration of the compound past form of *hablar*. The use of "Responsables:/El gran responsable y los pequeños responsables" echoes from the first stanza. Obviously, Felipe has a strong point to make about those who are responsible, which reminds us of those dining on putrid food in Neruda's "Almería." The repetition emphasizes his scorn.

There is a highly dramatic effect produced as Felipe lists in repetitive form those among the dead whom he had counted. Blood was Hernández' metaphor for all the war dead, comparable in emotional impact with Felipe's counting of corpses. Vallejo's metaphor for the death of Spain in "Masa" was one dead soldier, an equally powerful image. Felipe, by counting cadavers, is metaphorically holding up the bloody body of Spain.

Felipe subtitled the poem "Alocución poemática," which suggests a combination of poetry and prose. Spain and South America in the nineteenth century had a tradition of oratory, which they considered a distinct genre, and from which Felipe may well have inherited his oratorical style. An example of his style which combines poetic and prosaic elements begins "Un día morireis fuera de vuestra patria. En la cama tal vez./En una cama de sábanas blancas, con los pies desnudos . . ." Felipe has illustrated here the poetic technique of concretizing experience in a graphic way. An individual on a white bed makes vivid Felipe's general disdain for cowards who run away to hygienic refuge. The sarcastic tone is unmistakable. Poetic qualities of the passage are the concrete imagery, repetition, condensation, informal grammar, emotional tone, and adjectival descriptions. Some of these qualities would also be true of rhetoric. The extension and logic of the narrative, the form in which the poet arranged it as if in a paragraph, and the lack of flowery speech are prosaic elements of Felipe's technique. His artistry derives not from the complexity of his metaphors but from the dramatic use he makes of his rhetorical technique. The poem is very stirring but its dramatic effect comes more from its structure than from its dramatic imagery. The structure could be considered architectural.

The poet often uses an irregular rhythm of short lines and short words. Some of the lines consist of only one word. He plays with length of line, gradation, and progressively lengthening (or short-

ening) repetition. Shrinking and expanding, his lines build up to
a crescendo (or decrease) in which the last line is the culmination
or diminution:

La curva histórica del aristócrata, desde su origen popular
   y heroico, hasta su última degeneración actual, cubre
   en España más de tres siglos.
La del burgués, setenta años.
Y la vuestra, tres semanas.

The length of the lines offers an imaginative parallel to the historical curve, a technique used by Walt Whitman also.

The vocabulary is both simple and serious, less difficult than
that of Neruda or Vallejo. It is almost unpoetic in its everyday,
straightforward syntax. Felipe is an austere poet who has been
described by Luis Cernuda as avoiding the "halago de la palabra
y la magia del verso." Felipe matches his bare words with what he
hopes is a naked rhythm. The words, phrases, and framework are
often repetitive. There is also a humble simplicity to the form and
theme of "La insignia."

There is a development or progression of ideas in the poem as
the poet introduces his role and explains what is wrong with the
Republican side, which is precisely what he finds right about the
Nationalist side. The bloody body of Spain is present throughout
the poem. He distinguishes between the Spanish people and its
divided leadership, and condemns the traitorous Nationalists, the
fascists who side with them, and England, who remains neutral
and thus tips the scales in favor of the Nationalists. The single
insignia he recommends to the Republicans would represent Justice. He makes a clear distinction between the values of true Spain,
the Spanish revolutionary, Man, Don Quijote, and Justice, and
the values of their enemies—values of business and pragmatism.

"La insignia" is an intellectually critical poem as opposed to
the emotionally empathetic poems of Hernández and Vallejo.
While Neruda's poems are subjective, Felipe's vision is the most
historically realistic. He predicted the outcome, he predicted the
reasons for it, and he was right.

In sum, "La insignia" is a tremendous tour de force. It is not subtle and it is not especially metaphorical; the conception and technique of the poem are not so much poetic as rhetorical. It plays with repetition and cadence and has an architectural structure. The poem concretizes generalizations; for example, Felipe takes the fall of Málaga and the likely defeat of Valencia and makes them the metaphor for the larger death of Spain.

In his early works, Felipe was a human poet, a sad one, who saw human sorrows and society's evils. As he himself said, "no hay más que una causa: la del hombre." He later adopted a more belligerent tone, almost declamatory, but filled with both epic and lyric force which can be seen in "La insignia." He viewed what he felt was a disintegrating world where positive, constructive efforts were futile and where, perhaps, "nos salvaremos por el llanto." [7]

Miguel Hernández (1910-1942) was born in Orihuela, in the province of Alicante, in southeastern Spain.[8] His father was a goatherd and farm laborer, as was Miguel until the age of seven or eight. It is important to an understanding of his poetry that he had such direct contact with natural surroundings. Between the years 1920 and 1925 he studied near home at the Colegio de Santo Domingo, where he was educated by Jesuits. He received there a basic Christian education and was a good student. But he was hardly given a rigorous literary education, which he later achieved himself. He became familiar with poetic forms from Garcilaso through Góngora and, before the outbreak of the Spanish Civil War, published some Gongoristic poetry. In 1925 he left school to devote himself to the land, but wanting to broaden his literary horizons, he left for Madrid in 1931. He was given no immediate accolades, was unable to earn a living, and soon returned home. After the publication of a collection of his verse *Perito en lunas* in 1933, he went again to Madrid. This time he was well received and became friendly with such poets as Pablo Neruda and Vicente Aleixandre, to whom, out of appreciation, he later (1935-36) dedicated odes. He was also acquainted with Alberti, García Lorca (for whom he wrote an elegy), and Altolaguirre, and was encouraged by Antonio Machado and Juan Ramón Jiménez. His financial difficulties forced him to work in a notary's office in 1934. *El rayo que no cesa,* written in 1934, was published in 1936.

The Spanish Civil War found him in Madrid, where he immediately enlisted in the Republican army from a deep sense of social obligation and patriotism. He fought in the trenches, read his verses to fellow-soldiers, and escaped when he could to visit his fiancée, Josefina, in Orihuela. She inspired his passion, expressed in such lines as:

> . . . capaz de despertar calentura en la nieve . . .
> ¡Ay que ganas de amarte contra un árbol,
> ay qué afán de trillarte en una era . . . !
> (from "Mi sangre es un camino"
—1935-36)

> (. . . capable of awakening fever in snow . . .
> Oh what wishes to love you against a tree,
> oh what desire to thrash you (like wheat) on the
>   ground . . . !)

In 1937, in the middle of the war, he married Josefina. In *Viento del pueblo,* published that same year, his style became graver and simpler.

In 1938 his first child was born but died a few months later. As part of his education and to study foreign theatre (Hernández wrote plays as well as verse) he traveled to Russia, Paris, London, and Stockholm. In 1939, close to the end of the war, another child was born, and another collection of his verse *El hombre acecha* was published. After the war, he was confined by the Franco Government in the Torrijos jail in Madrid and condemned to death for his political attitude during the war. Only at the intervention of some friends was his sentence commuted to thirty years' imprisonment.

In the long years of imprisonment, he wrote poems of great economy, simplicity, and feeling. He addressed many poems to his wife and to his son, whom he had never seen. When his wife wrote him that she had only bread and onions to feed their son, he composed one of his most moving poems "Nanas de la cebolla." His son's small life enhanced Hernández' unfortunate existence:

Tu risa me hace libre,
me pone alas.
Soledades me quita,
carcel me arranca.

                    (from "Nanas
                    de la cebolla")

(Your smile makes me free,
gives me wings.
It takes away loneliness,
wrenches the cell from me.)

He was moved to the prison of Palencia and later to Penal de
Ocano, where he wrote *Cancionero y romancero de ausencia*. After
Ocano he was confined in the prison of Alicante, where he arrived
in July of 1941. He died in prison—early in 1942, at the age of
thirty-one—of typhoid fever and tuberculosis. His premature death
cut short one of the most promising poetic careers of his day. His
poetry remained uncollected for ten years, at the end of which
time a volume was published; it omitted, however, some of his
finest pieces.

From 1936 on, his main themes were his country, love, and
death. The war in Spain elicited from him a passionate response
and a loyal dedication. Recognizing the tragedy, he was still able
to sustain inspired hope throughout the war. Even up to his own
last miserable days, his unquenchable spirit conflicted with the
despair of his real situation, as in his poem "Vuelo":

Un ser ardiente, claro de deseos, alado,
quiso ascender, tener la libertad por nido.
Quiso olvidar que el hombre se aleja encadenado.
Donde faltaban plumas puso valor y olvido.

Iba tan alto a veces, que le resplandecía
sobre la piel el cielo, bajo la piel el ave.
Ser que te confundiste con una alondra un día,
te desplomaste otro como el granizo grave.

(An ardent being, clear of desires, winged,
wanted to ascend, to have liberty as a nest.

He wanted to forget that man goes away chained.
Where feathers were lacking he put bravery and
   forgetfulness.

He went so high at times, that the sky reflected
on his skin, the bird below his skin.
Being who thought yourself a lark one day,
another plummeted down like heavy hail.)

The two poems chosen for analysis here are from his collection
Viento del pueblo, written and first published in 1937: "Vientos
del pueblo me llevan" and "Recoged esta voz," which is in two
parts. This is the order in which they appear among his collected
works.

VIENTOS DEL PUEBLO ME LLEVAN [9]

1   Vientos del pueblo me llevan,
           vientos del pueblo me arrastran,
           me esparcen el corazón
           y me aventan la garganta.

5   Los bueyes doblan la frente,
           impotentemente mansa,
           delante de los castigos:
           los leones la levantan
           y al mismo tiempo castigan
10   con su clamorosa zarpa.

           No soy de un pueblo de bueyes,
           que soy de un pueblo que embargan
           yacimientos de leones,
           desfiladeros de águilas
15   y cordilleras de toros
           con el orgullo en el asta.
           Nunca medraron los bueyes
           en los páramos de España.

           ¿Quién habló de echar un yugo
20   sobre el cuello de esta raza?

¿Quién ha puesto al huracán
jamás ni yugos ni trabas,
ni quién al rayo detuvo
prisionero en una jaula?

25   Asturianos de braveza,
vascos de piedra blindada,
valencianos de alegría
y castellanos de alma,
labrados como la tierra
30   y airosos como las alas;
andaluces de relámpagos,
nacidos entre guitarras
y forjados en los yunques
torrenciales de las lágrimas;
35   extremeños de centeno,
gallegos de lluvia y calma,
catalanes de firmeza,
aragoneses de casta,
murcianos de dinamita
40   frutalmente propagada,
leoneses, navarros, dueños
del hambre, el sudor y el hacha,
reyes de la minería,
señores de la labranza,
45   hombres que entre las raíces,
como raíces gallardas,
vais de la vida a la muerte,
vais de la nada a la nada:
yugos os quieren poner
50   gentes de la hierba mala,
yugos que habréis de dejar
rotos sobre sus espaldas.

Crepúsculos de los bueyes
está despuntando el alba.

55   Los bueyes mueren vestidos
de humildad y olor de cuadra:
las águilas, los leones

60

y los toros de arrogancia,
y detrás de ellos, el cielo
ni se enturbia ni se acaba.
La agonía de los bueyes
tiene pequeña la cara,
la del animal varón
toda la creación agranda.

65

Si me muero, que me muera
con la cabeza muy alta.
Muerto y veinte veces muerto,
la boca contra la grama,
tendré apretados los dientes

70

y decidida la barba.

Cantando espero a la muerte,
que hay ruiseñores que cantan
encima de los fusiles
y en medio de las batallas.

—Miguel Hernández

Written in 1937, when the poet was only twenty-seven, "Vientos del pueblo me llevan" is an intensely emotional poem. In the title and first stanza, Hernández conceives of his people as "vientos del pueblo," a hurricane wind of pervasive and violent strength. Like the wind, his people are a strong, natural force—a force of nature unstoppable until death. Hernández is inspired by them:

Vientos del pueblo me llevan,
vientos del pueblo me arrastran,
me esparcen el corazón
y me aventan la garganta.

"Pueblo" means the common people who together share a country. Their dynamic quality is conveyed by such verbs as "llevan," "arrastran," "esparcen," and "aventan."

After the opening image of wind, Hernández turns to the physical and psychological posturing of oxen, lions, eagles, and bulls. He relates these images to the Spanish people. Oxen—domesticated, enslaved, and submissive—are unlike the Spaniards and are not even bred in Spain. Hernández sees the essence of Spain in certain animals. Bulls, of the same family as oxen, are completely different from them; they are immensely brave and strong and are even a national (Spanish) symbol. Spaniards also applaud wild lions that stand up to punishment with force, and eagles that swoop in disorder. Eagles, bulls, and lions are not easily dominated. Spaniards, too, fight with courage and dignity, even when challenging the unchallengeable. Spain's heritage is one of pride and bravery in the face of the impossible and of death. The poet conveys this quality of courage and determination through his metaphors.

The poem is presented from a first-person point of view, but this "I" represents a collective identity. There is identification between the poet and the people, making the "I" Spanish and proud of his people:

> Asturianos de braveza
> vascos de piedra blindada,
> valencianos de alegría
> y castellanos de alma . . .

There follows an enumeration of Spaniards from different provinces, with the characteristics of each. Hernández goes through all the provinces, evoking the way of life in each. This long list gives the impression of epic proportions. Fittingly, the reconquest of Spain after the Moorish invasion began with Asturias, whose people did, indeed, fight for the recovery of their pride there. Castilians, being in the heart of Spain, would represent its soul.

Hernández carefully weighs his metaphors, for example, in lines 33 and 34: "forjados en los yunques/torrenciales de las lágrimas." Anvils are the opposite of tears and the inconsistency helps create a striking image. Line 47 expresses the leitmotif of the poem, that of inevitability: "vais de la vida a la muerte."

The listed types are men of "hambre" and "sudor," rooted in Spain, and Spanish roots are proud. Hernández builds up in his poem to the climax of the surging forth of masses.

According to Hernández, the Spanish people are not to be subjugated. The comparison this time is with the impossible harnessing of a hurricane or imprisoning of a thunderbolt. The Spaniards are a force gathering like wind to throw off the yokes of enslavement.

At times the poet speaks about himself in particular (although always nationalistic in spirit) and, at times, he directly addresses his countrymen. He reminds them of their bravery and warns them not to acquiesce. He wants them to fight to the death rather than be conquered. He exhorts them to martyrdom. This poem is a far cry from Wordsworth's "emotion recollected in tranquillity." He wants them to break the yokes of their (unnamed) enemy across their enemies' backs:

> vais de la vida a la muerte
> vais de la nada a la nada:
> yugos os quieren poner
> gentes de la hierba mala,
> yugos que habréis de dejar
> rotos sobre sus espaldas.

Again the metaphor of the oxen is used. Oxen are bowed, subjugated, and degraded, and are yoked by their owners. Even the agony and death of oxen is of little consequence, while that of such virile animals as bulls, eagles, and lions can rock the universe. The poem has cosmic proportions like Vallejo's "España, aparta de mí este cáliz." The crepuscule is symbolic of the death of oxen.

The final stanzas are powerful and beautiful:

> Si me muero, que me muera
> con la cabeza muy alta.
> Muerto y veinte veces muerto,
> la boca contra la grama,
> tendré apretados los dientes
> y decidida la barba.
>
> Cantando espero a la muerte,
> que hay ruiseñores que cantan
> encima de los fusiles
> y en medio de las batallas.

To rephrase the ending of T. S. Eliot's "The Hollow Men," Hernández would die "not with a whimper but a bang."

The poet's voice is of the people, and speaks to and of them. Hernández is willing to die along with his people rather than be enslaved. Projecting himself into the struggle, he switches back to his first-person presentation with "Si me muero . . ." If he is to die, let it be proudly and decisively, the poet singing in the face of death. The metaphor here is sharp as he compares such a fateful circumstance to nightingales who sing hovering above rifles in the midst of battle. The incongruity between the beauty and life of the nightingale and its song, on the one hand, and the horror of war and death, on the other, is grotesque. It is reminiscent of the title of Roy Campbell's poem "Flowering Rifle."

The poem is sad because Hernández does not expect the Spaniards of whom he speaks to survive, but if death is the price of freedom, he advocates death, glorifying the reason for such a death. His people are not to be humbled; to die fighting is not a pessimistic prospect. What would be unforgivable would be to live on having given in and not having fought for freedom.

The contrast at the end is between oxen with bowed heads and free men "con la cabeza muy alta." They are all committed to the cause, not like slaves but free men.

To summarize, the poem is about people facing war. There is consistency in its imagery as Hernández characterizes the people of Spain. The natural force of hurricane winds points to the strength and determination of his people. They are a growing, surging force and the "llevar" of the title would mean "carry" or "push." They will stop when they have won either liberty or death. This is a martial poem, revealing a sense of fervor—the fervor of commitment—and dedication to something beyond oneself. It stresses the importance of collective freedom, not of individual death.

The poem is direct and straightforward, as Hernández faces the possibility of death with candor and says exactly what he thinks. The poem, a kind of ballad, could easily be memorized and recited to inspire soldiers. Hernández wished to encourage a people at war. He is able to write about the war without effort or affectation.

Being the son of a goatherd may not have been a disadvantage; it may have contributed to his natural and convincing poetry. The poem makes clear that Hernández felt close to the people and the land.

RECOGED ESTA VOZ [10]

1 Naciones de la tierra, patrias del mar, hermanos
 del mundo y de la nada:
 habitantes perdidos y lejanos,
 más que del corazón, de la mirada.

5 Aquí tengo una voz enardecida,
 aquí tengo una vida combatida y airada,
 aquí tengo un rumor, aquí tengo una vida.

 Abierto estoy, mirad, como una herida.
 Hundido estoy, mirad, estoy hundido
10 en medio de mi pueblo y de sus males.
 Herido voy, herido y malherido,
 sangrando por trincheras y hospitales.

 Hombres, mundos, naciones
 atended, escuchad mi sangrante sonido,
15 recoged mis latidos de quebranto
 en vuestros espaciosos corazones,
 porque yo empuño el alma cuando canto.

 Cantando me defiendo
 y defiendo mi pueblo cuando en mi pueblo imprimen
20 su herradura de pólvora y estruendo
 los bárbaros del crimen.

 Esta es su obra, ésta:
 pasan, arrasan como torbellinos,
 y son ante su cólera funesta
25 armas los horizontes y muerte los caminos.

 El llanto que por valles y balcones se vierte,
 en las piedras diluvia y en las piedras trabaja,

y no hay espacio para tanta muerte,
y no hay madera para tanta caja.

30   Caravanas de cuerpos abatidos
Todo vendajes, penas y pañuelos:
todo camillas donde a los heridos
se les quiebran las fuerzas y los vuelos.

Sangre, sangre por árboles y suelos,
35   sangre por aguas, sangre por paredes
y un temor de que España se desplome
del peso de la sangre que moja entre sus redes
hasta el pan que se come.

Recoged este viento,
40   naciones, hombres, mundos,
que parte de las bocas de conmovido aliento
y de los hospitales moribundos.

Aplicad las orejas
a mi clamor de pueblo atropellado,
45   al ¡ay!, de tantas madres, a las quejas
de tanto ser luciente que el luto ha devorado.

Los pechos que empujaban y herían las montañas,
vedlos desfallecidos sin leche ni hermosura,
y ved las blancas novias y las negras pestañas
50   caídas y sumidas en una siesta oscura.

Aplicad la pasión de las entrañas
a este pueblo que muere con un gesto invencible
sembrado por los labios y la frente,
bajo los implacables aeroplanos
55   que arrebatan terrible,
terrible, ignominiosa, diariamente,
a las madres los hijos de las manos.

Ciudades de trabajo y de inocencia,
juventudes que brotan de la encina,
60   troncos de bronce, cuerpos de potencia
yacen precipitados en la ruina.

Un porvenir de polvo se avecina,
se avecina un suceso
en que no quedará ninguna cosa:
65   ni piedra sobre piedra ni hueso sobre hueso.

España no es España, que es una inmensa fosa,
que es un gran cementerio rojo y bombardeado:
los bárbaros la quieren de este modo.

Será la tierra un denso corazón desolado,
70   si vosotros, naciones, hombres, mundos,
con mi pueblo del todo
y vuestro pueblo encima del costado,
no quebráis los colmillos iracundos.

II

Pero no lo será: que un mar piafante;
75   triunfante siempre, siempre decidido,
hecho para la luz, para la hazaña,
agita su cabeza de rebelde diamante,
bate su pie calzado en el sonido
por todos los cadáveres de España.

80   Es una juventud: recoged este viento.
Su sangre es el cristal que no se empaña,
su sombrero el laurel y el pedernal su aliento.

Donde clava la fuerza de sus dientes
brota un volcán de diáfanas espadas,
85   y sus hombros batientes,
y sus talones guían llamaradas.

Está compuesta de hombres del trabajo:
de herreros rojos, de albos albañiles,
de yunteros con rostros de cosechas.
90   Oceánicamente transcurren por debajo
de un fragor de sirenas y herramientas fabriles
y de gigantes arcos alumbrados con flechas.

A pesar de la muerte, estos varones
con metal y relámpagos igual que los escudos,

95   hacen retroceder a los cañones
        acobardados, temblorosos, mudos.

        El polvo no los puede y hacen del polvo fuego,
        savia, explosión, verdura repentina:
        con su poder de abril apasionado
100   precipitan el alma del espliego,
        el parto de la mina,
        el fértil movimiento del arado.

        Ellos harán de cada ruina un prado,
        de cada pena un fruto de alegría,
105   de España un firmamento de hermosura.
        Vedlos agigantar el mediodía
        y hermosearlo todo con su joven bravura.

        Se merecen la espuma de los truenos,
        se merecen la vida y el olor del olivo,
110   los españoles amplios y serenos
        que mueven la mirada como un pájaro altivo.

        Naciones, hombres, mundos, esto escribo:
        la juventud de España saldrá de las trincheras
        de pie, invencible como la semilla,
115   pues tiene un alma llena de banderas
        que jamás se somete ni arrodilla.

        Allá van por los yermos de Castilla
        los cuerpos que parecen potros batalladores,
        toros de victorioso desenlace,
120   diciéndose en su sangre de generosas flores
        que morir es la cosa más grande que se hace.

        Quedarán en el tiempo vencedores,
        siempre de sol y majestad cubiertos,
        los guerreros de huesos tan gallardos
125   que si son muertos son gallardos muertos:
        la juventud que a España salvará, aunque tuviera
        que combatir con un fusil de nardos
        y una espada de cera.
                                        —Miguel Hernández

Highly emotional in tone and full of vivid hyperboles, "Recoged esta voz" may be classified as a wartime recruiting poem, its imagery derived from the passion of the battlefield. Discouraged by the course of the war (by 1937), Hernández asks for action by kindred spirits all over the world. He sees the war, then, not as a purely Spanish struggle. He feels the situation very intimately, as a Spaniard or Latin American would, and describes it from a firsthand point of view. Like Walt Whitman, he was there, but not just as a spectator—he had participated. His life was threatened and he, too, is being destroyed. It is a poem written out of the immediate circumstances of battle, revealing the poet's passionate, emotional involvement with no perspective of distance in time and space:

> Hundido estoy, mirad, estoy hundido
> en medio de mi pueblo y de sus males.

He is sunk in the midst of his people, as if in mire. Hernández notices bleeding wherever he goes—bleeding which is both physical and spiritual. There is an inundation of blood:

> Sangre, sangre por árboles y suelos,
> sangre por aguas, sangre por paredes
> y un temor de que España se desplome
> del peso de la sangre que moja entre sus redes
> hasta el pan que se come.

The vision of blood is vivid: "sangrando por trincheras y hospitales."

Hernández presents his people as violated and dying: the "¡ay! de tantas madres." These valiant people are being left "sin leche ni hermosura." Sweethearts find themselves alone, without hope or occupation. Cities are "de trabajo y de inocencia." Those who fight are snatched daily from the hands of their mothers, to fight with farm tools against powerful weapons and die bravely.

On the other hand, the enemy is described as barbaric, criminal, and unconscionable, wanting Spain to be nothing but a vast graveyard. The image of the enemy is that of an animal predator living off weaker animals. They have hooves and fangs and destroy "como torbellinos," while the poet's allies are like innocent children. Such a black-and-white vision shows the emotionality of the poet's commitment to the cause of the Republic. His poem shares with political cartoons an oversimplification and an intensity of the polarization between the two forces involved in the war, although political cartoons tend to be intellectualized while the poems of Hernández are not.

All around him Hernández sees chaos, mutilation, and death. Blood permeates everything, including the bread. There is a plethora of death images; Spain's life blood is being sapped, and Spain might collapse. The pervasive wind, like the ubiquitous blood, emanates from trenches and hospitals. It is the disturbed breath of a violated, desperate people losing a war.

The future that Hernández warns against would be a disaster:

> Un porvenir de polvo se avecina,
> se avecina un suceso
> en que no quedará ninguna cosa:
> ni piedra sobre piedra ni hueso sobre hueso.

The only way to avoid total holocaust is:

> si vosotros, naciones, hombres, mundos,
> con mi pueblo del todo
> y vuestro pueblo encima del costado,
> no quebráis los colmillos iracundos.

"Recoged esta voz" is a passionate poem. Hernández claims it for himself ("tengo una voz enardecida") and pleads for it from others ("aplicad la pasión de las entrañas"). Pulling no punches, he appeals to the strongest instincts and loyalties of his public. The audience he addresses is much simpler than that of Vallejo or Neruda (whose poems are less logical and more difficult to understand). The constant reminders of death ("muerte los caminos," "tanta muerte," "tanta caja," "caravanas de cuerpos abatidos") stress the urgent need for action. Hernández is addressing peasant soldiers so the imagery is rural and stated in terms understandable to the laborer: "herramientas fabriles," "la mina," "el arado," "un prado," etc. Hernández, being of humble origin himself, felt very close to the proletariat.

The first-person presentation makes the poem personal and direct in its appeal. The poet's voice is the voice of Spain, its force derived from the clamor of Spain. Hernández directs the poem to a collective "you": "atended," "escuchad," "recoged," "ved," "aplicad." He defines his audience in the first lines: "Naciones de la tierra, patrias del mar, hermanos/del mundo y de la nada," and redefines it similarly throughout the poem. His final plea is outright and unmistakable: "si vosotros . . . con mi pueblo del todo/y vuestro pueblo encima del costado,/no quebráis los colmillos iracundos." His feeling for collective humanity is like Vallejo's.

As in "Vientos del pueblo," he stresses that he is singing as he fights—his song is the poem: "sangrante sonido," "latidos de quebranto." And it is a cry to fight.

The second part of the poem continues informally with "Pero no lo será," which contradicts the total disaster ("Será la tierra un denso corazón desolado") that had been foreseen in Part I. Part II is much more affirmative, for despite the unevenness of the battle, he sees hope. Spain's hope, as in Vallejo's "España, aparta de mí este cáliz," lies in the future and with a youth who will restore and beautify Spain. Not just chronological youth, but peasant and working youth; these peasants, because of their commitment, bravery, and passion, will overcome cannons and fighter planes:

> la juventud que a España salvará, aunque tuviera
> que combatir con un fusil de nardos
> y una espada de cera.

In his poetic vision, Hernández sees the disinherited masses pitted against force, but the strength of the people "shall overcome."

There are many images in the poem. In the first stanza of Pàrt II, youth is symbolized as a sea with the characteristics of a horse: "piafante" and "pie calzado." It is heroic, rebellious, and incorruptible. Hernández sees this vital force as composed of working men, and he eulogizes the common man with whom soldiers can easily identify.

In the second stanza, we have a variation of the title of the poem: "recoged este viento." This wind contains blood and breath —vital, essential ingredients. The title of the poem is significant as the voice and wind fill the atmosphere with a tremendous energy and force.

In the ninth stanza, the poet addresses the same audience as in Part I: "naciones, hombres, mundos." He looks on the war as offering some final hope—even if it brings temporary defeat and final death to some. He claims ultimate invincibility and victory for the brave youth of Spain, who are in perpetual and vigorous motion, communicating their dynamic qualities to everything they touch:

> El polvo no les puede y hacen del polvo fuego,
> savia, explosión, verdura repentina:
> con su poder de abril apasionado
> precipitan el alma del espliego,
> el parto de la mina,
> el fertil movimiento del arado.

A static element like "el polvo" contrasts dramatically with such dynamic elements as "fuego," "savia," "explosión," and "verdura repentina." Furthermore, the verb "precipitar"—and with respect to "verdura," the adjective "repentina"—implies abruptness to the aroma of the lavender plant, to the digging of the mine, and to the movement of the plow. Hernández sees the young Spaniards as colts, bulls, and flowers, and he and they believe that to die is the highest achievement. They will be victors, even if dead; they will die proudly, saviors of Spain no matter what the odds, even if fighting with flower guns and wax swords—metaphorical terms of futility rather than effectiveness. The poem ends on a note of inspiration and idealism. The ending reaffirms the martyrdom the poet sees as the necessary and only possible answer, and is very similar to the message of "Vientos del pueblo me llevan."

The poem is very visual:

30   Caravanas de cuerpos abatidos
34   sangre, sangre por árboles y suelos

66   España no es España, que es una inmensa fosa
67   que es un gran cementerio rojo y bombardeado.
87   Está compuesta de hombres del trabajo:
88   de herreros rojos, de albos albañiles,
89   de yunteros con rostros de cosechas.
90   Oceánicamente transcurren por debajo
91   de un fragor de sirenas y herramientas fabriles
92   y de gigantes arcos alumbrados con flechas.
113   la juventud de España saldrá de las trincheras
117   Allá van por los yermos de Castilla
118   los cuerpos que parecen potros batalladores,
119   toros de victorioso desenlace . . .
122   Quedarán en el tiempo vencedores
123   siempre de sol y majestad cubiertos,
124   los guerreros de huesos tan gallardos
125   que si son muertos son gallardos muertos:
126   la juventud que a España salvará, aunque tuviera
127   que combatir con un fusil de nardos
128   y una espada de cera.

The movement of large masses, growing in force, offers almost a muralistic vision. The tone is exalted and heroic, and the heroic, victorious youth will be "siempre de sol y majestad cubiertos."

Including many repetitions, the vocabulary is not extensive, its repetition characteristic of an oral style. Hernández speaks to soldiers as another soldier might. He has intentionally kept the poem simple in all ways and melodic in rhythm, because he has directed it to the common people. Since Hernández meant it to be a song, since it tells a sad tale of Spain with only romantic notions of victory, and since it is directed to the people, the poem might be considered a ballad. The structure is well defined, a rhyme scheme continues throughout. Hernández plays on the natural rhythm of the Spanish language, which tends toward the predominant accentuation on the penultimate syllable of words.

There is much repetition of words as well as sounds, which makes it easier to memorize. In the second stanza, "aquí tengo" plus an indefinite article is repeated four times, the second and fourth being exact duplicates: "aquí tengo una vida."

In stanza three the alliteration and repetition create a particularly lyrical effect:

> Abierto estoy, mirad, como una herida.
> Hundido estoy, mirad, estoy hundido
> en medio de mi pueblo y de sus males.
> Herido voy, herido y malherido,
> sangrando por trincheras y hospitales.

The rhythm and repetition help to spell out the relentless message. There is some progression as Hernández makes his strongest plea at the end of Part I, and his most poetic claim for youth at the end of Part II.

There is a conflict in this poem between what is real and what is imagined or hoped—which is reminiscent of Vallejo's three poems.

"Recoged esta voz" is not polemical, nor is it especially narrative. Rather it is descriptive of a certain course of events through the presentation of a series of images. The poem is rhetorical and dramatic. Death is a major consideration. Hernández is emotionally committed to the Republican cause, and Hernández is highly subjective as he exaggerates his case in order to motivate and inspire his readers or listeners. The poet, coming from the working class, identifies with it, and directs his poem toward it. The poem was written by a soldier/poet very much involved in the war.

César Abraham Vallejo (1892-1938) was born in the town of Santiago de Chuco, in northern Peru, within sight of the Andes Mountains.[11] Santiago de Chuco is a small town with more than its fair share of disease, undernourishment, and cold weather. No doubt his background made Vallejo conscious of the meaning of hunger:

> . . . si no hubiera nacido,
> otro pobre tomara este café!
> Yo soy un mal ladrón . . . A dónde iré!
>   (from "El pan nuestro,"
>   *Los heraldos negros,* 1918)

(. . . If I had not been born,
another poor man could have drunk this
    coffee!
I feel like a dirty thief . . . where will I
    end!)

Both his grandmothers were full-blooded Indians. The youngest of eleven children, César was raised with strong Catholic training. As he grew older (by 1931 he was a communist) he renounced formal religion, but his poetry reveals his essential Christianity in its imagery and profound truth. Vallejo's poems frequently include God and Jesus:

Hay golpes en la vida, tan fuertes . . . Yo no sé!
Golpes como del odio de Dios.
                    (from "Los heraldos negros")

(There are blows in life, so hard . . . I don't
    know!
Blows as if from the hatred of God.)

Many of his poems depict the life of his native Andean town. Moving to Trujillo, he entered the University there and earned his Bachelor's degree two years later in 1915. He became involved in politics and was even imprisoned briefly. In Trujillo, too, he came into contact with and began to imitate the French poetic styles of the twenties, which he could not absorb.

By 1916 Vallejo was publishing poems in a small poetry magazine—poems that were collected in 1919 under the title, *Los heraldos negros*. One of these poems eulogizes his brother Miguel ("A mi hermano Miguel: in Memoriam"). His suffering for everyone and everything pervades all of his poetry. Vallejo could react to the plight of a spider with deep feeling:

. . . Y, al verla
atónita en tal trance,
hoy me ha dado qué pena esa viajera.
                    (from "La araña,"
                    Los heraldos negros)

(. . . And upon seeing it
confused in such danger,
what a strange pain that traveler has
given me today.)

Trilce, which contains surrealist poems, was published in 1923.
After *Trilce,* Vallejo left his country (he never returned to Peru)
for Europe, and for a while politics obsessed him to the exclusion
of poetry. In Europe he wrote short stories, novels, and dramas,
but lived mostly from his newspaper articles. He had frequent
financial difficulties, was often in a state of poverty and distress,
but had long-standing Spartan habits.

In 1930 he and his wife traveled to Spain, where he met such
writers as Salinas, Alberti, Unamuno, Gerardo Diego, and Lorca.
By 1931 he was a communist and his writing became Marxist
revolutionary propaganda. He became one of the founders of the
Spanish communist cells. After another trip to Russia, he returned to Spain, going from there to Paris in a destitute state.
He felt a deep nostalgia for Peru and his family and great indignation at the treatment of the Indian peasants.

The fascist uprising in Spain in July of 1936 disturbed him
profoundly. He soon left Paris for Barcelona and Madrid. Returning to Paris at the end of December, he was completely
absorbed in the Spanish cause. He left again for Spain in July
of 1937. It was after this final visit to Spain, and after nearly fifteen years of poetic silence, that he turned his energy toward
writing and revising the poems that comprise *Poemas humanos.*
As the title suggests, he had a strong sense of human compassion
and wished to extend his hand to anyone he felt needed it:

> Quiero ayudar al bueno a ser su poquillo de malo
> y me urge estar sentado
> a la diestra del zurdo, y responder al mudo,
> tratando de serle útil en
> lo que puedo, y también quiero muchísimo
> lavarle al cojo el pie,
> y ayudarle a dormir al tuerto próximo.
> . . .

querría
ayudar a reír al que sonríe,
ponerle un pajarillo al malvado en plena nuca,
cuidar a los enfermos enfadándolos,
comprarle al vendedor,
ayudarle a matar al matador—cosa terrible—
y quisiera yo ser bueno conmigo
en todo.

(untitled poem from *Poemas humanos*)

(I want to help the good man to be a little bad
and I need to be seated to
the right of the lefthanded and respond to the mute,
trying to be useful to him in
some way, and also I want very
much to wash the cripple's foot,
and to help my one-eyed neighbor sleep.
. . .
I'd like
to help whoever smiles to laugh,
to put a little bird on the knave's neck,
to care for the sick exasperating them,
to buy from the salesman,
to help the killer to kill—terrible thing—
and to have been in everything
honest with myself.)

Either during this time or shortly afterwards, he wrote fifteen
poems inspired by the Republican cause, entitled *España, aparta
de mí este cáliz*. It was printed by Republican soldiers, but the
entire edition was lost in the disaster of Cataluña. These poems
and the poems that comprise *Poemas humanos* are much more
clearly expressed than the previous volume of poems, *Trilce*
(1923), whose obscurity attached it to the surrealist movement in
poetry. Perhaps, as in the case of Neruda, the brutal facts of the
war jolted him into an interest in having his poems communicate
a forthright message. On April 15, 1938, before the war came to
an end, Vallejo died in Paris. In 1940, almost three years after his
death, this same volume of poems was published in Mexico.

Of the three poems (from *España, aparta de mí este cáliz*) which I have chosen to analyze, the first, "Pequeño responso a un héroe de la República," is numbered IX in his collection. The second, "Masa," is XII; and the third, "España, aparta de mí este cáliz," is XIV. The themes of motherhood, death, and Man's isolation, suffering, and love are central to his poetry. It is clear that, although Vallejo cherished some inspired hope, he was skeptical and despairing over the outcome of the conflict. He had experienced at firsthand the horrors of Spain's Civil War, and was deeply concerned and involved. On his deathbed in Paris, in his final delirium, he said: "Voy a España . . . Quiero ir a España . . . ." [12]

PEQUEÑO RESPONSO A UN HÉROE DE LA REPÚBLICA [13]

1   Un libro quedó al borde de su cintura muerta,
un libro retoñaba de su cadáver muerto.
Se llevaron al héroe,
y corpórea y aciaga entró su boca en nuestro
     aliento;
5   sudamos todos, el ombligo a cuestas;
caminantes las lunas nos seguían;
también sudaba de tristeza el muerto.

Y un libro, en la batalla de Toledo,
un libro, atrás un libro, arriba un libro, retoñaba
     del cadáver.

10   Poesía del pómulo morado, entre el decirlo
y el callarlo,
poesía en la carta moral que acompañara
a su corazón.
Quedóse el libro y nada más, que no hay
15   insectos en la tumba,
y quedó al borde de su manga el aire remojándose
y haciéndose gaseoso, infinito.

Todos sudamos, el ombligo a cuestas,
también sudaba de tristeza el muerto

20   y un libro, yo lo ví sentidamente,
        un libro, atrás un libro, arriba un libro
        retoñó del cadáver exabrupto.

                                    —César Vallejo

The "responso" of the title is a responsory, part of a church service sung in response to the reading of a text, but the poem itself hardly offers a formal religious context. There are, however, mystical circumstances, a religious occasion (a funeral), and a religious form to the poem. The poem concerns a small ritual (funeral) ceremony and offers a tribute to an unnamed, dead soldier of the Republic. The framework is localized and, basically, convincing. Vallejo's sentiments are clearly Republican; and the fateful battle at Toledo, where Republican forces failed to recapture the Alcázar, claimed many a hero.

The poem is not sequential. Rather, it is a succession of visual images that narrate an event. Many of the details emphasize physical and living aspects of the dead body and of those carrying it. Only remotely may it be considered a responsory: they go through the ritualistic motions of carrying the corpse during a funeral procession. Presumably, the body is buried. It may be supposed that some sort of anthem was sung on the same occasion—praising the enduring message of the "hero's" life and death, which is the main subject of the poem.

The hero is, in a sense, doubly dead: "cadáver muerto." His dead body is described in fragments: "cintura," "boca," "ombligo," and "mango." Fragmentation seems appropriate to the shattering of a life. His navel may symbolize part of the heritage that his poetry offered. From his sleeve his writing hand is missing. His mouth would have offered his word. His body is dead, but his words (his poetry, his message, and perhaps the meaning of his whole life) which he gave birth to live on—in this way, too, the umbilical cord is related. What remains is his book, his testament: "Quedóse el libro y nada más." What this book symbolizes is debatable. It may represent more than one man's lifetime. Since the poetic sequence (*España, aparta de mí este cáliz*) centers on the murder of Spain, the book may represent, in a broad sense, whatever value Spain may have which would survive were she destroyed.

Presumably, the body has been taken away, but the book which fell with the body on the battlefield insists on staying alive. It is already sending out sprouts to spread the meaning which had been within his heart: "poesía en la carta moral que acompañara a su corazón." If we limit the body to that of one individual, he died because he was a hero, but he will live on because of his poetry—a not unhappy idea for a fellow-poet to advance.

In lines two and nine the verb "retoñaba" has the force of continuing action, while in the last line the action has been accomplished: "retoñó." The finality is intensified by "exabrupto." But does this final word refer only to "retoñó," or to the book, or to the corpse? Or, does it mean all three?

The first stanza reports that a book remained at the side of the corpse, having emerged from it. The deceased shared the breath of those who carried his body. It is a strange corpse that still has breath and perspiration. Perhaps "sweating" is a sign of suffering. The derivation of "sudor" may be related to "sudario," which means a shroud. And it is a strange book that exudes from a body as if it, too, were a form of perspiration or, even more miraculously, of birth. The burden which they all feel is a burden of sadness, death, perhaps even mortality, as well as the burden of the body.

The first stanza is anguished, showing the passage of time through visual images. The two-line second stanza repeats that a book was sprouting from all over the corpse. A living book is thus deriving from the deceased. "Retoñaba" connotes quick development and budding, so that the extracted book is not only animate but also flourishing. The poetry is spreading, perhaps both in memory and influence. It multiplies in the sense that it becomes a greater part of the surrounding people.

The third stanza defines the book as poetry. The book reveals the dead man's very essence. The description here is condensed and suggestive rather than explicit. The body, decomposing, becomes infinite vapor as it enters into spirit.

The last stanza returns to the image of the first. "Todos sudamos" but this time a first-person narrator, who has evidently been giving us a firsthand report, interjects "yo lo ví sentidamente." The ending is sudden and definitive: "retoñó del cadáver exabrupto."

The responsory offers consolation to those who attend a funeral and reaffirms the power of his poetry. The word "responso" also denotes a service for the dead where a verse is repeated many times. Typical of religious chants and prayers, in general, is their repetitious and impressive drone. The poem contains many repetitions. "Libro" appears ten times; "cadáver," twice; "muerto," four times; and "retoñar," three. The phrase "el ombligo a cuestas" is repeated, the first time following "sudamos todos," the second time following its reverse, "todos sudamos." The seventh and ninth lines are exactly the same: "también sudaba de tristeza el muerto." This personification of the dead man magnifies his suffering whose source may be not only his death but also the pangs of creating (or giving birth). From everywhere the book asserts his message: "un libro, atrás un libro, arriba un libro." The repetition of the same occurrence in lines nine and twenty-one emphasizes the prevalence of the book and its message.

In line five, "el ombligo a cuestas" literally means "our navels on our shoulders, or back." Why navel? Is it because this anatomical part, through which the unborn child is nourished, is still central to us? Does the line then suggest that we bore away with us the very core and burden of our lives, after the hero's breath had entered our breath?

In lines ten through thirteen the poetry intended is halfway between telling and keeping silent:

> Poesía del pómulo morado, entre el decirlo
> y el callarlo,
> poesía en la carta moral que acompañara
> a su corazón.

It is the poetry that he was bearing in his heart when he performed his last act of sacrifice.

In lines fourteen and fifteen, "que no hay/insectos en la tumba" calls attention to the insects by negation. Their absence insures that the book will not be gnawed away by them; the poetry will endure.

There are many obscurities in this poem, for instance, the referent of "exabrupto" and the meaning of "pómulo morado."

Its relation to the sequence of poems among which it is included
is also uncertain. Is it really just about a poet, or does it represent
Spain, as do most of the fifteen poems of this Spanish Civil War
collection? It is the most complex and difficult of the three poems
of Vallejo to be analyzed.

MASA [14]

1   Al fin de la batalla,
        y muerto el combatiente, vino hacia él un hombre
        y le dijo: "¡No mueras; te amo tanto!"
        Pero el cadáver, ¡ay! siguió muriendo.

5   Se le acercaron dos y repitiéronle:
        "¡No nos dejes! ¡Valor! ¡Vuelve a la vida!"
        Pero el cadáver, ¡ay! siguió muriendo.

        Acudieron a él veinte, cien, mil, quinientos mil,
        clamando: "¡Tanto amor, y no poder nada contra
            la muerte!"
10   Pero el cadáver, ¡ay! siguió muriendo.

        Le rodearon millones de individuos,
        con un ruego común: "¡Quédate hermano!"
        Pero el cadáver, ¡ay! siguió muriendo.

        Entonces todos los hombres de la tierra
15   le rodearon; les vió el cadáver triste, emocionado;
        incorporóse lentamente,
        abrazó al primer hombre; echóse a andar . . .
                                        —César Vallejo

"Masa" informs us immediately that the battle is over and the
combatant dead. We know that the poem was the twelfth of fifteen
written by Vallejo in his Spanish Civil War collection. It is obvious
that when he wrote it (1937) he was in despair over the outcome
of Spain's war.

The first man to approach says to the dead man, "¡No mueras,"
because "te amo tanto!" Two others approach and make the same

plea with the same result: "Pero el cadáver, ¡ay! siguió muriendo."
Then steadily increasing numbers surround the corpse, begging
it not to leave them. Finally, when everyone in the world is there,
with one common desire, the body resurrects, embraces the first
man, and begins to walk.

The narrative is simple but its symbolism has large dimensions.
A single dead soldier magnifies not just to the great body of all the
war dead, but even to Spain itself. Spain's fall is Spain's death, but
Spain, dead and dying (sic), resurrects (metaphorically, not literally). Spain in this poem symbolizes crucified humanity and, like
the traditional figure of Christ, died for mankind and rose from
the dead. The difference, however (and here lies the rub), is that
Christ, being God-like, always had within him the power to be immortal. Spain had no such option. The cadaver views all of mankind sadly and, moved by their solidarity in love, faith, and hope,
revives. It walks again as if out of pity for suffering humanity. But
could this miracle happen?

The title, "Masa," meaning "a mass of people," presents the
poignantly romantic notion that Spain could be revivified by the
love and hope of all the people in the world collectively. It is both
idealized in its hoping and despairing in its impossibility. It is in
its impossibility that it is so moving. It is the fantasy of a poet
yearning to believe. Vallejo poeticizes the dream romantically,
passionately, hopelessly.

But, from another viewpoint, an Hispanic poet could look at
the total image of Spain, of its cities, of its people, dying and being
destroyed, as the promise of a new Spain (this message underlay
"España, aparta de mí este cáliz" also). Vallejo agreed with Hernández that death is inevitable, and Vallejo could further regard
the war dead as not just dead and gone, but as part of a living
army, sharing in the struggle and in the future with the people
with whom and for whom they had fought.

The refrain, "Pero el cadáver, ¡ay! siguió muriendo," is a formal
part of the structure of the poem and produces a cumulative effect
of irony. It is like an undertow of fate and sadness. It is the last line
of every stanza until the end, when the trend is reversed with
"abrazó al primer hombre; echóse a andar . . . ." The reversal
would lead us to believe that the love and religious faith (in the

possibility of resurrection and in the individual Christ-figure) of all the people in the world (which is in itself impossible) could produce a miracle and save Spain. If this is what Spain's salvation depends upon, we are not much comforted.

The presentation of "Masa" is straightforward and relies on direct quotations. The structure of the brief poem is neat and simple. The vocabulary is limited to simple words and the dialogue is informal. There is a discrepancy between the mysterious, miraculous subject matter and the matter-of-fact tone.

It is curious that although Spain is "muerto" as of the second line, it continues dying in the refrain, as if it is in the process of becoming, and therefore retrievable, rather than an accomplished fact. The association of inanimate objects with animate qualities and vice versa is typical of Vallejo's (and Neruda's) poetry. In "Pequeño responso" the corpse sprouted and breathed ("retoñaba . . . entró su boca en nuestro aliento").

It is a very human poem, resulting from the personal anguish of Vallejo, registering his ironic protest against injustice: Spain deserves to be transformed. Vallejo obviously had a strong impulse for human solidarity, and this poem reveals his interest in man individually and collectively; after all, there is no landscape in the poem, only people and feelings. It is a sad, lyrical poem, expressing high idealism.

ESPAÑA, APARTA DE MÍ ESTE CÁLIZ [15]

1   Niños del mundo,
       si cae España—digo, es un decir—
       si cae
       del cielo abajo su antebrazo que asen
5   en cabestro, dos láminas terrestres;
       niños, ¡que edad la de las sienes cóncavas!
       ¡qué temprano en el sol lo que os decía!
       ¡qué pronto en vuestro pecho el ruido anciano!
       ¡qué viejo vuestro 2 en el cuaderno!

10   ¡Niños del mundo, está
       la madre España con su vientre a cuestas;

está nuestra maestra con sus férulas,
está madre y maestra,
cruz y madera, porque os dió la altura,
15   vertigo y división y suma, niños;
está con ella, padres procesales!

Si cae—digo, es un decir—si cae
España, de la tierra para abajo,
niños, ¡cómo váis a cesar de crecer!
20   ¡cómo va a castigar el año al mes!
¡cómo van a quedarse en diez los dientes,
en palote el diptongo, la medalla en llanto!
¡Cómo va el corderillo a continuar
atado por la pata al gran tintero!
25   ¡Cómo váis a bajar las gradas del alfabeto
hasta la letra en que nació la pena!

Niños,
hijos de los guerreros, entretanto,
bajad la voz, que España está ahora mismo repartiendo
30   la energía entre el reino animal,
las florecillas, los cometas y los hombres.
¡Bajad la voz, que está
con su rigor, que es grande, sin saber
qué hacer, y está en su mano
35   la calavera hablando y habla y habla,
la calavera, aquélla de la trenza,
la calavera, aquélla de la vida!

¡Bajad la voz, os digo;
bajad la voz, el canto de las sílabas, el llanto
40   de la materia y el rumor menor de las pirámides, y aún
el de las sienes que andan con dos piedras!
¡Bajad el aliento, y si
el antebrazo baja,
si las férulas suenan, si es la noche,
45   si el cielo cabe en dos limbos terrestres,

si hay ruido en el sonido de las puertas,
si tardo,
si no véis a nadie, si os asustan
los lápices, sin punta, si la madre
50   España cae—digo, es un decir—
salid, niños del mundo; id a buscarla! . . .

—César Vallejo

The title (the same as that of the volume which contains the poem, along with fourteen others by Vallejo on the Spanish Civil War) is from the Bible. It is taken from Christ's words in the garden of Gethsemane: "O my Father, if it be possible, let this cup pass from me" (Matthew XXVI: 39; Mark XIV: 36; Luke XXII: 42). Vallejo changed it to "España, aparta de mí este cáliz," replacing Father with Mother Spain. The story behind the Biblical quotation is that Christ had had a premonition that he would be betrayed and that he would soon die. He had also prophesied that the next time he drank from the cup he would be beyond death, in the Kingdom of God. The chalice, then, symbolizes death. The night that Christ was apprehended, in a moment of weakness, as if he might change his fate, he asked that the cup be taken away. It was not and he went on to fulfill his divine destiny. A comparison is being made between his position—what he stood for, what he died for, carrying his own cross, being resurrected—and that of Spain, whose fate the poet is anguishing over, and would challenge if he could, Spain might be said to be dying for the sins of mankind, and Spain looks to its children as Christ might have looked to his disciples.

Vallejo addresses the poem to the future, to the "Niños del mundo." Spain's war has international implications. These children are "hijos de los guerreros" who represent multifarious nationalities. The war has cosmic overtones, also:

que España está ahora mismo repartiendo
la energía entre el reino animal,
las florecillas, los cometas y los hombres.

Vallejo means children who are children not only by age, development, activities, but in a sense, too, children of the Spanish world.

Latin American countries may be considered children of Mother Spain. As a Peruvian, Vallejo would have such a perspective.

The poem is a personification of Spain—in the first stanza as a huge image in the sky whose forearm is held in the grip of two earthly metal plates, which literally may refer to "armaments" or "engravings" that are opposing one another, and symbolically allude to the two distinct camps into which Spain, and the world, too, is divided. The poet then captures, by a series of images, some universal qualities of children:

> ¡qué edad la de las sienes cóncavas!
> ¡qué temprano en el sol lo que os decía!
> ¡qué pronto en vuestro pecho el ruido anciano!
> ¡qué viejo vuestro 2 en el cuaderno!

Whatever fate flesh is heir to is always part of us. The poet ascribes this mythical instinct to children: "el ruido anciano." One can visualize generations of school children laboriously forming the number "2" in their notebooks—a number difficult for them to draw.

Vallejo describes "la madre España" as most vulnerable and uncomfortable "con su vientre a cuestas," which recalls Christ's carrying his cross. She is mother and teacher, religious and secular. Again, there is grade-school terminology: "maestra con sus férulas . . . división y suma." This mother and teacher, "cruz y madera," reminding us again of Christ's cross and of Spain's being a source of religion, offers spiritual "altura" as well as physical "vertigo y división y suma." Spain, extended to represent the world, is divided and may or may not become united and whole again ("suma").

If Spain falls (and the repetition of this possibility makes it more likely), the consequences would be horrendous. In stanza three Vallejo lists some of the deleterious effects it would have upon the children. It would stunt their growth and the development of their teeth. All their learning would be arrested at the letter of the alphabet "en que nació la pena," which reminds us of line eight's ". . . en vuestro pecho el ruido anciano."

"¡Bajad la voz!" is perhaps a necessary admonition to boisterous children, but to hear what? Vallejo lists silent aspects of Spain's heritage and presents them in audible forms: ". . . el canto de las sílabas, el llanto/de la materia y el rumor menor de las pirámides . . . ." The comparison to the Pyramids suggests Spain's civilization. The fall of Spain brings with it the silent crumbling of centuries of history as well as its audible wreckage.

The poem personifies the image of Spain throughout. Spain represents to Vallejo not just the mother country, but the mother language, the source of civilization and religion as well. It is both a terrestrial image and a celestial one. Spain falls from above in the beginning, but from the earth in stanza three.

In the third stanza we return to the metaphor of stanza one: "si/el antebrazo baja," another way of hypothesizing Spain's fall, and if, thereby, the wooden rulers in the hand of this "madre-maestra" are lowered with a bang; and if it is night, a time particularly frightful for children; and if the sky is divided between two earthly states of limbo, where all are unbaptized and stagnating; and if doors slam on you as if you have been abandoned; and if "I" (the narrator) am late, a traumatic experience for children; and if you don't see anyone—which can be terrifying to children; and if your pencils without points scare you, then the scene is set for the final tragedy. Vallejo has led up to the climax in such a way, with the repetition of "if" this and "if" that, that the tragedy seems inevitable. It is as if a crescendo were created in which the climax is the death of the mother. This sequence of images has been carefully selected for its impact upon children. The final and ultimate loss is that of the mother. Vallejo ends the poem in the imperative. "Si la madre/España cae, . . . ¡salid niños del mundo; id a buscarla!" Not only will they look for "España," but, in a way, they will recreate her, for children recreate their parents by living on in their images.

Despite its tragic circumstances, there is hope in the poem that Spain can be saved. Reviewing the image of Spain, we may conclude that she extends up to the sky and down to the earth and that she is divided between two forces. Her fall is impending. She is in the clutch of the power of these opposing forces. She is both mother, familial and religious, and teacher of religion, language, culture. Mother connotes security, comfort, sustenance, nonabandonment. Teacher suggests learning, mental development, language, religion. In these two capacities, Spain would suggest to Spaniards and Latin Americans a long association of love, tradition, and civilization. Spain's energies are being drained, and in her hand is the skull of life. If she falls, life falls. The choice of children as part of the imagery in this poem is especially apt. Vallejo is able to play upon the powerful bond between children and their mother. Also, in their vulnerability and innocence, children and mothers evoke our emotions.

The poem is well unified in its imagery, the metaphors consistent with childhood. There is the pervasive, hovering image of Spain, and the reiteration of her possible fall. There is the focus of the poem toward the children, and the successions of images to represent the various aspects of Vallejo's vision. In the first stanza the children are presented. Spain, whose image has been suggested in stanza one, is further clarified in stanza two. In stanza three the fall of Spain is indicated by the effects it would have upon the children. Stanza four symbolizes the dimensions of the war. Here, for the first time, the "I" (the narrator and the poet himself, I presume) directs the children. Stanza five expresses other fatal implications of Spain's fall: "está en su mano/la calavera . . . aquélla de la vida." The final stanza offers the crux of his message to the children. The poet lists the contingencies upon which to base their (the children's) decision to take over. He exhorts that if the tragedy does occur, they should go forth and reclaim Spain, with all of its implications for the world. There is hope that the surviving children of the world will provide a better future.

The poem's five stanzas are of unequal length. The length of individual lines varies also, but with frequent repetition of words and sounds. There are numerous images in series, both visual and auditory, each with its own repetitive framework. Thus, we have, for example, "si cae" repeated five times and "si" alone introducing many instances; "que" precedes others.

There are many exclamatory sentences, the poem ending with an exclamation point. The tone of the poem is highly emotional; the personification of Spain as the mother figure and of those who are, in a sense, from her womb and under her influence as her children is effective and moving. The underlying assumption is that

Spain is in serious, terrible danger, but Vallejo places his hope upon the children and the future.

Neftali Ricardo Reyes y Basoalto, who was to assume the pseudonym Pablo Neruda, was born in Parral, a remote village in southern Chile, on July 12, 1904.[16] There he lived close to nature, an association especially apparent in his early poetry. His father was a railway employee, and Neruda knew what it was to be poor in a country noted for its poverty. In Parral he studied at the Liceo de Técnico, but at the age of sixteen he went to the capital, Santiago, to continue his studies at the Instituto Pedagógico of the University of Chile. In Santiago he spent most of his time in cafés talking about literature and writing poetry, and at the age of seventeen he won first prize in a poetry contest.

Neruda left Chile in 1927, proceeded to Europe, traveled in the Orient, where, between 1927 and 1932, he lived successively in Rangoon, Colombo, Singapore, and Batavia, visiting adjacent areas of Asia and Oceania, and was Chilean consul in Calcutta. On his return to Chile in 1933, Neruda was assigned first as consul to Buenos Aires (1932-1933) and then to Madrid (1933-1937), where he was received with admiration and acclaim by a generation of Spanish poets: Federico García Lorca, Rafael Alberti, Luis Cernuda, Miguel Hernández, and Manuel Altolaguirre. In Madrid, too, his first and second *Residencias* first appeared together, with enormous success, in 1935.

When the Civil War broke out in Spain in 1936, Neruda, heedless of diplomatic protocol, made no secret of his antifascist convictions. His active role in radical politics from 1936 on was to result in conflict with the Chilean government, expulsion, and, finally, exile. He was recalled to Chile in 1937, but a new President soon sent him off to Europe to expedite the emigration to America of Republican Spanish refugees. From 1939 to 1943, he served as Chilean consul to Mexico. He enrolled in the Communist Party of Chile in 1943, although his conversion to communism antedated this time.

The enumerative bibliography of his works is a long one, beginning with *La canción de la fiesta*, published in Chile in 1921, when he was seventeen years old. *Crepusculario*, consisting of poems written in 1919, was published in 1923. His romantic vein was most apparent in *Veinte poemas de amor y una canción desesperada,* published in 1924:

> Puedo escribir los versos más tristes esta noche. . . .
> Yo la quise, y a veces ella también me quiso.

> (I can write the saddest verses tonight.
> I loved her, and at times she also loved me.)

Tentativa del hombre infinito was published in 1933. *Residencia en la tierra,* Volume I, containing poetry from 1925 to 1931, in 1935. *Las furias y las penas,* written in 1934, was published in 1939. *Tercera residencia,* covering 1935 to 1945, appeared in 1945, and *Alturas de Macchu Picchu* in 1948.

At first he wrote in romantic and surrealist styles. After his war poetry in honor of the Spanish Republic, he began his lengthy and uneven *Canto general,* published in 1950. It was an attempt to portray his own country and continent in its place in time and political development. *Odas elementales, Estravagario,* and *Navegaciones y regresos* were published in 1954, 1958, and 1959, respectively. A volume of political verse, *Las uvas y el viento,* was published in 1954.

Neruda felt close to Vallejo and reacted to his death in a poem called "Pastoral":

> Sufro de aquel amigo que murió
> y que era como yo buen carpintero.
> Ibamos juntos por mesas y calles,
> por guerras, por dolores y por piedras.
> Cómo se le agrandaba la mirada
> conmigo, era un fulgor aquel huesudo,
> y su sonrisa me sirvió de pan,
> nos dejamos de ver y V. se fué enterrando
> hasta que lo obligaron a la tierra.
> (from Estravagario, 1958)

> (I mourn for that friend who died
> and who was, like myself, a good carpenter.

We walked together through plateaus and
  streets,
through wars, through sorrows, and
  through stones.
How he widened his gaze
with me, an intense fire was that boney
  man,
and his smile was my bread,
we parted and he was burying himself
until they forced him into the ground.)

In 1956 *Nuevas odas elementales* appeared; and the following
year *Obras completas* and *Tercer libro de las odas* were published.
In 1960 came *Cien sonetos de amor* and *Las piedras de Chile*.
Neruda, considered Chile's major poet of the twentieth century,
was awarded the Nobel Prize for Literature in 1971. He died September 23, 1973.

Throughout his poetic career, Neruda exhibited a variety of
styles: symbolic, straightforward, lyrical, polemical, detached, sarcastic, fantastic, realistic, and surrealist.

The poems of my selection are contained in Neruda's collection
España en el corazón, written between 1936 and 1937, when he
was thirty-three. These hymns to the glories of the Spanish people
during the Spanish Civil War form part of the third volume of
Residencia en la tierra. The spectacle of death and injustice in
the crushing of the Spanish Republic by the military awakened
the political conscience of Neruda and forced him into a more
engaged stance; his voice began to be heard less and less hermetically and more and more didactically. The poems analyzed here
are "Explico algunas cosas," "Llegada a Madrid de la Brigada
Internacional," and "Almería."

EXPLICO ALGUNAS COSAS [17]

1   Preguntaréis: Y dónde están las lilas?
       Y la metafísica cubierta de amapolas?
       Y la lluvia que a menudo golpeaba

sus palabras llenándolas
5   de agujeros y pájaros?

Os voy a contar todo lo que me pasa.

Yo vivía en un barrio
de Madrid, con campanas,
con relojes, con árboles.
10   Desde allí se veía
el rostro seco de Castilla
como un océano de cuero.

         Mi casa era llamada
la casa de las flores, porque por todas partes
15   estallaban geranios: era
una bella casa
con perros y chiquillos.
         Raúl, te acuerdas?
Te acuerdas, Rafael?
20   Federico, te acuerdas
debajo de la tierra,
te acuerdas de mi casa con balcones en donde
la luz de junio ahogaba flores en tu boca?

         Hermano, hermano!
25   Todo
era grandes voces, sal de mercaderías,
aglomeraciones de pan palpitante,
mercados de mi barrio de Argüelles con su estatua
como un tintero pálido entre las merluzas:
30   el aceite llegaba a las cucharas,
un profundo latido
de pies y manos llenaba las calles,
metros, litros, esencia
aguda de la vida,
35   pescados hacinados,
contextura de techos con sol frío en el cual
la flecha se fatiga,
delirante marfil fino de las patatas,
tomates repetidos hasta el mar.

40   Y una mañana todo estaba ardiendo
        y una mañana las hogueras
        salían de la tierra
        devorando seres,
        y desde entonces fuego,
45   pólvora desde entonces,
        y desde entonces sangre.

        Bandidos con aviones y con moros,
        bandidos con sortijas y duquesas,
        bandidos con frailes negros bendiciendo
50   venían por el cielo a matar niños
        y por las calles la sangre de los niños
        corría simplemente, como sangre de niños.

        Chacales que el chacal rechazaría,
        piedras que el cardo seco mordería escupiendo,
55   víboras que las víboras odiarían!

        Frente a vosotros he visto la sangre
        de España levantarse
        para ahogaros en una sola ola
        de orgullo y de cuchillos!

60   Generales
        traidores:
        mirad mi casa muerta,
        mirad España rota:
        pero de cada casa muerta sale metal ardiendo
65   en vez de flores,
        pero de cada hueco de España
        sale España,
        pero de cada niño muerto sale un fusil con ojos,
        pero de cada crimen nacen balas
70   que os hallarán un día el sitio
        del corazón.

        Preguntaréis por qué su poesía
        no nos habla del suelo, de las hojas,
        de los grandes volcanes de su país natal?

75   Venid a ver la sangre por las calles,
        venid a ver
        la sangre por las calles,
        venid a ver la sangre
        por las calles!

—Pablo Neruda

The title, "Explico algunas cosas," is intimate in the first person. Although one might expect the poem to be defensive, Neruda explains his change in poetic aesthetics aggressively and even bitterly. In part the poem represents a coming to terms with himself and his readers about his new aesthetics, and in part it offers a particular perspective on the war. Neruda was in Spain both as a poet and as a man, and the war had a profound effect upon him in both capacities. Neruda sees himself in the role of a poet in the war (Felipe does, too) and translates the Spanish catastrophe into a personal one. In this respect this poem is the most personal in tone and content of the three I shall deal with. Neruda begins on an intimate key, conversationally, with "preguntaréis," which is addressed to a familiar, collective "you." It is a confession to fellow poets and students since it is they who would read his poetry. "Os voy a contar todo lo que me pasa"—it is what is happening that is forcing him into a reappraisal of himself as a poet.

"Explico algunas cosas" is a poem transitional in his career from an earlier poetry ("las lilas," "la metafísica cubierta de amapolas," "la lluvia" filling his words with gullies and birds) which he echoes in the first stanza, only to reject in favor of a new poetic style. It is a re-examination of where he stands and where his poetry stands.

In his early poetry, before the *Residencias,* Neruda had demonstrated a lyric inclination, while concerned as a human being with problems of coping with love, death, abandonment, and loneliness. Elements of nature, very personal emotions, and artistic consciousness affected this poetry. His later experience aroused his political conscience. His commitment (to communism) was ideological, not artistic, but caused priorities within his verse to shift. His vision became less introspective and more outward-directed toward experience which involved him as a person and as a poet. Some critics have condemned the prosaic qualities they saw in his later works, for example, in *Canto general* (1950). Typical of his later development was his choice of such subjects in *Odas elementales* (1954-1957) as a lemon and an artichoke:

> La alcachofa
> de tierno corazón
> se vistió de guerrero,
> erecta, construyó
> una pequeña cupula . . .
> > (beginning of
> > "Oda a la alcachofa"
> > from *Odas elementales*)

> (The artichoke
> of delicate heart,
> erect
> in its battle-dress, built
> a small cupola . . .)

But really Neruda has always been a poet. This particular poem is a critical point in the evolution of Neruda as a poet and as a social animal. And his decision is to put his poetry at the service of his commitment—which is clearly implied in his poem.

Typical of Neruda's poetry (as of Vallejo's) had been the juxtaposition of animate and inanimate objects, such as, from the first stanza: "la metafísica cubierta de amapolas." The fragrance, color, and life force of poppies contrast strikingly with the philosophical abstraction of metaphysics. Both Vallejo and Neruda had the knack of making disparate things live with each other, their logic often deriving from emotion rather than intellect.

In the third stanza, "Yo vivía en un barrio/de Madrid, con companas,/con relojes, con árboles" is near to conversation made rhythmic. While his description of Madrid as being arid and withered is not surprising, his use of simple analogies has a powerful effect, for instance: "el rostro de Castilla/como un océano de cuero." His quotidian experiences and the flowers are ordinary, but they make the impact of his later "Y una mañana" that much greater. The poem has religious, sacramental symbols, such as flowers and blood.

As in Auden's *Spain*, the poem is presented in three tenses: past, present, and future. In the past, Neruda's poetry had been metaphysical, with adornments from nature. In the past, too, the poet had lived in a beautiful house in Madrid in an idyllic situation. He reports in a conversational way that all was lovely and, then, asks intimately, in the present tense, if three particular friends who would have visited his house remember: Raúl (González Tuñón [18]), Rafael (Alberti), and Federico (García Lorca). He recollects the two living and one dead poet. (Lorca was shot at the outbreak of the Spanish Civil War in 1936 by adherents of Franco, although he had had no political interests.) Appropriately, lines 22 and 23 contain images like those of Lorca's poetry.

In line 24 Neruda addresses his audience "Hermano, hermano!" but more in the sense of brother poets than as comrades. He shared a fraternity with Lorca based on their mutual suffering because of the war—Neruda in the sense of uprooting his past life and poetry and Lorca in the total sense of giving his life. He may then have been asking if they remember the sense of life they shared. He continues in the past, telling how things were: business went on in the marketplace, a microcosm of prewar life in Madrid. The imagery is auditory and visual. There is the interchange of food and appropriate imagery related to food. The olive oil is integral to Spanish cuisine. He hears the movement of hands and feet like the throb of a heart. He captures the sheer sensuality of the feeling of life and a tremendous sense of movement and sound. This sense of physical force and dynamism is typical of Neruda's poetry. The hands and feet are performing daily tasks of life. Despite the ordinariness of the day, he is getting at the very essence of daily life and people: food sale and preparation, nourishment, and the palpitating sound of human beings. The configuration of rooftops and tiles is brought out in sharp, cold relief by an intense sun. Neruda makes the scene somewhat sacred by including the metaphor of a marble statue: "delirante marfil fino de la patatas." Included in this picture is the same disorder that pervades living: "aglomeraciones," "llegaba," "llenaba," "tomates repetidos hasta el mar." Despite the mundane subject, the imagery is far from common (much like Vallejo's): "su estatua/como un tintero pálido entre las merluzas." The rich imagery appeals to all of our senses.

One can taste, smell, hear, feel, and see what Madrid had been and meant to him.

And then there is a sudden reversal. "Y una mañana," still in the past, everything that has meant life is completely obliterated:

> Y una mañana todo estaba ardiendo
> y una mañana las hogueras
> salían de la tierra
> devorando seres,
> y desde entonces fuego,
> pólvora desde entonces,
> y desde entonces sangre.

The life/death contrast of the imagery of the poem is striking. It is as if someone came along and knocked over and leveled everything, leaving nothing. This image of destruction leads up to the total holocaust of the final stanza, consisting of the repetition three times of "venid a ver la sangre por las calles." Blood is a frequent image of Neruda's poetry as we see also in Almería" and "Llegada." The image is as terrifying as that of Hernández in "Recoged esta voz": "un porvenir de polvo se avecina,/se avecina un suceso/en que no quedará ninguna cosa:/ni piedra sobre piedra ni hueso sobre hueso." In contrast with the geometrical imagery of the market scene, this negation of life is generalized.

There follow political caricatures with characteristic imagery. He designates the enemy as "bandidos" with airplanes and names their accomplices: the Moors, the wealthy ("sortijas"), the aristocracy ("duquesas"), and the Church, represented by black (in dress and character) friars who go through the motions of their office perfunctorily. Neruda is alluding to the following facts: During the uprising that began the Spanish Civil War, General Franco declared war in Tenerife (Canary Islands) on July 17, 1936, flew to Casablanca (French Morocco), and then on to Spanish Morocco on July 19 to take command of the Army of Morocco. This army of Africa was transported to Spain across the Strait of Gibraltar, and became a formidable battalion for the Insurgent side.[19] Of the Franco forces in 1937, 100,000 were Moors, 70,000 were Italians,

several thousand were Germans and Portuguese, and 250,000 were
Spanish troops in Carlist and Falangist militia units. Thus, the
Moors made the major contribution quantitatively.[20] In addition,
the word "Moros" has negative connotations.

"Niños" are pitted against these forces and "por las calles la
sangre de los niños/corría simplemente, como sangre de niños" is a
powerful repetition. In this poem as well as in "Llegada" and
"Almería," Neruda sees children as being particularly vulnerable
(as had Vallejo in "España, aparta de mí este cáliz"): "chiquillos,"
"venían por el cielo a matar niños/y por las calles la sangre de los
niños/corría simplemente, como sangre de niños."

The class struggle is emphasized in line 48: "bandidos con sortijas y duquesas." This ideological vision of the war as a product of
particular economic interests is reminiscent of Spender's "Ultima
Ratio Regum." In line 49 the Church is on the side of the rich.
Neruda sees the rich versus the poor here as well as in "Almería."

Neruda calls the enemy by despicable names: he thinks in terms
of things that feed on dead matter. Jackals are carnivorous and
prey upon other animals. Vipers are venomous. Neruda challenges
the enemy, "generales/traidores," to look upon the destruction
they have wrought. Again he is aware of the historical fact that
certain generals did revolt against the Republic to ignite the war.
Lines 64 and 65, "pero de cada casa muerta sale metal ardiendo/en
vez de flores," suggest line 15 of Spender's "Ultima Ratio Regum":
"The unflowering wall sprouted with guns." But Neruda adds the
twist that "de cada hueco de España sale España." Neruda had
confidence in the ultimate retribution on the part of the victims:

> Frente a vosotros he visto la sangre
> de España levantarse
> para ahogaros en una sola ola
> de orgullo y de cuchillos!
> . . .
> pero de cada casa muerta sale metal ardiendo
> en vez de flores,
> pero de cada hueco de España
> sale España,
> pero de cada niño muerto sale un fusil con ojos,

        pero de cada crimen nacen balas
        que os hallarán un día el sitio
        del corazón.

It is as if all of Spain were arising to smother the jackals and
traitors. This vow and cry for vengeance suggests in language and
spirit the call to arms of Hernández.

Again Neruda speaks of his past poetry's having dealt with "el
suelo . . . las hojas . . . los grandes volcanes . . . su país natal."
Then he asks scornfully how they might have the audacity to
wonder why his poetry does not speak of these trivialities (this is a
most liberal transliteration), after the incalculable monstrosity, the
overwhelming crime against children and against people with
whom he has lived. The tone here is very different from before.
He had begun the poem conversationally and with restraint. There
had been a progressive gradation of emotional intensity, leading to
his promise of revenge and his sense of outrage. His outrage and
emotional reaction take precedence over the artist. The experience
makes his new aesthetics unavoidable, and he answers his own
question:

        mirad mi casa muerta
        mirad España rota:
        . . .
        Venid a ver la sangre por las calles,
        venid a ver
        la sangre por las calles,
        venid a ver la sangre
        por las calles!

In the final stanza, there is repeated play upon the same words,
again as in Lorca's poetry (for example, "a las cinco de la tarde"
and "verde . . . que te quiero verde"). Like the imagery of Hernández, the poem offers a growing crescendo of destruction.

Neruda is considering his own poetry in relation to what is
happening (1937), but it is not an intellectual exercise. In the
heat of a traumatic experience, the poem offers a re-evaluation of
how the poet stands in relation to the large, collective experience

outside himself. In view of the overwhelming facts, everything else becomes essentially academic. His style has changed from being obscure, metaphysical, and inner-directed to being a poetry of emotional, as well as ideological, commitment. Putting his poetry at the service of his beliefs, he wishes to present his doctrine clearly and simply. He uses fewer images, and there is an emphasis upon direct communication. Between 1936 and 1939, when the Spanish Civil War exploded upon the world of his tradition, culture, and language as well as upon the routine of his life in Madrid, Neruda offered to the world a changed heart and a new source of perception firmly aligned with suffering and embattled mankind. His communist affiliation engaged his political conscience and artistic talent on the side of the Republic.

There is poetic intensity in the choice of strong words to dichotomize the opposing factions (Nationalist vs. Republican), in the careful repetitions, bitter accusations, and acid declaration of Spain's tragedy as well as his own. There is artistic tension in terms of language and imagery.

Neruda chose to cast this most personal poem in the form of a soliloquy. It is as if he were thinking aloud in reordering his values and life. The poem includes a re-evaluation of his poetry in view of the Spanish tragedy and a nihilistic picture of devastated Spain. It indicates an ideological background and offers a battle cry of revenge.

The twelve stanzas, of varying length and form, condense his emotional and intellectual response, but also allow him a flexible framework in which to build up the intensity of the poem.

LLEGADA A MADRID DE LA BRIGADA
INTERNACIONAL [21]

1   Una mañana de un mes frío,
         de un mes agonizante, manchado por el lodo y por
            el humo,
         un mes sin rodillas, un triste mes de sitio y
            desventura,

cuando a través de los cristales mojados de mi casa
se oían los chacales africanos
5   aullar con los rifles y los dientes llenos de sangre,
entonces,
cuando no teníamos más esperanza que un sueño
de pólvora, cuando ya creíamos
que el mundo estaba lleno sólo de monstruos
devoradores y de furias
entonces, quebrando la escarcha del mes de frío
de Madrid en la niebla
del alba
10   he visto con estos ojos que tengo, con este corazón
que mira,
he visto llegar a los claros, a los dominadores
combatientes
de la delgada y dura y madura y ardiente brigada
de piedra.
Era el acongojado tiempo en que las mujeres
llevaban una ausencia como un carbón terrible,
15   y la muerte española, más ácida y aguda que otras
muertes
llenaba los campos hasta entonces honrados por el
trigo.

Por las calles la sangre rota del hombre se juntaba
con el agua que sale del corazón destruído de las
casas:
los huesos de los niños deshechos, el desgarrador
20   enlutado silencio de las madres, los ojos
cerrados para siempre de los indefensos,
eran como la tristeza y la pérdida, eran como un
jardín escupido,
eran la fe y la flor asesinadas para siempre.

Camaradas,
25   entonces
os he visto,
y mis ojos están hasta ahora llenos de orgullo

porque os ví a través de la mañana de niebla llegar
a la frente pura de Castilla
silenciosos y firmes
30   como campanas antes del alba,
llenos de solemnidad y de ojos azules venir de lejos
y lejos,
venir de vuestros rincones, de vuestras patrias
perdidas, de vuestros sueños
llenos de dulzura quemada y de fusiles
a defender la ciudad española en que la libertad
acorralada
35   pudo caer y morir mordida por las bestias.
Hermanos, que desde ahora
vuestra pureza y vuestra fuerza, vuestra historia
solemne
sea conocida del niño y del varón, de la mujer y
del viejo,
llegue a todos los seres sin esperanza, baje a las
minas corroídas por el aire sulfúrico,
40   suba a las escaleras inhumanas del esclavo,
que todas las estrellas, que todas las espigas de
Castilla y del mundo
escriban vuestro nombre y vuestra áspera lucha
y vuestra victoria fuerte y terrestre como una
encina roja.
Porque habéis hecho renacer con vuestro sacrificio
45   la fe perdida, el alma ausente, la confianza en la
tierra,
y por vuestra abundancia, por vuestra nobleza, por
vuestros muertos,
como por un valle de duras rocas de sangre
pasa un inmenso río con palomas de acero y de
esperanza.

—Pablo Neruda

Neruda wrote "Llegada a Madrid de la Brigada Internacional"
about a particular event. On October 20, 1936, Franco issued
the general order for the capture of Madrid. On November 8

the first units of the International Brigades, formed at Albacete, arrived in Madrid. Some 3000 men, mostly Germans and Italians, many of them veterans of World War I and of fascist concentration camps, marching with absolute precision and singing revolutionary songs, paraded across the embattled capital. In total, there were to be twenty-odd nations represented in the International Brigades.[22] The poem enshrines a moment, and without that moment the poem would not live.

November would then be the cold month of the first line. It was a dying month because Madrid had by then been under siege for almost three weeks. It was a month without knees because its defenders would not acquiesce. The jackals are aptly "African" because Franco had come over from Africa, bringing the Moors. These African soldiers comprised the main force of the attack.

The enemy is called "chacales" (as in "Explico algunas cosas") in line 4, "monstruos devoradores y de furias" in line 7, and "bestias" in line 35. On the other hand, Neruda is so enthusiastic about the International Brigade that he cannot use enough adjectives: "la delgada y dura y madura y ardiente brigada de piedra." There is an interplay among the adjectives as the qualities of "fragility in numbers," "strength," "determination," and "burning commitment" are combined. The brigade is variously described. In line 11 the soldiers are "los claros" and "los dominadores." They are "camaradas" and "hermanos," "silenciosos y firmes," "llenos de solemnidad y de ojos azules." They come from all over the world, some having forfeited passports and, thus, their countries to do so. But they come not so much from country or group as from individual commitment to something in which they believe strongly. They come with "sueños" and out of true generosity of self ("abundancia").

In lines 13 and 14 "las mujeres/llevaban una ausencia como un carbón terrible." The simile suggests the intense burning within these solitary women left behind as they suffer frustration and unhappiness. In line 15 "la muerte española" is distinguished from other deaths. Death has often been the morbid preoccupation of Spaniards. Unamuno's "tragic sense of life" derives from a simultaneous awareness of mortality and yearning for eternal life. Death was all around—concretely manifested. It filled every corner: "llenaba los campos hasta entonces honrados por el trigo." It was amidst all this death that a vision of hope, in the form of the International Brigade, arrived.

In line 17 "la sangre rota" offers a mixed metaphor. It is as if the plumbing system of the human body had joined in broken chaos with that of the devastated houses.

Line 28's "la frente pura" of Castille alludes to Castille's location on high ground in relation to the rest of Spain, and its geographical centrality within the Iberian Peninsula.

The word "companas," in line 30, frequently used by Neruda, is one of beauty and clarity of sound, and Neruda plays upon it. The arrival of this Brigade was as stark and striking as the sound of bells in the otherwise utter silence before dawn. The analogy is further that the bells herald the coming of dawn as the Brigades herald the coming of a new day.

In the first stanza Neruda refers to the Brigade in the third person. Stanza two describes the destruction to the city and its inhabitants before their arrival. In stanzas three and four the poet calls them "camaradas" and "hermanos," expressing increasing gratitude. He is expressing a comradeship based on the commitment of one human life to another. In the final lines the soft quality of "un inmenso río con palomas" is juxtaposed with the hardness of "un valle de duras rocas" and "acero." This represents the very essence of hope: the illusion or ideal combined with the hard determination which gives it the ability to survive.

The poem expresses tremendous gratitude. It has an epic, larger-than-life quality and an ode-like tone. The whole vision of the Brigade filing into an embattled Madrid is panoramic and mural-istic. Neruda describes the city prior to their arrival: the sense of apprehension and doom, the unhappy circumstances, the physical climate. Then he presents his proud feelings upon their arrival in glorified, idealistic terms. The Brigade's arrival is an inspiring experience, and one can almost hear martial music in the background.

The language is like that of a Spanish Civil War campaign song. The song/poem offers a hymn of gratitude to the volunteers who have come to help defend Spain. It is the intent which is of primary importance, and the language is the product of an intent both hyperbolic and glorifying. The combative elements of the language are like those of Hernández.

But the language is not especially original. The evocative details of Neruda's previous poetry are not present here. He is dealing in semantic generalities. The epithets are designed to evoke an emotional reaction not so much from their graphic suggestiveness as from the subjectivity of their connotations. Neruda has given us his highly emotional response to the ideological potential of the circumstances, and his canvas is huge. But the resulting poem is politically more stirring than poetically.

ALMERÍA [23]

1   Un plato para el obispo, un plato triturado y
              amargo,
         un plato con restos de hierro, con cenizas, con
              lágrimas,
         un plato sumergido, con sollozos y paredes
              caídas,
         un plato negro, un plato de sangre de Almería.

5   Un plato para el banquero, un plato con mejillas
         de niños del Sur feliz, un plato
         con detonaciones, con aguas locas y ruinas y
              espanto,
         un plato con ejes partidos y cabezas pisadas,
         un plato negro, un plato de sangre de Almería.

10   Cada mañana, cada mañana turbia de vuestra
              vida
         lo tendréis humeante y ardiente en vuestra mesa:
         lo apartaréis un poco con vuestras suaves manos
         para no verlo, para no digerirlo tantas veces:
         lo apartaréis un poco entre el pan y las uvas,
15   a este plato de sangre silenciosa
         que estará allí cada mañana, cada
         mañana.

Un plato para el Coronel y la esposa del
      Coronel,
en una fiesta de la guarnición, en cada fiesta,
20   sobre los juramentos y los escupos, con la luz de
      vino de la madrugada
para que lo veáis temblando y frío sobre el
      mundo.

Sí, un plato para todos vosotros, ricos de aquí
      y de allá,
embajadores, ministros, comensales atroces,
señoras de confortable té y asiento:
25   un plato destrozado, desbordado, sucio de sangre
      pobre,
para cada mañana, para cada semana, para
      siempre jamás,
un plato de sangre de Almería, ante vosotros,
      siempre.

—Pablo Neruda

On May 29, 1937, the German battleship *Deutschland* was attacked off Ibiza by two Republican aircraft. Thirty-one of the
ship's company were killed and many others wounded. The Germans (especially Hitler) were furious, and at dawn on May 31
the Germans took their revenge. A cruiser and four destroyers
appeared off Almería, on the southeastern coast of Spain, and fired
200 shots into the town, destroying thirty-five buildings and caus-
ing nineteen deaths. The Republic considered bombing the German fleet in the Mediterranean in retaliation, but there was too
much pressure against it from fear of setting off world war. For
reasons, then, mostly political, the incident of Almería was "forgotten." [24]
    Pablo Neruda did not forget. The destruction to an innocent
Almería, chosen as a convenient victim by such powerful adver-
saries, enraged the poet. Neruda metes out his particular retribution in an extravagantly ironic manner. He carefully sidesteps the
German involvement and names the types of people he held responsible for the inception and maintenance of the war: "el

obispo," "el banquero," "el coronel y la esposa del coronel," "ricos de aquí y de allá," "embajadores, ministros, conmensales atroces,/ señoras de confortable té y asiento" (the religious leaders, financial controllers, army officials and their wives, the rich from all over who lend support to the Nationalist side, and the political leaders and idle aristocracy whose activity as well as neglect help to destroy the Republic). Neruda emphasizes the class struggle underlying the war, as Spender suggests it in "Ultima Ratio Regum." It is the rich against the poor, the powerful minority with its material and social advantages against the masses. In line 24 ("señoras de confortable té y asiento"), Neruda is criticizing the bourgeoisie. He is accusing the system—the Establishment. The poem is political and sounds socialistic in its criticism of the higher echelons of the social hierarchy.

Neruda uses the metaphor of a variety of nauseating "edibles," such as garbage and suffering-thickened blood, to express his own revulsion toward those he holds responsible for the tragedy. This particular punishment suggests Cronos of Greek mythology, who ate his own children, as well as Atreus, who killed Thyestes' young children and had them served up at a banquet. Ironically, Neruda is concentrating on those who might, ordinarily, take sensuous pleasure in what they were eating. The food he introduces is calculated to curdle in their stomachs and to send a shiver through their flesh. The blood he would offer them is hardly meant with sacred and mysterious reverence, but with hate, contempt, and horror. Neruda is telling the beneficiaries of his contribution to their breakfast table (the first food of the day) that they will eat the results of what they have created for the rest of their lives. That particular philosophy is reminiscent of the Bible's "what you sow, you shall reap" and "by their fruits shall ye know them," and also of the Mosaic law "an eye for an eye, a tooth for a tooth."

The imagery is visual and olfactory ("humeante y ardiente"). These potential gourmands will be made to smell, see, and swallow the carrion of their making. The poem is unflinching in its viewpoint and unsparingly graphic in its cannibalism. The recipients will sit there as mute victims of their own atrocities.

The ideological vision is of those with wealthy interests feeding on the innocent bodies of children and other victims to sustain themselves. This vision is Goyaesque (cf. his war sketches) in grotesqueness. Neruda transforms his ideological commitment into a plastic one which is overwhelming. It reminds me, also, of Jonathan Swift's "A Modest Proposal," in which instead of abstracting the problem of starving people, Swift suggests that the children of the poor be served up to their parents in a cannibalistic orgy.

In the first stanza, the "o" sound predominates like a sorrowful backdrop as Neruda insistently serves up a select menu for the chosen guests. There is much repetition not only of the "o" sound but of the word "plato," which appears six times in the brief quatrain. The refrain "un plato de sangre de Almería" concludes the first, second, and fifth stanzas.

It is obvious that Neruda meant the poem to be repetitious as well as inexorable. It is undoubtedly part of Neruda's irony that the poem should be stated with a variety of metaphors rich in adjectives, and frequent alliteration, assonance, and repetition. The sharp contradiction between the apparent generosity and the obvious bad faith of the giver is strengthened by the simplicity of the images. The poetic devices and lyrical qualities jarringly emphasize his bitterness. The poem's ironic vituperation is as strong as that of the Bible's Psalm 137.

"Almería" is epic in its larger-than-life imagery and Neruda speaks not of individuals but of broad categories of types. The imagery is much more graphic than that of "Llegada." There is a richness not only of emotional commitment, but also of language and imagery. The strength of its poetic language gives "Almería" a raison d'être that rises above its meaning, which is not true of "Llegada." "Llegada" is a poem of a particular time and place. "Almería" is more powerful and durable.

All four poets (Felipe, Hernández, Vallejo, and Neruda) sympathized with the Republican side, sharing deep reactions to the war. All of their poems analyzed here in depth were written, by coincidence, in 1937. Vallejo's presentation was in most personal terms. Neruda ("Llegada" and "Almería") wrote about specific events, as did Felipe in "La insignia" (the fall of Málaga and the threat to Valencia). Hernández had a more generalized approach, with insinuations about political background. He saw the need to

unite the nations of the world ("Recoged esta voz"). Vallejo included mention of Toledo in "Pequeño responso" but mostly
generalized. Felipe had the most transcendental view, but Neruda,
too, saw the war in international dimensions. Felipe was able to
criticize the Republican side for a lack of unity, while admiring
the cohesion of the Franco side. He bitterly condemned England
for her motives in failing to intervene on the side of justice. He
is the most historically realistic of the four. The Republican side
was, indeed, hopelessly divided, which weakened its effectiveness
and helped bring on its defeat. The prophetic ending of "La
insignia," however, intimates that Spain and Justice will somehow
resurrect. By 1939 Felipe's poems became completely pessimistic.

Felipe is more didactic than the other poets, having been a
teacher and a translator. He was understandably more concerned
with his message than with imagery, but all four made an effort to
create their war poems with a minimum of vague language and
obscure imagery ("Pequeño responso" is the most obscure). They
were trying to be understood. This came naturally to Hernández
whereas Vallejo and Neruda had to change their styles.

At the explosion of the war, Hernández enlisted immediately
to serve "la España de las pobrezas." He was attracted and drawn
by the "viento del pueblo" to the defense of their cause—the Republican cause. Like Vallejo he had a capacity for suffering—not
just for himself but for others—and a feeling for the solidarity of
his people. We can see his close identification with the common
man through his own first-person inclusion in the poems.

The poems are not strictly religious, but some of their elements
(the pervasive blood, for example) are true to the ritual of the
Catholic religion. They do not deal outrightly with politics or
economics, but they do show a class of peasants and workers fighting against enslavement. In "Vientos del pueblo me llevan" the
enemy is trying to put a yoke on the working and peasant class.
Hernández sees the conflict as the enslaved against the enslaver
more than as a civil war. His awareness of the economics and politics of the war is insinuated in a way that reminds us of the poems
of Stephen Spender. The two analyzed poems by Hernández are
not argumentative, but his patriotic and ideological commitment
is unmistakable. They are sometimes rhetorical and their purpose

is to move, encourage, and motivate the peasant soldiers and other forces for the Republic. He wrote for the common people who are most representative of the people of Spain. He spoke out directly, simply, and with understanding and empathy. He empathized from a deep sense of common humanity. Hernández and Neruda had in common this empathy for the people, but their perspective in time and space differed. Hernández was much closer to the people. But Neruda, also, had a definite sense of commitment to his theme and a sense of the responsibility and role of the poet.

Hernández put a personal and original stamp on his poems and was able to write vividly and vivaciously. His poetry is rich in images, virile passion, and humanity. The power of his poems derives from his strong emotional commitment. He wrote with the passion of immediate experience of the war. His poems reveal the inspiration and awareness of tragedy of the twenty-seven-year old poet whose courage and dedication cannot be doubted.

In comparison, Vallejo is a more academic poet who writes less vivacious, but more complex poems for more educated audiences. In Vallejo's poems there is no class confrontation. Rather he presents the trauma and death of Spain in war in intimate terms.

The three analyzed poems of Vallejo have religious elements, but they are not held in any orthodox way. They are dramatic and rely upon striking symbols and imagery. They are directly, simply, and forcefully expressed, disclosing a very vigorous hand. The poetry is sincere as well as passionate. Vallejo was deeply involved, and his poems about Spain are subjective, emotional, and inspiring.

Taken in the order in which they appeared in *España, aparta de mí este cáliz,* the first, "Pequeño responso," offers some hope (about poetry or, more broadly, about Spain) even during such a war. Its concept is romantic, although its imagery contains physical details—some of which are surrealistically expressed. The second poem, "Masa," is very lyrical, also romanticized, and, in its way, more despairing than "Pequeño responso." One can conceive of the enduring nature of a man's poetry, though Vallejo's imaginative conception of it is far from realistic. But to imagine a dead soldier, representative of Spain, resurrecting is both ironic and heart-breaking in its historical context. The third poem, "España, aparta de mí este cáliz," offers a more tangible hope than "Masa," although here again the imagery is very subjective. Vallejo looks to the children of all mankind for salvation. It is as if he had had the premonition that the fight would be prolonged and the hour of salvation delayed until the future. Vallejo was offering his prophetic words on the outcome.

"Pequeño responso" is expressed in brief images, abruptly (a word from the poem), and perhaps could be compared to the measured and abrupt steps of the funeral procession it depicts. "Masa" is beautiful both in sound and meaning, the miracle it concerns and the casual tone of its expression in contradiction to one another. It is the most ironic of the three poems. "España" is written in very long, periodic-type sentences, but also includes brief images. As in "Pequeño responso," some of its referents seem very obscure. "Masa" is the simplest of the poems.

Vallejo's tone is striking—firmly masculine despite his humility as a human being. His poems have an oral power (as do those of Hernández), and he uses common speech to lyrical advantage. His manipulation of language is both careful and original, with frequent repetition of sounds and words.

The poems are not doctrinaire, but deeply felt and forcefully, movingly expressed. Especially in "Masa" and "España" Vallejo exposes his desire for human solidarity, and one senses his feeling of brotherhood toward the oppressed and suffering. The hope of Vallejo was a hope for mankind—all those he acknowledged as brothers and with whom, along with Neruda, he took common cause.

It is most natural that the Spanish Civil War would have an impact on the poetry of Vallejo and Neruda because, from the start, they concerned themselves with the social realities with which they had lived. There was a common denominator between the tensions at home (Peru and Chile, respectively) and the Spanish Civil War. Vallejo could equate the Indians and miners of his homeland with the oppressed of Spain. This war was an extension of the confrontation between the disinherited and those who wield political, economic, and social power. The Spanish Civil War as a theme, therefore, occupied an understandable place in their vision.

Neruda's "Explico algunas cosas" is a personal poem, showing his close identification with the misfortunes of Madrid. At the same time he explains his new attitude about writing poetry, a change from inner- to outer-directedness, certainly in line with communist philosophy. The holocaust he describes is reminiscent of that which Hernández had predicted if the war went against the Republic. The poem is political; the method remains poetic. The enemy whom he does not hesitate to call derogatory names has the support in his conception, as well as in reality, of the Moors, the aristocracy, the Church, and moneyed interests. He calls the generals of the enemy side traitors.

"Llegada a Madrid de la Brigada Internacional" shows Neruda's awareness of the international context of the war. He is also aware of the dangers at the time (1936 in Madrid) but is suddenly hopeful, proud, and grateful because of the arrival of the first of the International Brigades.

"Almería" is the most ironic of the three poems, its form and rhythm the most regular. Its venom incriminates those he holds responsible for the war. The political implications of the poem are clear and have a factual basis. His nightmare-like punishment is for the Church, the economic leaders, the military, the rich, the aristocracy, and the political forces of the Nationalist side. He retaliates for the masses of Spanish Republicans, namely for the "niños del Sur feliz" and the poor. All three poems include bitter protest against a tragic course of events, but "Almería" has the sharpest answer.

Neruda's general condemnation (he has not named the offenders specifically) is very strong. There is no doubt about Neruda's strong convictions about the war and his deep involvement. He became politically minded at the time of the war, and we see the depiction of the class struggle clearly in his poems. The historical relevance of specific details is more apparent than in the poems of Hernández and Vallejo. There are some religious elements in his poems (the prevalence of blood and flowers) but also skepticism about the actual institution of the Church.

His close identification with the cause of the Spanish Republic comes not just because he was a Chilean with strong allegiance to Spain, but also because he was an antifascist (later to join the Communist Party) and because he had lived in Madrid among Spaniards and was there during the first few years of the war.

Neruda wrote political poems conscious of class struggle. He was aware of himself as a poet ("Explico algunas cosas") as Felipe was conscious of his role at the beginning and end of "La insignia." Vallejo's poems are of the tragedy of Spain in a personal, though generalized, context. Felipe had a very independent slant on the circumstances of the war, being critical of both sides and stubbornly demanding elimination of Republican dissension, materialism, and cowardice despite the course of events by 1937. Hernández praised and inspired the Spanish soldiers and had a fatalistic idea about death that Felipe held. Both encouraged martyrdom. Vallejo's poems contain emotional imagery and a sense of abandonment, desperation, and loneliness. Felipe intellectualized. His anguish came not so much from the military confrontation as from the intrigues and rivalries within the Republican group. Unlike Hernández and Vallejo, but in common with Neruda, Felipe is declamatory. Hernández speaks as a soldier to other soldiers. Felipe speaks as a poet/prophet, a gigantic figure astride the world, looking down at the people. Vallejo is more humble. Felipe is intellectually critical (as opposed to emotionally empathetic).

While Vallejo speaks in a muted, one-to-one dialogue, Neruda may be said to declaim. While Vallejo scaled down an experience (in tone, not in meaning), Neruda's voice has epic reverberations. Neruda is always conscious of being a poet. Vallejo, on the other hand, does not impose his own literary personality. Vallejo exposes an anguished soul in a personal way. Hernández offers a battle cry to fellow-soldiers, and at moments both he and Neruda present nihilistic visions.

Being Latin American affected the imagery of Vallejo and Neruda. Having a mother complex in relation to Spain, Vallejo called Spain mother ("España, aparta de mí este cáliz"). Both featured children in their poems as being most vulnerable ("España, aparta . . . ," "Almería," and "Explico algunas cosas")—which, of course, they are.

For Felipe the war was a sobering experience which aroused a more hostile and declamatory tone than he had adopted previously. He went into permanent exile after the war and died in exile.

Hernández fought in the war, felt very close to his fellow-soldiers, and wrote tragic and inspired (as well as inspirational) poems. He died as a result of his prison experience after the war. At the time of the war, Vallejo had not written poetry for almost fifteen years. As meaning increased in importance to him, he abandoned the obscure surrealism of his earlier poems (*Trilce*, 1923) for more simplified expression in his last two (war) volumes. He died in Paris before the end of the war. Neruda changed considerably as a result of the war and, perhaps for the same reason as Vallejo, developed from obscurity toward didacticism. He never returned to Spain and remained a communist.

As to the durability of these war poems, we might ask whether they would survive outside their historical context. Although Felipe's poetic speech deals with particular circumstances, it is elevated to a transcendental plane. It derives its value from the fact that the poet does not speak through the mouths of certain men or names, but represents Man and is addressed to Man. Felipe is essentially concerned with Man. Felipe's poem goes beyond the Spanish Civil War to the hopelessness of all war. He is concerned with the ultimate brutality and horror of all war ("eran sesos humanos que tuve por mucho tiempo pegados a las suelas de mis zapatos."). He points to the grotesque discrepancy between the horrible carnage and the political in-fighting. His poetry has ideological survival value, being based on political truth, and his understanding of human nature (though cynical) rings true. The poem has artistic survival value in the form of its dramatic elements, architectural form, skillful repetition, vivid images, emotionally-suggestive language, and emotional impact. His concern for the Republicans can be compared to his feeling for the loneliness and anguish of the exile in "Español del éxodo y del llanto"; both have universal application.

Being completely caught up in the situation, Hernández wrote of the desperation and carnage of any war, with feelings of brotherhood, despair, and inspiration. His poems are exciting, full of energy and ideals, and have lyrical qualities which suggest they will last. The nature of Vallejo's poetic conception transcends the Spanish Civil War to include all of mankind. Besides, his poems are lyrical, intense, vivid, and beautiful in any context. His poems will survive because they are poetically conceived and because his message of compassion, feeling, and frustration-hope has universal meaning. His capacity for suffering reaches all humans. Of the three poems by Neruda considered here, "Explico" has the most artistic quality and "Llegada" the least. "Llegada" is the most limited of the three both in scope and artistry, but it does contain insights into human nature. Readers can identify with the bitterness and resentment of "Almería" with or without knowing the historical circumstances.

Notes

1. The phrase is Unamuno's.

2. Opening lines of "Heces," *Los heraldos negros* (Buenos Aires: Editorial Losada, 1918), p. 36.

3. Biographical material came mostly from the Prólogo by Guillermo de Torre to *Obras completas* by León Felipe (Buenos Aires: Editorial Losada, 1963); but also, in part, from the following: Angel del Río, *Historia de la literatura española,* Tomo II (New York: Holt, Rinehart and Winston, 1963) and Angel Valbuena Prat, *Historia de la literatura española,* Tomo II (Barcelona: Editorial Gustavo Gili, S. A., 1946).

4. León Felipe, *Obras completas* (Buenos Aires: Editorial Losada, 1963), pp. 927-44.

5. The Fifth Column refers to a clandestine subversive organization working within a given country to further an invading enemy's military and political aims. It was first applied in 1936 to the Franco supporters and sympathizers in Madrid by General Emilio Mola, who was leading four rebel columns of troops against that city.

6. Jackson, *The Spanish Republic and the Civil War, 1931-1939,* pp. 342-44.

7. This is the title of a poem in his collection "Español del éxodo y del llanto: Doctrina de un poeta español en 1939."

8. Biographical data was compiled from Juan Cano Ballesta: *La poesía de Miguel Hernández* (Madrid: Editorial Gredos, 1962); Juan Guerrero Zamora: *Miguel Hernández, poeta (1910-1942)* (Madrid:

Colección El Grifon, 1955); the Introduction (by José Luis Cano) to *Poemas: Miguel Hernández* (Barcelona: Editorial Gredos, 1964); and the Prologue (by María de Gracia Ifach) to *Obras completas: Miguel Hernández* (Buenos Aires: Editorial Losada, 1960).

9. Hernández, *Viento del pueblo,* pp. 95-97.

10. Hernández, *Viento del pueblo,* pp. 108-12.

11. Sources for biographical information were: Translator's Foreword to *Poemas humanos: Human Poems* by César Vallejo, translated by Clayton Eshleman (New York: Grove Press, 1969) and André Coyné, *César Vallejo* (Buenos Aires: Ediciones Nueva Visión, 1968).

12. Quotation appears on p. 311 of *César Vallejo* by André Coyné.

13. César Vallejo, *España, aparta de mí este cáliz* (Mexico: Editorial Séneca, 1940), pp. 69-70.

14. Vallejo, *España, aparta de mí este cáliz,* p. 81.

15. Vallejo, *España, aparta de mí este cáliz,* pp. 89-90.

16. Biographical details were obtained from: Introduction to his poems in *Antología de la poesía hispanoamericana,* Julio Caillet Bois, ed. (Madrid: Aguilar, 1958); and Amado Alonso, *Poesía y estilo de Pablo Neruda* (Buenos Aires: Editorial Sudamericana, 1966).

17. Pablo Neruda, *Poesía política* (Santiago de Chile: Editora Austral, 1953), I, 57-60.

18. Suggested in footnote 9, p. 354, of *Poesía y estilo de Pablo Neruda* by Amado Alonso.

19. Facts are from Jackson, *The Spanish Republic and the Civil War, 1931-1939,* pp. 231-33.

20. Jackson, p. 428.

21. Neruda, *Poesía política,* I, 66-68.

22. Jackson, pp. 327-28.

23. Neruda, *Poesía política,* I, 70-71.

24. Facts from Hugh Thomas, *The Spanish Civil War,* pp. 440-42.

CHAPTER III

Spanish Civil War Poets in the English Language

The five poets in this grouping are linked not just by the English language but by their culture as well. These poets are representative of their various backgrounds and countries and, at the same time, have written poems resulting from the Spanish Civil War which may, in their own right, be considered important. There is only one poet to be discussed on the Nationalist side, Roy Campbell, because I could find no other who made a significant poetic contribution. That also accounts for there being only one woman, Muriel Rukeyser.

The focus of these non-Spanish, non-Latin poets is not the dead center of the Spanish Civil War. Their motivations and interests were, at least partially, elsewhere. None of them actually bore arms. Rukeyser was in Spain by chance at the opening of hostilities. W. H. Auden was there for only three months; and Stephen Spender made three brief visits in a literary capacity. Campbell, despite his claims, is said to have been evacuated in August of

1936 and to have returned only as a well-protected war correspondent. Hugh MacDiarmid did not go to Spain at all.

MacDiarmid was the oldest (forty-four in 1936) of the five poets at the time of the war, while Rukeyser was the youngest (twenty-three in 1936). MacDiarmid was a well-read intellectual, educated at Edinburgh University, who held radical socialistic views. He used his poetry as a weapon in his general political struggles and was able to assimilate the political thinker and the artist in himself. His background was not dissimilar to that of Neruda and Vallejo. He came from a working-class family and knew physical and economic hardship. His socialistic and communistic sympathies immediately sided him with the Republic. But the primary concern of his life was for Scottish unity and nationalism, so that he identified with the kindred nature of the struggle in Spain, not so much with its particular time, place, and circumstances.

Campbell was thirty-five in 1936. He had the least formal education of the five and was, probably, the most active physically. A convert to Roman Catholicism (in 1936), he staunchly supported the Nationalist side. He was anti-intellectual and antiliberal, and his lack of formal education perhaps influenced his subjectivity. His background was rural and his imagery favored nature over science and technology. His life and personality were entangled in his egocentric poetry and he harbored bitter grudges. Very emotional, his viewpoints were fanatically maintained.

The most similar backgrounds are those of Spender and Auden, who came from urban environments, were two years apart in age, went to the same college at Oxford, and had mutual friends. Both came from successful middle-class families of culture. Auden (the older) came from the industrial North, where he had witnessed economic depression. He was scientific in inclination and interests. Marx and Freud attracted his attention, and his political orientation gradually gave way to an interest in the psychology and sociology of man. His conversion to Anglo-Catholicism (1940) caused a more optimistic outlook and affected his thinking and writing.

Spender was twenty-seven in 1936. His poetry was personal, more subjective than Auden's, and removed from politics and propaganda. His attitude was humanitarian, antiwar, and antiromantic.

He joined the Communist Party but, like Auden, resented some of its practices and later disassociated himself. He was critical of the Party's regimentation ("Two Armies") and propagandistic deception ("Two Armies" and "Ultima Ratio Regum").

Rukeyser, American born, Jewish, urban, and liberal, was educated at Vassar. She had wide contemporary interests: social, political, and scientific. Her poetry suggests a passionate nature and there are frequent sexual allusions.

Her volume *A Turning Wind* was published in 1939 but only some of its poems refer to the Spanish Civil War. This was also the year of World War II's outbreak—which influenced her poetry. Her poem "Mediterranean" was published in 1937 in *New Masses* magazine.[1] Her antiwar attitude was a reaction to the times more than to one specific war. She was part of the group movement mobilized in America against militarism and fascism. Her viewpoint is humanitarian, and she includes many personal allusions in her poems, extending their focus beyond the war.

MacDiarmid's poem *The Battle Continues* is in reaction to Campbell's *Flowering Rifle*. Though Campbell and MacDiarmid have diametrically opposed philosophies, the two have much in common: vigor, egocentricity, strong views, verbosity. Campbell wrote eleven poems on the Spanish Civil War which, by far, comprise the largest poetic contribution by any of these five poets.

Auden's only poem on the war was *Spain*. His logical, objective approach to the subject reflects his scientific background. Spender included ten short poems in his *Collected Works* under the subtitle "Poems about the Spanish Civil War."

To repeat my main contention, not one of these poets was caught up in the war emotionally or intellectually to the extent that the Spanish-writing poets were. Campbell had many axes to grind. MacDiarmid retaliated against Campbell and was attracted to Republican Spain through its cause, kindred to that of Scotland. Each was working out personal feuds and personality idiosyncrasies. Rukeyser shared the pacifistic sentiments of many humanitarians of that time in history. Her poems are interwoven with personal considerations and there is only limited mention of Spain. Auden's contribution was a single poem in a detached, objective tone. Spender from a broad, humanitarian viewpoint extracted from the larger panorama individual, anonymous sufferers. While Auden's poem is political, Spender's are less obviously so. Campbell's and MacDiarmid's poems in their verbosity include many matters not germane to the war.

Since MacDiarmid's poem reacts to Campbell's, discussion of MacDiarmid follows that of Campbell. With that exception, the poets are discussed in chronological order, in accordance with their birthdates: Campbell, MacDiarmid, Auden, Spender, and Rukeyser. As in Chapter II, close analyses of selected poems follow each biographical-literary sketch.

While the Oxford poets (Auden, Day Lewis, MacNeice, Spender) were products of the old English university and of an urban and industrial milieu, Campbell (1901-1957) came from South Africa.[2] (Ignatius) Roy (Dunnachie) Campbell was born in Durban, Natal, a British colony in what became the Union of South Africa, in 1901, and left for England seventeen years later. The South Africa in which he grew up had not yet experienced its Industrial Revolution. His background had scarcely made him conscious of the problems of an urbanized society, post World War I economic problems, revolution (Russia, 1917), and social protest. The poetic images of his early poetry come from an ambience in which nature is close at hand (those of Auden, Day Lewis, MacNeice, and Spender allude much more often to the modern world, history, and science). Campbell's attitude toward life was optimistic, combative, direct, and simple. His vigorous, extroverted verse contrasted with the uneasy self-searching of the more socially conscious poets of the 1930s. Campbell was a romantic in the sense that he upheld the individual, the personal, and the value of imaginative and intuitive faculties, as opposed to technology, standardization, bureaucratization, and the anonymous millions. Politically he was a reactionary (antiliberal) and culturally he was an anti-intellectual.

His anti-intellectual attitude most likely stemmed from his having failed the entrance examinations for Oxford. In any case, he sustained a belief in the superiority of practical knowledge gained from action rather than from reading:

And reading without wisdom is to blame
For half the world destroyed with blood or flame—
By Left-wing reading incapacitated
Either to tolerate or be tolerated;
Experience better serves the most Unread
Who carry no Boloney home to bed.[3]

Campbell expressed contempt for nearly all leftist writers. He considered them too cerebral, too mincing and fussy, too fearful of the cruder elements of life, and, worst of all, too far removed from life itself.

In the Twenties Campbell took no interest in politics, social causes, or proletarian reforms, and stayed clear of leftist groups. Between 1928 and the outbreak of war in 1936, Campbell provided for his growing family by raising olives in Martigues, bullfighting in Provence, fishing off southern France, and steerthrowing and horsebreaking in Toledo. The intensity, excitement, and demands of this life did little to quicken an interest in politics, although his hostility toward the Bloomsbury group and their politics grew stronger, especially after he learned that a few of them had banned his poem "The Georgiad." [4] But his political detachment ended around 1935. As signs of unrest increased in Spain, Campbell, then living in Toledo, was forced to recognize the power of an ever more daring and hostile Left. To the frequent outbursts of lawlessness, he reacted vehemently, accusing the Spanish communists of deliberately creating disorder preparatory to launching an attack on the state. Their goal, he believed, was a communist-dominated Spain. He openly proclaimed his allegiance to the Church, which had already become a target of leftists. In June, 1936, Campbell and his wife were officially converted to Roman Catholicism, a defiant act in those times.

Campbell often expressed unpopular convictions. His combative, individualistic temperament kept him apart from literary movements of the day, and some of his lyrics express his sense of isolation and independence amidst the hostile forces of nature. His literary output was copious and uneven.

The best of Campbell is contained in his lyrics, epigrams, and translations. Of his verse, his reputation rests mainly on two early volumes "The Flaming Terrapin" (1924) and "Adamastor" (1930), both lyrical works. The former exalts the instinctive vital force that brings forth intelligent human effort out of apathy and disillusionment:

> . . . Old Ocean growls and tosses his grey mane.
> Pawing the rocks in all his old unrest . . .
> Then to my veins I feel new sap return,
> Strength tightens up my sinews long grown dull,
> And in the old charred crater of the skull
> Light strikes the slow somnambulistic mind
> And sweeps her forth to ride the rushing wind,
> And stamping on the hill-tops high in air,
> To shake the golden bonfire of her hair.

These poems were remarkable for energy, rhetorical power, and striking imagery. He followed these with many other volumes of verse. Among them are two long satires, "The Wayzgoose" (1928), which ridicules South African intellectuals, and "The Georgiad" (1931), which attacks the "Georgian" poets who were in vogue during the Twenties and anticipates the level of attack of *Flowering Rifle:*

> And in a Bloomsbury accent it could yodel . . .
> Unlike our modern homos, who are neither,
> He could be homosexual with either
> And heterosexual with either, too—
> A damn sight more than you or I could do!

He wrote poems of the Spanish Civil War, "Mithraic Emblems" (1936) and the long polemical satire *Flowering Rifle* (1939); and poems of the Second World War, "Talking Bronco" (1946), which attacks the literary figures of the Bloomsbury group. His *Collected Poems* (3 volumes) appeared 1949-1957. He published three autobiographical books, *Broken Record* (1934), *Light on a Dark Horse* (1951), and *Portugal* (1957).

Campbell translated St. John of the Cross (1951), Lorca (1952), Baudelaire, and other Spanish, French, and Portuguese writers. He also wrote five or six prose books, including the above-mentioned autobiographies and critical studies of Burns, Taurine Provence, and Lorca.

Campbell wrote only eleven poems based on the Spanish Civil War, but, in all, they offer perhaps the most extensive treatment of the war by a single poet. Campbell was almost the only poet writing in English who was on the fascist side, and I have chosen to analyze *Flowering Rifle,* a 157-page poem which he subtitled "from the Battlefield of Spain."

Repeatedly, Campbell tried to give the impression that he had fought in the front ranks of Franco's army, and in one footnote to *Flowering Rifle* he actually stated as much (p. 224 of Volume 2 of *Collected Works,* London: The Bodley Head, 1957). There is, however, some evidence that Campbell was not the front-line combat soldier he claimed to be. Robert Graves wrote that Roy Campbell "was evacuated from Spain early in August, 1936 . . . and returned there only as a well-protected war correspondent." [5]

Since he had just become a Roman Catholic, and since the Nationalist rebels proclaimed themselves anticommunists and saviors of the Catholic Church, it was not surprising that Campbell chose the side of the "Christian Crusade against Communism." The Thirties had been a decade of unemployment and hunger marches, of the rise of fascist tyrannies; to almost all writers and intellectuals the only hope at the time seemed to lie with the forces of socialism and even communism. The emotional partisanship generated by the Spanish Civil War was intense. When in the middle of all this, Campbell produced *Flowering Rifle,* a fanatical view of the Spanish Civil War in which he jeered at those "pinks" and "wowsers" who supported the "Reds," he was fiercely attacked and his books boycotted.

This was a continuation of Campbell's famous feud with the young Thirties poets, Auden, Spender, MacNeice, and Day Lewis. Cliques, groups, and movements in poetry were anathema to Campbell, quite apart from his disagreement with the left-wing political attitudes held by these four, whom he later satirized under the acronym of MacSpaunday in "Talking Bronco," which is no more than an epigraph to *Flowering Rifle.*

Campbell's bias probably derived, in part, from his South African birth and half-pastoral upbringing. He accounts for other sources of his prejudice in the Author's Note to the 1939 edition of *Flowering Rifle:* "Like all English writers on Spain I am biassed, but . . . I am biassed, unlike any of the others, by a thorough first-hand experience of life under both regimes as one of the working population." While it is probably true that Campbell was more familiar with the workaday world of Spain than most other English-speaking poets who became involved in the war, religion also motivated his Spanish Civil War poetry. Campbell, especially as a new convert, was sensitive to attacks on the institution for which he obviously held an intensely emotional respect.

During World War II he (paradoxically) fought against fascism with the British Army in Africa. In the post World War II years, Campbell wrote less original poetry. The injuries he sustained during World War II forced him to lead a more sedentary life. Action, with Campbell, was accessory to poetry; the one stimulated the other. He died in a car accident near Setubal, Portugal, on April 22, 1957.

The fruit of Campbell's experience in the war, his aversion to the communist ideology, his contempt for British Intellectualism of the Left, and his loyalty to the Church were combined in *Flowering Rifle,* which was first published at the end of the Spanish Civil War. What provoked Campbell's sizable reaction to the Spanish Civil War was the poet's firm belief that the Nationalist cause embodied most of the values and ideas which he as a man and poet profoundly agreed with or, at least, respected; and that, on the other hand, the Loyalist cause of "freedom and democracy" was nothing but camouflage to conceal the ambitions of a ruthless group of communists to seize control of Spain. Furthermore, he believed the Republican leaders had attracted nearly every enemy he had ever made, including particular left-wing poets.

Campbell found his values, disbeliefs, friends, and enemies felicitously arranged into opposing camps. To divide the combatants into groups representing right and wrong was probably an easier task for him than it had been for most poets. His personal designations for the combatants expose his prejudice: "Wowsers" and "Reds" for the Republicans and the simple but ennobling epithet

"Men" for the Nationalists. At the beginning of Part II Campbell
clarifies his bias:

> A hundred years of strife with warring vans
> Had winnowed Spain in two distinctive clans
> Upon the left, inflammable, the chaff,
> Corn to the right, the vulnerable half,
> And thus in Spanish history began
> The war between the Wowser and the Man—
>   (p. 31)

His admiration for the Carmelite fathers of Toledo, who had
heard his confession and received him into the Church, is suggested in his description of the part they played in defending the
Alcázar:

> With iron valour vascoing their ship,
> The Carmelites rose up to show the way:
> For martyrdom their eagle spirits burned
> As fierce as angry captains for the fight—
>   (Part III, p. 85)

Campbell attributed determination and courage to the Church
that warred against the "godless horde" (p. 50) of Republicans. He
conceived of the Church as a church-militant, forced to fight for
its own survival and determined to resurrect a new Spain out of
the ashes of war. He fashioned the heroic defense of the Alcázar
into a symbol of "Resurrected Spain" (p. 87). He saw the Nationalist cause as a great crusade to expel the heretics whose "dogma-
tized Utopias" (p. 36) threatened to destroy the religious as well as
social and political traditions of the country. The Church alone
gave purpose and symbolic value to the cause:

> The Army of the Peoples of the World,
> The hoarse blaspheming of the godless hoard
> Against the Cross and Crescent of the Lord,
> The Cross, our Hammer, and the Quarter Moon
> Our Sickle, and Hosanna for our tune!
>   (Part II, p. 50)

Campbell often stated that when Spain would again be ruled by the Right, it would experience an unprecedented economic revival. Under the Nationalists, he foresaw a much improved standard of living for everyone, an abundance of food, more work, and even greater international prominence. In fact, he declared that the economic transformation had already begun wherever Franco's soldiers had won victories—wherever, that is, the influence of the Church had been restored—for he believed that a fruitful economy simply could not exist under the Left. The wealth of Spain flowed only where "Christ is King" (p. 28), but:

> Where the Red Curse is, there will Hunger be!
> . . .
> They gasp to see our half-ton bullocks bleed
> Whom wealth of mighty nations failed to feed,
> To see the flocks of fat merinos spring
> From some poor provinces where Christ is King,
> Where loaves are multiplied from scanty grain
> And fishes seem deserters from the main.
> (Part I, p. 28)

Not only would the starved survivors of "Red" domination be taught the science of agriculture, but having seen the prosperity of their former enemies, they would themselves set about laboring to improve their conditions:

> Now through the Nation as our legions spread
> The richer by the poorer half is fed:
> Beside the lewd inscription, where they sprawl,
> From loafing idly charcoaled on the wall
> Hammer and Sickle to their labour fall.
> Storks to the steeples, rollers to the wires
> Return, and swallows to the broken spires—
> And men to the religion of their Sires!
> (Part I, p. 28)

Such was the restorative power of the Church that it would effect not only a religious but an economic recovery. Campbell viewed the whole Nationalist effort as an "extraordinary awakening of a national consciousness in a ruined and prostrate country" (Author's Note). It represented the needs and desires of the majority of the Spanish people, including most of the workers; only the "literate lounging class . . . that first conceived this Rabies of the brain" (p. 41), or communism, tried to obstruct this demonstration of the people's will. But the help this class received from alien "Reds" or "Wowsers" amounted to almost nothing. When they did not run away from battle, they either surrendered or defected; their very presence in Spain, Campbell contended, augured the defeat of the Republic:

> Vultures and crows so rally to the field
> And where they "group" you know the doom
>   is sealed,
> Before it hits our nostrils ripe and hot
> They've long ago divined the inward rot,
> And as by sympathy I sense the rose
> Of Victory before its buds unclose,
> So they (before it trumpets to the nose)
> Anticipate the maggot on its way,
> With it co-operate in swift decay,
> And so with one more carcass strew the way:
>   (Part I, p. 20)

The occurrence in *Flowering Rifle* which Campbell claimed he foresaw was the capture of 300 British volunteers at San Mateo (it did happen in 1938). Campbell refers to the incident repeatedly throughout *Flowering Rifle,* always in a snickering and vindictive manner. He evidently believed that they were captured because Campbell had willed it. He believed that his prophetic words had somehow directed the volunteers to their ignominious fate:

> But let these prisoners speak for my precision
> And answer for my range and drive of Vision,
> Who promised this before the war begun,
> And drilled them with my pen before my gun
>   . . .

Surrendering without a single blow
For nothing, save that I foretold it so—
. . .
The British International Brigade,
And twice predicted clearly in advance . . .

(Part I, pp. 22-23)

Claiming nature as a colleague, he maintained that nature also contrived to frustrate the labor of the Republicans by refusing to allow grass and corn to grow in their territory:

But nature's elements, except for gold,
Will shun the Yiddisher's convulsive hold,
And it's an axiom that mere eyesight yields—
Grass hates to grow on communist fields!

(Part I, p. 15)

Corn, out of shame, refused for them to grow . . .

(Part II, p. 34)

For still where Marx's influence is least,
Red fields with vestiges of grass are fleeced,
But where his lore we trample and oppose
Reviving Nature thanks us with the rose . . .

Part III, p. 79)

(The former is also one of many examples of Campbell's derisive equating of Jews and Communists.) Matter in Campbell's animistic universe does its part, too, to defeat the enemy, by showing a sort of natural hostility toward those whose insensitivity to order would force it into incongruous forms:

In its behavior, Matter proved no dolt,
And that it has opinions of its own—
. . .
Whether it's guns to fire, or bricks to pile,
Matter is always sensitive to style
(Which is the breathing rhythm of the soul)

And shows itself Devout from pole to pole:
. . .
But when democracy begins to soar
To whom the jail, the brothel, and the store,
Stand for the Church, and tries for like proportions
Matter complies with sorrowful distortions,
And rather as a slave than an ally
"Co-operates" to raise them to the sky,

                                        (Part II, p. 58)

Even the sun is made a fascist ally, and on one occasion literally bakes Russian tank crews into surrendering:

We needed tanks: as if they knew the road,
They came like bakers' vans to orders booked,
When the fierce sun their crews of Russians cooked
Who have to be like convicts bolted in—
Surrender being their one besetting sin:
And with the Centigrade at sixty-seven
Their brains were baked and yeasted in their leaven,
And what the sun began, the iron heated,
The Fahrenheit and Centigrade completed,
To save us any need of work more fiery,
As they came nosing to our mazed inquiry,
For the good sun, our ally and physician,
Had kept those dread-vans in the best condition,

                                        (Part II, p. 57)

As if it were not enough to have the natural universe take sides, Campbell declares that even the Loyalists' war machinery rebelled: "For even their machinery rebelled/And as by miracles, our armouries swelled:/Till we could almost pray for what we wanted/And take the answer to the prayer for granted," (p. 56).

This all-out effort to consecrate the Nationalists by claiming that nature, matter, and even God actively intervened on their behalf to defeat the Republicans exposes Campbell's fanatical determination to win support for his side. *Flowering Rifle* really develops no argument that might conceivably persuade anyone that the Nationalists had a better cause. For Campbell cannot conceive that any logical argument about logistics, for example, could outweigh the fact (and for him it was a fact) that the Nationalists had been blessed with holy sanction. To dispute about politics, land reform, social rights, or about the respective merits of the belligerents was irrelevant: the Nationalists were "holy crusaders," the Loyalists were "godless marauders," and this distinction, in Campbell's opinion, not only superseded debate but also made all the difference between Right and Wrong.

What is objectionable about Campbell is not just his boasting, which frequently sounds hollow, but also the tediousness of the ex-cathedra tone in which his predictions and views are uttered. And the monotony is intensified by the regularity with which these prophecies are recited or defended. Campbell's determination to impress us with "the constant certitude of his pen" (p. 26) has led to a tedious tirade in his own defense, which all but overshadows his primary purpose, which was to herald the supremacy of the Nationalist cause. Repetition is one of the propagandist's most effective tools, but it is fatal to poetry when it is used as a means of self-glorification, having little to do with the principal subject of the poem. Prejudicial is not just the absence of political neutrality (although this would be unacceptable to the impartial reader) but also the personal and spiteful tone which sparks so much of his satire. *Flowering Rifle* is uncontrolled in form and emotion.

Campbell wished to give the impression that the substance of his verse was authentic, that it was the work of one who, having lived in Spain ("As I who've lived beneath the two regimes," Part II, p. 40), had thoughtfully chosen to defend the side that was fighting to preserve Spain's best traditions. *Flowering Rifle* has the subtitle "A Poem from the Battlefield of Spain" and contains myriad details about the war and the poet. The poem has scanty explanatory notes (and those appear only in the *Collected Poems* edition of 1957). What this mass of details (including names, nicknames, places, events, etc.) does is to give it the appearance of a trustworthy document where all the information has been meticulously gathered. However, beneath the apparent factuality are extravagant claims, some of which contradict objective evidence and most of which would be difficult to corroborate: [6]

1. that the Republicans, besides having foreign aid before Franco, received alien soldiers who outnumbered foreign enlistees on Franco's side four to one:

> Such foreign aid as, later, we were lent,
> The Reds already to the front had sent,
> Out-numbering still, to-day, by four to one,
> And antedating with four months to run:
> (Part II, p. 39)

2. that whatever aid Franco received—less substantial than on the Loyalist side—"was proffered, not entreated":

> Although in foreign aid by one to four
> Outnumbered as preceded months before,
> Which on our side was proffered, not entreated
> (Part II, p. 50)

3. that the Moors, first solicited by Azaña, preferred to serve as mercenaries with Franco, even at lower pay:

> As to the Moors, whom they were first to bribe
> With their Autonomy—that Spanish tribe
> Whom they invited first . . .
> To swell the People's Army on the plain.
> Azaña's ten pesetas to refuse
> And fight for five—the Moors were free to choose
> And be called "Mercenaries" as are we
> Who in the Legion are content with three,
> . . .
> Without Autonomy, without more pay,
> They chose with us the clean equestrian way,
> (Part II, pp. 50-51)

4. that the Nationalists, by nature peace-loving, were forced to fight in order to preserve Spain from the "Red Curse" (p. 91), often only having arms captured from the Reds themselves:

> Upon the Right his would-be victim stood,
> Armed chiefly with a sense of Bad and Good,
>   (Part II, p. 32)

> When with our cities blown about our ears
> We bore in silence what they bawl in tears
> Before we had a bomber fledged to fly,
> And months before we ventured to reply;
>   (Part II, p. 34)

> Many besides myself have touched no gun
> Or cutlery, but what from them was won.
>   (Part II, p. 37)

5. that Mussolini's invasion of Ethiopia was simply a matter of settling an account with an old enemy:

> Now thanking old allies for rendered aid
> He bombs the Arabs, whom his Jews invade,
> Yet turns on Mussolini censures venomous
> Because he does the same to his old enemies.
>   (Part IV, p. 117)

6. that the Left, inclined toward "filth and famine," was completely devoid of morality, but that the "clean hands" of the Nationalists would purify the "filth and dirt" of these sham reformers:

> Invariably they side with filth and famine,
> Morality for them has never mattered,
>   (Part I, p. 21)

> Our own clean hands accept the filth and dirt,
>   (Part III, p. 74)

7. that the Left was guilty of the most callous sort of aerial bombing and of killing their own forces:

> Who bombing their best allies to their shame,
>   (Part II, p. 51)

It was natural that it (Humanitarianism) should side with the party that, at the very beginning, had slaughtered more unarmed victims than the whole war has yet slain . . .

(Author's Note, p. 8)

8. that the destruction of Guernica was the work of Loyalists who tried to blame the Nationalists for the tragedy:

> To blame us for the Reds' Subhuman crimes,
> Guernica dynamited from within
> He lays to Franco's aeroplanes the sin,
> And with humanitarian fuss makes bold
> To "save Bilbao's children" (and its gold!)
> (Part IV, pp. 114-15)

9. that, in contrast to the heroic defense of the outnumbered Nationalists, the Reds were not only uncommonly cowardly but afraid even to save their own wounded:

> And at the sight (of aurora borealis), the foe half-
>   dead with fright,
> Fled howling in their Gadarene stampede,
> Nor stop to help their comrades when they bléed
> But downwards to the ocean hurl their flight,
> And shed their arms, in mountains, on the plain,
> (Part VI, p. 156)

10. and, finally, that Franco clearly foreshadowed his greatness by bidding "the epic years begin" (p. 44), while the Red leaders revealed their cowardice by escaping Spain before the war ended.

The first edition of 1939 *Flowering Rifle* extends for 157 pages and contains six parts including more than 5000 lines. Part I is a satire of British intellectuals of that period, of their leftist tendencies and their conduct in war. Campbell criticizes the sympathies of the English generally toward Red Spain. He satirizes the contradictions of their reasoning and attacks certain individuals (Day Lewis, Auden, Spender), ending with a lyrical meditation of political and religious character.

Part II ridicules some of the established values in British society of 1920 to 1940—institutions, customs, concept of life—in the light of Spain and the Spanish war. He alludes to some traditional misconceptions of the English and eulogizes the heroic Nationalists for singlehandedly sweeping away Reds and Jews. He extracts social and moral consequences from the differing payments that the red militia and the Nationalist soldiers receive.

Part III begins with a juxtaposition of the beliefs that were conflicting in the Spanish Civil War, frequently blaming Marx and Freud. He describes the burning of the Carmelite convent of Toledo, alluding to the massacres and searches of the days of terror, and comments on the death of García Lorca, whom he considers his poetic inferior (cf. footnote on p. 199 of the 1957 edition), and of José Antonio Primo de Rivera, whom he reveres.

Part IV returns to the charge against certain personalities who have helped corrupt modern British thinking. He satirizes capitalism as much as communism and criticizes what he considers British hypocrisy and cowardice in misconstruing such incidents as Guernica and the Basque children.

Part V describes the disruption of social life induced by the Left to gain their objectives of power, and satirizes "liberty" as it is understood by them. It praises the discipline, order, and hard work of the Nationalists while deriding the stagnation, confusion, and materialism of the Republicans.

The last part begins with a description of a bloody battle that symbolizes the clash between Nationalist and Red Spain, and is suggestive of *Gulliver's Travels:* the tanks become black beetles and the men become ants. Campbell ends his poem with a description of the symbolic phenomenon of the aurora borealis that took place at the end of the war.

In its first edition (1939) *Flowering Rifle* was in six parts, prefaced by an Author's Note. Its length and heroic conception of the Nationalists are epic. The poem extends to more than 5000 four-beat lines of rhymed (heroic) couplets. There is an almost total lack of form except for the division into six parts. The poem suffers from extreme repetitiveness, even in one or two instances repeating the same lines without representing some artistic design:

> In its behavior, Matter proved no dolt,
> And that it has opinions of its own—
> As any one who's worked in wood and stone
> Can tell you . . .
>
> (Part II, p. 58)

> For Matter has opinions of its own
> As any one who's worked with wood and stone
> Can tell you . . .
>
> (Part VI, p. 154)

It appears that Campbell simply piled one contention on top of another indiscriminately, without any careful consideration to the shape of the finished poem. For instance, an argument favoring the Nationalists suddenly ends, a passage of autobiographical boasting begins (shifting to the first person), which, in turn, stops, and a section of satire on British intellectuals commences—all perhaps within a page or two, and without transition.

Like his contentions, Campbell's images are presented one upon the other, the accumulation massive. Like his ideas, many of his images are repetitive, the fat bourgeois representing the self-indulgent Republicans and gold representing their acquisitiveness. Charlie is his name for the typical left-winger. He speaks frequently of right and left hands to distinguish between the sides. But there are no encompassing images to unite the expansive poem, which suffers from diffuseness. Many of its metaphors are clichés, for example, "kill-joy parents" (p. 105), or downright antipoetic, like "banana peel" (p. 76) and "baloney" (p. 41), but such wording is perhaps appropriate to his purpose.

The poem is very uneven in thought and quality due both to its extreme length and to Campbell's lack of restraint and talent. Campbell does not achieve, nor does he aim for, sustained narration, description, or logic. The flow of thought is choppy, and the emotion fluctuates—indeed it would be impossible to sustain a sometimes hysterical tone.

While Campbell had force and humor, produced original and often witty rhymes, and while his diction could be racy and colloquial and nearly always vivid and alive, he did not have the

subtlety of ear which the manipulation of the heroic couplet re-
quires, nor could he manage the delicate variations of pace and
beat with which Dryden and Pope were able to avoid the monotony which is the chief peril of the form. Worse, writing in heroic
couplets encouraged Campbell's great weakness, a tendency to the
prolix; and it may be said that all his poems in this meter suffer
from monotony and go on far too long.

Verse is, perhaps, the worst vehicle for argument, and, in particular, political argument. *Flowering Rifle* is more tedious than
most political poems because of its enormous length, its intermi-
nable tirades, and its savage vituperation, in which Campbell, in
political and emotional isolation (from everyone else I have read
on the subject), often seemed to lose all sense of proportion.

His battle scenes, especially those describing the siege of the
Alcázar, are brilliant pageantry and reveal his attitude about war
as a glorious contest. He felt an overwhelming ecstasy marching
into battle:

> How thrilling sweet, as in the dawn of Time,
> Under our horses smokes the pounded thyme
> As we go forward; streaming into battle
> Down on the road the crowded lorries rattle
> Wherein the gay blue-shirted boys are singing,
> As to a football match the rowdies bringing—
> But of this match the wide earth is the ball
> And by its end shall Europe stand or fall:
>
> (Part VI, p. 138)

Considered one of Scotland's greatest modern poets, Hugh
MacDiarmid (the pseudonym of Christopher Murray Grieve) was
born in Langholm, Dumfriesshire, near the Scottish-English border, in 1892.[7] His native language was Scots. His father was a rural
postman whose people had been mill workers. His mother's people had been agricultural workers, but Christopher's faith lay with
the industrial, not the rural, and in the growth of the third factor
between Man and Nature—the Machine. His development owed
a great deal to his growing up in a working-class family. He spent

his childhood in the Scottish Border country, where he came into contact with a life which, in his own words, was "raw, vigorous, rich, bawdy, and simply bursting with life and gusto." He was later to bring his broad awareness of natural phenomena and love of color into his poems.

The Langholm Public Library was housed in the same building as the Grieve family, and he had free access to a collection of "upwards of twelve thousand books." By his own account he had "certainly read almost every one of them" by the time he left home for Edinburgh at the age of fourteen.[8] He was an omnivorous reader and note-taker, as the eclecticism of his works testifies. Nothing was wasted upon the boy—his nearness to neither the land, working people, nor books.

Such difficulties as came about between the adolescent boy and his family seem to have centered on the "ambitious gentility" of his mother and the opposition of both parents to his early decision to become a poet. His break with their devout religion appears to have been accomplished with a minimum of recrimination, perhaps because he retained a deep awareness of religious issues while rejecting all the orthodoxies.

He was educated at Langholm Academy, Broughton Junior Student Centre (Edinburgh), and Edinburgh University. When his father died in 1911, Grieve had already joined various local socialist societies. His political nationalism grew out of his reading of Scottish history and literature, and the search for Scottish unity became one of the main concerns of his life. In 1912 he turned to journalism and worked until 1920 as editor-reporter of *The Montrose Review*. When World War I erupted, he served as a member of the Royal Army Medical Corps. Again in Montrose, he edited three issues of the first postwar Scottish verse anthology, *Northern Numbers* (1921-1923). In 1922 he founded the monthly *Scottish Chapbook,* in which he advocated a Scottish literary revival (or "Renaissance") and published the lyrics of "Hugh MacDiarmid," later collected as *Sangschaw* (1925) and *Penny Wheep* (1926). Grieve's first book, entirely of his own work, was *Annals of the Five Senses* (1923), in which poems alternate with prose pieces. Rejecting English as a medium for Scottish poetry, Grieve wrote in "synthetic" Scots, an amalgam of elements from various dialects and literary sources, and he achieved notable success both in his lyrics and in *A Drunk Man Looks at the Thistle* (1926), a long, semiphilosophical poem, ranging from investigation of his own personality to exploration of the mysteries of time and space. Later, as he became increasingly involved in metaphysical speculation and accepted the philosophy of dialectical materialism, he found it difficult to express his themes adequately in modern Scots, which had lost most of its intellectual terminology. After writing Scotticized English in *To Circumjack Cencrastus* (1930) and archaic Scots in *Scots Unbound* (1932), he returned to "King's English" and sought to produce a "poetry of fact" in *Stony Limits* (1934) and *Second Hymn to Lenin* (1935), where his treatment of Scottish scenes and social circumstances has all the verve and penetration, though less of the ironic humor and the formal dexterity, of his earlier work in Scots. He realized the frustration of readers because of his alternation between Scots and English: "I write now in English, and now in Scots/To the despair of friends who plead/ For consistency: sometimes achieve the true lyric cry,/Next but chopped up prose . . ."

In 1929 he went to London to become London editor of *Vox*, a radio critical journal. He then spent a year in Liverpool as publicity officer, returning to London a little later to join a publishing firm. His domestic affairs were in a bad state and led to divorce in 1931. He married again shortly thereafter, but with little money or income. His determination early in life was to avoid the acquisition of money, a principle on which he seems not to have compromised. He and his family endured extreme physical hardship and poverty, and his physical and psychological suffering resulted in a serious, general breakdown in 1935.

He thought of communism as the hope of downtrodden humanity, and by the end of 1932, he was describing himself in print as a communist, though he did not join the Party until 1934. After much trouble with the Scottish Nationalists because of his communism, and with the communists because of his nationalism, he was expelled from the Communist Party in 1938, the reason ascribed to his nationalistic deviation in regard to the Spanish Civil War. He did not rejoin until 1957, precisely when so many members were leaving the Party because of the Hungarian uprising.

The reason for his timing is unclear considering the nature of the Hungarian suppression, but MacDiarmid has written in his prose work *The Uncanny Scot* (London, 1968, p. 170) that only a convinced communist would have remained loyal at such a time.

He moved from London to Whalsay (Shetland) in 1933 and remained until 1941. There he wrote *The Golden Treasury of Scottish Poetry, Lucky Poet,* and *The Islands of Scotland.* After the outbreak of World War II, he returned to Scotland to work first for a large engineering firm and then entered the Merchant Service as a First Engineer. He was fifty-three years old at the war's end.

After the war he lived on dole, and only after about twenty years of struggle did his life assume some comfort and security. He was awarded an honorary LL.D. from Edinburgh University in 1957, but it was in 1962 that the real breakthrough came, the occasion being his seventieth birthday, celebrated all over the world.

In almost all MacDiarmid's thought and work, two or three interrelated themes have been constant: Scottish Nationalism (which includes anti-Englishism), the literary revival of Scots and Gaelic, and communism. His work falls into three main categories—lyrical poetry, nonlyrical poetry, and prose criticism and polemical writing. His lyrical poetry is MacDiarmid's richest and most permanent contribution to literature. There is a directness of statement in both the longer and shorter works that is both moving and unusual, revolutionary, yet deeply traditional.

His poetry was political from the outset, though he is outside the Auden-Spender-Day Lewis group. In "Lo! A Child is Born" (from *Second Hymn to Lenin*) the marvel of the birth of a child is stated against a political background of the unemployed and hungry:

> Then I thought of the whole world . . .
> There is a monstrous din of the sterile who con-
>   tribute nothing
> To the great end in view, and the future fumbles,
> A bad birth, not like the child in that gracious home.

While such poets on the Left as Auden, Spender, and Lewis left barely one unquestionably outstanding piece of Marxist writing, there are among Hugh MacDiarmid's poems twenty pieces in which his Marxism or communism found a style, an imagery, and a rhythm, that drew upon the very fabric of that movement. MacDiarmid's poems combined a truly Marxist intellectual content and a truly vernacular speech-idiom. He was the first important communist poet in Britain (his *First Hymn to Lenin* preceded any of the so-called communist poetry of the Auden group). Passionate admirer of Lenin though he was, his communism is not doctrinaire and he is no man for a party line. Rather it is the expression of his revolt against modern capitalist civilization and what it has done to Scotland:

> For I am like Zamyatin. I must be a Bolshevik
> Before the Revolution, but I'll cease to be one quick
> When Communism comes to rule the roost,
> For real literature can exist only where it's produced
> By madmen, hermits, heretics,
> Dreamers, rebels, sceptics,
> —And such a door of utterance has been given me
> As none may close whosoever they be.[9]

It would have been surprising if a man who despised mere logical consistency in every other respect were to be a party-liner in his politics; and, in fact, he interpreted communist doctrine in his own highly individualistic way: "I am a poet; our fools ask me for logic not life." [10]

Between 1935 and the appearance of his *Collected Poems* in 1962, very little poetry by MacDiarmid was published in book form, and nearly all of it is fragmentary. *The Battle Continues,* published in 1957 in Edinburgh, was an exception and seems something of an anomaly, appearing almost twenty years after the event which inspired it, the Spanish Civil War. He kept voluminous notes for his works over the years, and it seems likely that he had written *The Battle Continues* long before getting back to it and having it published. MacDiarmid had not been in Spain prior to or during the war. His long, polemical poem was a reaction mainly against Campbell's *Flowering Rifle,* fascism, and capitalism. The book went unnoticed and unreviewed in the United States. There is much that corresponds between his poem and Campbell's, making its inclusion here essential.

His *Collected Poems,* brought out first in America, was published belatedly in Scotland, where Edwin Morgan wrote in the *Glasgow Herald:*

> . . . What he may lose to T. S. Eliot in fastidious precision of language or to Ezra Pound in music and cadence, he gains in the greater interest of his subject-matter . . . what he loses to Wallace Stevens in brilliance of metaphor and symbol he gains by command of simile and analogy. Why then has he not achieved the estimation these poets have achieved? [11]

The Battle Continues, inspired by the Spanish Civil War and impelled glaringly by a negative, hostile reaction to Roy Campbell and his *Flowering Rifle,* is 107 pages long. It is lengthy in keeping with its "impetus," the even longer *Flowering Rifle.* Mac-Diarmid has written a devastating denunciation, putting an enormous amount of energy into this work and displaying an excess of vituperation.

There is in the nature of the man a suitability to the type of poem he chose to write. Although their beliefs were diametrically opposed, MacDiarmid and Campbell shared certain tendencies which encouraged them to produce similar poems. They were both passionate, talkative, strongly opinionated, outspoken, energetic, and practically fanatical. Their egos seem immense. But although they both wrote long, subjective, denunciatory poems, there are fundamental, important differences.

The Battle Continues is a major reaction in 1957 (publication date) to Campbell's stand in *Flowering Rifle.* It may be a parody of Campbell's poem, which would account for its similarity in form and structure. But it has an additional twist, philosophically, against everything Campbell represented. If MacDiarmid wrote the poem prior to 1957, it is not clear why he waited so long to publish it. Epistolary inquiry produced no answer from the poet.

MacDiarmid is basically an idealist with a philosophical bent toward polemics. Though he clings to communism as man's hope, his belief in man's justice has frequently been shattered—which accounts for his bitterness and disillusionment, though never pessimism. The epigraphs to the book are, not surprisingly, cynical: ". . . O God, giver of Light, hater of Darkness, of Hypocrisy and Cowardice, how long, how long!" and "Chrétiens d'Espagne, vous êtes abandonnés." MacDiarmid was a Scottish nationalist with a deep feeling and affinity for the common, working man. He could, therefore, identify with the masses of Spaniards in their fight against oppression, greed, crime, cant, and possible extinction. He looked at Spain from the overview of a Scottish nationalist and, in a sense, took Spain out of its time and place, seeing the universality of the fight.

The poem begins with a direct, caustic attack upon Campbell:

> Anti-Fascism is a bit out of date, isn't it?
> All just yesterday's pancakes now?
> And all the Spanish War newspaper clippings
> Dried out like the lives of so many of my friends?
> Forgotten—that's the way you would like it,
> Calf-fighter Campbell, I have no doubt,
> But there's an operation to do first
> —To remove the haemorrhoids you call your poems
> With a white-hot poker for cautery,
> Shoved right up through to your tonsils!
>
> (p. 1)

The attack is ad hominem, with insult heaped upon insult with little reasonable development of ideas: "Campbell, they call him —'crooked mouth,' that is—" (p. 1). The attack on Franco is equally personal:

> A lock of lank hair falls over an insignificant
> And slightly retreating forehead. The back head is
>   shallow.
> The nose is large but badly shaped and without
>   character.
> His movements are awkward, almost undignified.
> There is no trace in his face of any inner conflict

Or self-discipline. Fit generalissimo, Campbell,
    For conscript armies armed with flowering
        rifles!

(p. 52)

The language is abusive, unrelenting, and can be scatological: "speaking with a voice not only banal/But absolutely anal" (p. 1). MacDiarmid manipulates gross, unpoetic language to convey the nature of his emotion. According to MacDiarmid, Campbell has brutally betrayed "Everything noble and disinterested,/Everything that elevates the life of man" (p. 6) and MacDiarmid attacks him:

The same dislocation affects, it's clear,
His eyes and brain and so-called soul as well,
While if his rifle flowers it only bears
Such roses as in syphilis a penis wears.

(p. 6)

His picking up of such terms as "penis" and "syphilis" is a direct retort to Campbell's overbearing assertion of *machismo,* and MacDiarmid plays on Campbell's virility problem.

The quotations to support the poet's views are well chosen and appropriately inserted. A "Mickiewicz" has somewhere stated what MacDiarmid considers true of Campbell:

Sunk in tyranny—he who once was human,
Abandoned by the Lord to slow corruption,
He has driven from him like an evil thing
His last resource of conscience.

(pp. 1-2)

MacDiarmid presents analogies and disparities by direct statement or in the form of metaphors, anecdotes, and quotations. For example, MacDiarmid compares the massacre of a vulnerable Spanish people to the sport of a bullfight, with Campbell fulfilling a "degrading thirst after outrageous stimulation":

To have an indomitable great pain-blinded people
To torture in your bloody bull-ring for a change!

. . .

For who can add insult to injury more deftly than
   you
Or salt an open wound to please the afficionados
   better?

(p. 3)

MacDiarmid sustains a sarcastic tone: "You (Campbell) are indeed an honourable man" (p. 3). He further jibes:

And I am perfectly entranced for my part
Not only with your expertise but even more
With your genial courtesy and largeness of heart,

(pp. 3-4)

There is no doubting that Campbell is anathema, for MacDiarmid keeps the words in proper perspective. When he quotes Edmund Blunden's praise of *Flowering Rifle*, "Nobody else could have struck such a blow in verse," the irony of his pun is unmistakable. The first line of the poem questions rhetorically a situation which MacDiarmid would not have admitted nor permitted to be true: "Anti-Fascism is a bit out of date . . ." (p. 1). But there are other times when the poet is less coy and gives full vent to his bitterly ironic attack: "All that's diseased, malformed, obscene,/Mankind accepts and guards" (p. 11) and "Rien que la mediocrité est bon./ C'est sortir de l'humanité/Que de sortir du milieu." (p. 11).

Among the images of the poem is one of light and darkness. With the darkness-decay of Campbell, MacDiarmid juxtaposes the light-life of Lenin: ". . . Ah, Lenin,/Life and that more abundantly, thou Fire of Freedom!" (p. 10).

It is at first disconcerting that MacDiarmid should write in a poem published in 1957 on the subject of the Spanish Civil War: "The forces of 'life and that/More abundantly' will triumph in the end" (p. 10). And further:

It is impossible that Franco can win
Since his victory would represent
The abandonment of all human hope, . . .

(p. 11)

It is not until the third of the three parts of the poem that the
reader understands upon what MacDiarmid's hope is sustained.
And, furthermore, in the sense of his broad historical view, the
success or defeat of fascism is still a pregnant question.

MacDiarmid transfers his insults from Campbell the bullfighter
to Campbell the poet he claims to be. "Hitler the painter, Campbell the poet!" (p. 12). The analogy is pungent. He expands his
comparison to Republican and fascist poetry: "Poetry versus Animal Noises,/Our cause versus yours!" (p. 13). He denigrates Campbell's poetry by declaring that fascism can breed no true poets:
"You are no true poet that they (fascists) tolerate you./No poet
worth a damn is on your side." (p. 14), and "you, Campbell, stand
for all/The hypocrisy, falsity, and callousness of the Law, . . ."
(p. 14). This is not a developed argument, but the implication is
that poetry demands a commitment to life whereas Hitlerism leads
to death.

He considers Campbell the "Nadir of English Literature" (p. 16)
and includes Lorca as a dynamic contrast to Campbell: "Lorca
dead lives forever./Campbell, living, is dead and rots." (p. 15).

MacDiarmid attempts to define poetry:

Men of work! We want our poetry from you,
From men who will dare to live
A brave and true life.

(p. 19)

Again taking a broad view, MacDiarmid equates culture, poetry,
and people, stressing that Spanish art and culture have always been
close to the people. Of the two poetries, that of the Republic and
that of the fascists, he reaffirms that poetry can only be on the side
of the people—on the liberal Left.

The Battle Continues is largely political and didactic, and Mac-
Diarmid explains that the military insurgents of Spain are fascists,

"Supported by foreign states and marching hand in hand/With the catholic church and the capitalists" (p. 20). He prophesies the death of the bourgeoisie and the supremacy of communism and democracy over capitalism. He denounces the Moorish mercenaries and curses all fascists:

> It were better that you all should rot in your vices
> In the bottomless filth of damnation,
> And that they (Spanish comrades) should live!
>
> (p. 17)

He takes a final swipe against Campbell's manhood and poetry: "He's poor shakes as a soldier and poorer as a poet!" (p. 24).

Part II begins with the admonition that we should "endlessly boycott" the forces of evil that caused this Spanish tragedy and that among these forces Campbell is but an insignificant tool. Campbell had lived among the Spaniards and been proud of it. MacDiarmid relegates his relation to Spain to that of a tourist and aficionado. And as to Campbell's ability to make judgments, MacDiarmid contends that he had no intimate insights to offer and toyed with Spanish anguish in a superficial way. He continues his denunciation by contrast: "Lorca, not Campbell!/Christ, not Barabbas!" (p. 34).

Reminiscent of the open-mindedness of Felipe's *La insignia*, in which he criticized the factions of his fellow Spaniards, MacDiarmid here turns against the English and puts them on an even lower level than the Nazis and fascists:

> There is nothing the Nazis and Fascists have done
> That the English haven't done again and again
> In the name of very different ideals, of course,
> And are not repeating or trying to repeat
> Continually. The horrors of Czechoslovakia
> And China and Spain are the very stuff
> Our Empire is founded upon. We have nothing to
>   learn
> From Hitler or Mussolini. We've forgotten more
>   than they know . . .
>
> (p. 34)

But then we realize that MacDiarmid is for the Spanish masses, the Spanish Republic, all working people of the world, communism, nationalism (Scottish, especially), and that his bias is indeed consistent and is dead-set against fascism, Nazism, capitalism, colonialism, and oppression anywhere.

He pits his faith in the Spanish Republic ("I sing of the Spanish Republic,/Of men who went to their deaths not with the hope of victory," (p. 36)—which shows MacDiarmid had learned something from Walt Whitman) against his disdain for the fascists and, also, for the British: "Struggling to think and feel as little as possible" (p. 39). As for the Queen, he profanes her name, too:

> a great bloated watery mass,
> Safe in a dark cavity for underground,
> With nevertheless a power so all-pervading
> (pp. 39-40)

MacDiarmid expresses his pride over being Scottish and claims that 90 per cent of the Scottish had supported the Republican cause.

His next classification of Campbell is that of "Cheer-Leader of World Fascism" (p. 46). He sees Campbell as an active spectator, a sideliner with fervor and zeal at best, and not as an important participant. Athletic Campbell is for MacDiarmid a kind of world cheerleader/tourist/aficionado. He despises those who might applaud Campbell, such as Hitler, Mussolini, Franco, and Chamberlain. Chamberlain's gross capitulation is summed up by a brutal anecdote attributed to Tolstoy. MacDiarmid's anecdotes are potent weapons of abuse.

Again the poet asks a curious question for 1957: "if Fascism wins —who would wish to live?" (p. 56). He is not talking about only Spain now, but looking at fascism in a broad historical perspective and condemning it to extinction. MacDiarmid is applying his considerations to a contemporary, universal setting. The thrust of the poem is not to give a sense of time and place, but to present a broader perspective essential to both his title and his theme.

His extended criticism of bourgeois capitalism is based on its lack of creativity, spirit, spine, and substance. It is practical (a sin to an idealist), self-indulgent, and without culture, morals, or religion (in its ethical ramifications, presumably).

The end of Part II contrasts Campbell with Heine. Heine chose communism out of a "generosity of despair" because "every man has the right to eat" (p. 60). Like Heine, MacDiarmid believes:

> . . . the future belongs to Communism
> And that the present system is rotten from top
>   to bottom
>
> (p. 61)

He concludes, "But there is no generosity of despair in you, Campbell, . . ." and besides "Heine's a poet," the insinuation being clear.

Part III is the most ideological, idealistic, and hopeful of the three parts. It is also the part based most on reasonable arguments, and gives us a good indication of the political, economic, and social background of the Spanish Civil War, as well as of the poet's hope for the future. He generalizes about the human will and the cause for which the Spanish Republicans fought and died. But out of the defeat of the temporal battle, he praises their spiritual victory:

> I thank you, my Spanish comrades, for this most
>   timely
> And invaluable reassurance—
> For vouchsafing me so wonderful a spectacle
> Of the movement of individual will
> Towards a common beckoning good,
> Always distant, yet always implicit
> In love and in understanding,
> And the only alternative to callousness and
>   despair,
> And for all the glimpses you have given me of
>   the incredible beauty
> Of those who give themselves while they are yet
>   young
> Selflessly, to a noble Cause.
>
> (p. 63)

The imagery is abstracted, idealistic, and lyrical. The trajectory of the poem begins at the level of the sewer, with its anal cavities, and moves upwards, reaching the idealism of the Spanish people. Their sacrifice is juxtaposed with the hypocritical self-interest of Franco. The language alternates between coarse, gutter, street language and abstract, lyrical, idealistic language.

MacDiarmid prides himself on the Marxist philosophy Campbell had detested. MacDiarmid blames Franco for Guernica, the shelling of civilian Madrid, and "pointless wholesale cruelties" (p. 70).

Their lack of ethical values is disguised by the lip service the Nationalists give to religion: "Where is the humanitarian heart of the millions/Who go to Church and pray to God . . ." (p. 70). They are superstitious and lack understanding. Dictators are vile as evidenced by the ruthlessness with which Franco "handled" even fellow-Spaniards.

MacDiarmid glorifies the International Brigade ("Ideals of duty and sacrifice"—p. 77) and writes some of his most lyrical lines to commemorate them.

According to MacDiarmid, Franco, like Campbell, has no real significance, and will be forgotten by history. But he sees the Spanish people themselves as admirable and wishes that the British resembled them.

MacDiarmid distinguishes the Left from the Right, the Republicans from the Nationalists/fascists. He asserts romantically and idealistically that it is better to fail on the side of humanity than to win with Hitler, Mussolini, Franco, Chamberlain. The side of mankind is unlimited in potentiality and vitality while the other side is rotten or dead.

MacDiarmid also expresses strong anti-Bloomsbury sentiment:

> And Auden, Spender, Allott, Grigson,
> The Woolfs, the *New Statesman* clique,
> All Left Fascists, so very pointedly unrevolutionary,
> Writing nothing any "intelligent" Fascist
> Might not equally well write.
>
> (p. 85)

MacDiarmid felt that the work of Auden and Spender was completely antipopular and anti-Scottish as well. They do not belong to the working class while MacDiarmid does. He had no use for them or any of the English Literary Left. Their grasp of socialist theory was always inadequate—which characterized the English movement in general. Besides, the English Left is an incongruity since it arises in an oppressor-country.

Much like Felipe in *La insignia* and for the same reasons, Mac-Diarmid denounces in a definite order:

> I prefer the forthright brutality and aggression
>   of Hitler
> To the smug double-crossing and sanctimonious
>   hypocrisy
> Of Britain's umbrella-bearer.
>
>   (p. 85)

MacDiarmid presents his political values most clearly in this third and final part of the poem. The ideology of democracy encompasses social change and a search for truth. These values will survive "though my comrades themselves are slain" (p. 86). He shares their belief "in the philosophy/Of equality of opportunity" (p. 86). He understands "that the revolution had its roots/In the social life of Spain" (p. 88) and that "the Republic was justified in seeking/A drastic transformation of Spain's economic life" (p. 87).

In Britain, where all the Institutions work against the people, MacDiarmid predicts:

> I confidently believe that the day is near
> When Capitalism will be abolished here
> And Labour will rule the British Isles
> But . . . it won't come without a fight,
> And a bitter one!
>
>   (p. 89)

He fears the British proletariat could be betrayed, as the Spanish people had been.

After accusing Campbell of nursing an inferiority complex, he goes on, like Dante, to arrange people in Hell; he would place

Mussolini's supporters ("Hateful to God and to the enemies of God!"—p. 94) even below Mussolini.

He accepts the tragic past of Manchuria, Ethiopia, Spain, China, Austria, and Czechoslovakia, only because they are established facts. But he is optimistic about the future, because deliverance can come through wisdom and courage. According to him, we must demand truth. We must redouble our efforts for peace (*The Battle Continues*). And we must choose democracy, because "Democracy is the best form of government" (p. 96) and dictatorship is the worst.

He repeats some of his previous contentions: ". . . criminal and stupid murder/Of García Lorca who took no part in politics" (p. 98). The Spaniards were without illusions and "knew what they were fighting for." (p. 99).

The end of the poem offers an ecstatic eulogy to the Spanish workers who fought ("one against ten/Against World Fascism"— p. 105) and were killed. Their spirit transcends the temporal disaster and pervades the world (cf. poem's title).

He closes his poem with a renewed attack on Campbell's poetry:

> And your poetry is the sort of stuff one expects
> From a mouth living close to a sewer
> And smelling like a legacy from Himmler.
>
> (p. 106)

His final analogy by means of an anecdote is abrasive and unforgiving as he buries *Flowering Rifle* along with Campbell.

The poem is divided into three main parts and into many stanzas. Some of the stanzas are titled; others are simply quotations from other writers. The poem bristles with so many quotations from others that it looks like an anthology if one simply thumbs through the pages. Yet the diverse nature of the quotations—an indication of the astonishing range of MacDiarmid's reading and retention—and their order and arrangement in relation to the poet's presentation of his own ideas, gives the book some of its power and uniqueness. MacDiarmid makes eclectic use of widespread material. The poem combines quotations from other writers, expressions from foreign languages, dialogue, and references and allusions to worldwide figures—literary, political, and others.

MacDiarmid relies at times upon rhyme. His language varies from the clichés of pamphleteering to flights of beautiful expression. Some of his imagery is poetic; other images are purposely repulsive; and some of his lines lack images altogether. Some of his unpoetic language may parody Campbell's poem. But, when he chooses, MacDiarmid can manage a rich technique, deriving from emotional impetus, imagery, and lyric quality.

He abandoned traditional meter and allowed himself great rhythmic freedom. His tendency is to drop into prosaic rhythms— prosaic in the sense that our ear tells us they belong to prose contexts of a comparatively unimaginative order—for example:

> No man or group of men has any right
> To force another man or other groups of men
> To do anything he or they do not wish to do.
> There is no right to govern without
> The consent of the governed. Consent is not only
> Important in itself, and as a nidus for freedom
> And its attendant spontaneity, (clearly valuable
> As the opposed sense of frustration is detrimental),
>   but the sole
> Basis of political obligation. . . .
>
> > (p. 5)

Freed from traditional discipline, MacDiarmid lets the poem run on for too long. But some of its lyricism is striking, for example:

> Ah, Spain, already your tragic landscapes
> And the agony of your War to my mind appear
> As tears may come into the eyes of a woman very
>   slowly,
> So slowly as to leave them clear!
>
> Spain! The International Brigade! At the moment
>   it seems
> As though the pressure of a loving hand had gone,
> (Till the next proletarian upsurge!)

> The touch under which my close-pressed fingers
>   seemed to thrill,
> And the skin to divide up into little zones
> Of heat and cold whose position continually
>   changed,
> So that the whole of my hand, held in that clasp,
> Was in a state of internal movement.
> My eyes that were full of pride,
> My hands that were full of love,
> Are empty again . . . for a while.
>   For a little while!
>
>   (pp. 85-86)

There is more repetition and playing upon sound in this passage than in the previously quoted one. The first four lines contain a number of soft vowel sounds, mostly "a" and "o." There is skillful parallelism of presentation as he repeats Spain and other words ("hand," "that were full of," etc.). Here beauty and meaning are blended.

The support and illustrations for MacDiarmid's points include statistics although, as with Campbell's "facts," these are strongly stated and would be difficult to support:

> One out of every 25 Spaniards dead,
> And another one wounded;
> A million lives lost in all,
> A quarter of them civilians,
> At a cost of 22 hundred million pounds
> —(Enough to have given the whole population
>   of Spain
> Abundance in perpetuity
> Instead of the terrible distress
> That is all it has purchased).
>
>   (p. 2)

His facts are oversimplified: ". . . in Spain the arms were on one side" (p. 28). The exaggeration here appeals for an emotional reaction. However, much of his argument relies upon a reasonable, ideological basis. He names places, people, and events; he quotes others (though out of context). Such evidence lends credence to his views. He is certainly partisan, and he deviates from neutrality in the direction of liberalism, Marxism, and democracy, and, most importantly, toward humanitarianism. He believes in mankind. He is an idealist interested in changing the world. But, at the same time, he was very emotionally antagonized by Campbell and his fascist cohorts. Some of MacDiarmid's attack is as subjective as Campbell's, but as the poem progresses the poet relies more upon a reasonable argument.

His poem is often passionate. His abuse is sometimes humorous. He makes effective use of puns and includes powerful illustrative material.

The Battle Continues is an unforgiving, injustice-collecting effort. It is a long, bitter, accusing indictment, but with hope sustained through the enduring spirit of the working class. Mac-Diarmid addressed all of his works in the first place to his fellow countrymen. However, within the poem he verbally addresses Campbell, Blunden, his Spanish comrades, profascists, International Brigades, Spain, among others, depending upon his focus or point.

He juxtaposes his material, is somewhat repetitious of ideas, stoops to namecalling at times, uses nouns to categorize his opponents rather than more temporary adjectives, but manages, especially in Part III, to develop an argument that convinces and shows a broad basis of knowledge and understanding of the complexities of the Spanish Civil War.

Wystan Hugh Auden, Anglo-American poet, dramatist, and literary critic, was born on February 21, 1907, in York, England.[12] The son of refined, enlightened parents, he had what Campbell would have called a bourgeois upbringing. His father was a surgeon, his mother a cultured woman of Anglican learning. His grandfathers and four uncles were Anglican clergymen. His name was Nordic, and his background, affinities, and tastes Northern. He lived in the Midlands, where he came in contact with Britain's industrial area. From York his family moved to Birmingham, where he had firsthand experience of economic depression. Growing up during the

Great Depression, when unemployment was at a peak in England, Auden and his contemporaries, in sympathy with the problems of the working class, looked to Marxism as a possible solution to social conditions and to Sigmund Freud for answers to the spiritual barrenness resulting from these conditions. He received his education at Gresham's School and Christ Church, Oxford (1925-1928). His earliest interests were scientific (geology, machinery, and mining), and his specialty was biology. While at Oxford he developed an interest in psychology. Afterwards, from 1928 to 1929, he visited pre-Hitler Germany. When he returned to England, he became a schoolmaster.

Auden was fully conscious of the disintegration of values and the forces which were to produce Hitler and the Spanish Civil War. He visited Spain from January to March, 1937, from a desire at least "to do something" (cf. "Conversation with Claud Cockburn," *The Review,* No. 11/12, July, 1964, p. 51). *Spain,* the only poem he overtly wrote about the Spanish Civil War and his most famous political poem, resulted from his brief trip and was first published as a pamphlet in May of 1937, the proceeds being donated to the British Medical Unit in Spain.

But Auden's social and political concern was subordinate to his interest in the nature of man and in the roots of his social and individual problems (metaphysics). Several related themes run throughout Auden's work. He sees man as an individual isolated in society. "Musée des Beaux Arts" emphasizes this separation; suffering, says Auden, "takes place while someone else is eating or opening a window or just walking dully along":

> In Brueghel's *Icarus,* for instance: how everything
>   turns away
> Quite leisurely from the disaster; the ploughman
>   may
> Have heard the splash, the forsaken cry,
> But for him it was not an important failure . . .

As early as his undergraduate days, Auden had told Spender that the "poet must have no opinions, no decided views which he seeks to put across in his poetry" and that "poetry must in no way be concerned with politics." [13] Probably disgusted with the condition of Europe, Auden immigrated to America in 1939, with no intention of returning. In America he exchanged his inclination toward Marxism for a commitment to Christianity, becoming an Anglo-Catholic about 1940. This conversion to Christianity provided him with a conceptual and emotional framework.

In both his pre-Christian and Christian poems Auden wrote of love as the salvation of mankind, but both humanistic and Christian love in his poetry are extremely impersonal. Even the so-called love lyric "Lay Your Sleeping Head My Love" is strangely abstract:

> Beauty, midnight, vision dies.
> Let the winds of down that blow
> Softly round your dreaming head
> Such a day of sweetness show
> Eye and knocking heart may bless,
> Find the mortal world enough;
> Noons of dryness see you fed
> By the involuntary powers,
> Night of insult let you pass
> Watched by every human love.

Auden also wrote of the necessity for human relationships and mutual concern. His view is well expressed in these lines from *For the Time Being* (1944):

> Space is the Whom our loves are needed by,
> Time is our choice of How to love and Why.

While Marx and Freud were anathema to Campbell, Auden found in them a psychological approach to social evils and a philosophical conception of the condition of man which anticipated his later approach to existentialism. Based on the firm foundation of Marx and Freud, Auden had a keen, objective, reporter's sense of scientific observation.

His first volume of *Poems* (1930) combined ideas from Marx, Darwin, Freud, and Homer Lane, and celebrated in conversational rhythms the decay of middle-class society and his hopes for a new order. It showed Auden's versatile style and originality.

His next work, *The Orators—An English Study* (1932), dedicated
to Stephen Spender, gave a rather immature picture of the twentieth-century "hero" as a young airman. The book offered a prophetic picture of the idealists who were to fight in the Spanish
Civil War, and it showed a country in crisis. By this time, Auden,
though not a professed communist, was commonly considered one;
at least, he was one of the group of so-called leftist writers, including Spender, Christopher Isherwood, Louis MacNeice, and C. Day
Lewis, who directed their writing toward a search for meaning in
a world which seemed to them empty and mechanical.

The social criticism implicit in *The Orators* became explicit in
his most Marxist poetic play, *The Dance of Death* (1933), and in
the three dramatic works he composed with Isherwood, the most
notable being *The Dog Beneath the Skin* (1935) and *The Ascent
of F. 6* (1936). The gist of *The Dance of Death* is summed up in
the Announcer's opening words: "We present to you this evening
a picture of the decline of a class, of how its members dream of a
new life, but secretly desire the old, for there is death inside
them. . . ." The play was a satire on the decadence of the bourgeoisie in the 1930s. *The Dog Beneath the Skin,* a satirical parody
of ecclesiastical eloquence employed in the interest of political
propaganda, denounced upper-class hypocrisy, while *The Ascent
of F. 6* showed its hero, driven by the ambitious and false values
of his parents and their bourgeois social milieu, undertaking the
ascent of Mt. Everest. In *On the Frontier* (1938) Auden passed
from the concept of the individual versus society to the plane of
international catastrophe through a conflict of ideologies.

With Isherwood again, he wrote *Journey to a War* (1939), an
account of their visit to China. Gradually Auden's idiom became
less private and his technique more sure. *Look, Stranger!* (1936)
and in 1940 *Another Time* (which included a reissue of the poem
"Spain 1937," first published in 1937 as *Spain* and the text of
which varied slightly from the original edition) [14] encompass the
period covering the Spanish Civil War and the events leading up
to the Second World War.

After coming to the United States, Auden lectured at a number
of universities and, in 1946, became a U.S. citizen. Auden published over a dozen collections of poems after coming to America,

including *Nones* in 1951, *The Shield of Achilles* in 1955, and *The Old Man's Road* in 1956. He won the 1948 Pulitzer Prize for *The Age of Anxiety* (1947) and the 1953 Bollingen Prize in Poetry. From 1956 to 1961, he was Professor of Poetry at Oxford University, although his home remained the United States until 1972, when he returned to Oxford. He died in Vienna in 1973.

Auden was, from first to last, a moralist who wanted his poems to arouse his audience into critical self-awareness and to incite them to reform (at first politically and then religiously). His poems are characteristically ironic, indirect, impersonal, and largely "anti-poetic." They are composed of a bewildering mixture of flippancies and profundities. He can be witty, as in the following verse from "Law Like Love" (from Part III, 1939-1947, of his *Collected Shorter Poems, 1927-1957*):

> Law, says the judge as he looks down his nose,
> Speaking clearly and most severely,
> Law is as I've told you before,
> Law is as you know I suppose,
> Law is but let me explain it once more,
> Law is The Law.

And he can be gloomy, as in "Journey to Iceland" (from Part II, 1933-1938, of the *Collected Shorter Poems, 1927-1957*):

> Where is the homage? When
> Shall justice be done? O who is against me?
> Why am I always alone?

After the relatively free early poems, Auden's mature verse, starting in the middle 1930s, embodies a deep commitment to the precision of formal control as a means of controlling and stimulating the imagination.

According to Spender, "The effect of the turmoil of the 1930s on Auden's poetry was a tremendous inflow of new impressions, influences, and ideas, which he met with an ever-increasing virtuosity. Auden belonged more with his conscience than either with head or heart to the antifascist movement of this time. He felt, as others did, that fascism was wicked, political persecution a crime, and the Spanish Republic the best cause of the first half of the twentieth century." [15]

In *Spain* (1937) Auden revealed his reforming enthusiasm. By 1939 his poetry had gone a long way toward accepting life with all its imperfections. Auden's interest in changing the world faded and then disappeared entirely, while his emphasis on accepting life appeared in nearly every poem. This transition, already faintly noticeable in a few poems published between 1936 and 1939, was almost certainly speeded up by his discovery of Kierkegaard (who gave philosophical reasons for accepting life and a theology insisting that it must be accepted). Auden's cynical distrust of civilization gave way, then, to his religious hope for it. Also, by 1939 he showed a new interest in light verse and, as his form became more conventional, his meanings became more transparent.

Spain is Auden's one poem on the subject of the Spanish Civil War and it is analyzed here because of its high poetic quality and its illuminating viewpoint. Unfortunately, because of Auden's subsequent doubts about the value of the poem (discussed later), he extracted it from the final (in his lifetime) edition of his collected works, and it is not available for reproduction in toto. The quotations from *Spain* that follow are from the 1938 edition, published in London by Faber and Faber.

Spain resulted from Auden's visit to that country from January to March, 1937. Whatever merits it has as a poetic statement, afterward he neither wrote nor spoke publicly about Spain. It is one of his few poems to include communism conspicuously.

The poem's title pinpoints its subject matter as does Auden's brief description of the country's typography: "that arid square, that fragment nipped off from hot/Africa, soldered so crudely to inventive Europe;/On that tableland scored by rivers." The poem has three basic divisions: past, present, and future, with the refrain, "but to-day the struggle," infringing upon both the past and the future. Around the vision of past, present, and future, with the moment of struggle the highest achievement of the present, Auden molded his analysis of the Spanish problem. The poem's purpose is to call to arms Republican sympathizers to defend Spain against the fascist insurrection.

The poem consists of twenty-six quatrains of free verse, in each case the third line briefer than the other three. The beginning of the poem shows the pattern:

> Yesterday all the past. The language of size
> Spreading to China along the trade-routes; the diffusion
>   Of the counting-frame and the cromlech;
> Yesterday the shadow-reckoning in the sunny climates.

> Yesterday the assessment of insurance by cards,
> The divination of water; yesterday the invention
>   Of cartwheels and clocks, the taming of
> Horses. Yesterday the bustling world of navigation.

It opens with a rapid survey, in six stanzas, of the past civilization of Europe. Yesterday was sensible and exorcised superstition ("abolition of fairies and giants"). The past age of believing folklore was completely gone. This new age turned to science, based its knowledge on empiricism, and provided many of our basic inventions, explorations, and discoveries. Religion was still important enough to be discussed, and there were miracles. God was alive and well and so were heroes. Greek values were inviolate—standards were classical and there was restraint ("the taming of/ Horses").

We have the ending of an age. All the past, with its structures and its tensions, is gone and would be an anachronism "today." The poem's present (1937) epitomizes the struggle of the Spanish Civil War and the impossibility of a normal life without the triumph of the Republican cause. If the Republic wins, the future would rebound to a normality free from terror ("To-morrow, perhaps the future"), and there would be a return to romantic love, poetry, research, exploration, and reassuring trivial pursuits.

After building up tension with the repeated "But to-day the struggle," the poet, the scientist, and finally the nations of the world are shown raising their cry of protest and of prayer. They are averse to accept an unfavorable outcome and, at the same time, expect some deus ex machina to come to their rescue. The stricken nations appeal to the Life-force:

And the nations combine every cry, invoking the life
That shapes the individual belly and orders
    The private nocturnal terror:
"Did you not found the city state of the sponge,

"Raise the vast military empires of the shark
And the tiger, establish the robin's plucky canton?
    Intervene. O descend as a dove or
A furious papa or a mild engineer, but descend."

Although the poem aligns itself with the cause of the Spanish
Republicans, the speaker talks less of Spanish politics than of matters of general human nature, specifically the subject of freedom-
necessity-choice. He shows that in the middle of agonizing circumstances, when men are desperate for a change, they hope some god
will turn up fortuitously, thus relieving them of choice and responsibility: Christ, or a Freudian father figure, or an omnipotent god
("O descend as a dove or/A furious papa or a mild engineer").

Instead of coming, "Life" replies, in the guise of Spain, that life
can be whatever the nations choose to make of it, and that what
they make of it will depend on what they make of Spain. Each
man is responsible for what happens. Men make their own fate
and their own world ("I am whatever you do . . . I am your
choice"). Choices must be made, actions taken, and freedom won.
In the Spain of 1937, choices and actions were particularly painful:
"To-day the inevitable increase in the chances of death;/The conscious acceptance of guilt in the necessary murder . . . ."

    "O no, I am not the mover;
Not to-day; not to you. To you, I'm the

"Yes-man, the bar-companion, the easily-duped;
I am whatever you do. I am your vow to be
    Good, your humorous story.
I am your business voice. I am your marriage.

"What's your proposal? To build the just city? I will.
I agree. Or is it the suicide pact, the romantic
    Death? Very well, I accept, for
I am your choice, your decision. Yes, I am Spain."

The point is that a crisis has been reached and the human species has a political will to exercise. Men can become committed and critically involved. Without this, the Just City, the whole premise of civilized society, is an impossible dream. If the struggle fails (through the implied failure of the political will), then "History to the defeated/May say Alas but cannot help nor pardon." "History," the poem dramatically explains, means nothing without responsible, individual decisions.

Some understood the stakes and stood up to be counted, risking their lives in the fight against fascism ("but to-day the struggle"). These men of conviction and idealism comprised the international brigades and came from various parts of the world:

> . . . remote peninsulas,
> On sleepy plains, in the aberrant fisherman's islands
> Or the corrupt heart of the city,
> Have heard and migrated like gulls or the seeds of
> a flower.
>
> They clung like birds to the long expresses that lurch
> Through the unjust lands, through the night,
> through the alpine tunnel;
> They floated over the oceans;
> They walked the passes. All presented their lives.

While asserting the urgency of the Spanish struggle, Auden also fears that if the battle is lost in Spain the struggle will thereupon terminate ("History to the defeated/May say Alas but cannot help nor pardon."). The true Marxist would never agree that defeat in Spain meant the end of the struggle. Auden implies that history cannot be altered. This conclusion, while not exactly defeatist, is far from optimistic.

In stanzas twenty to twenty-three the poem passes to a consideration of the future, a return to normal life, only to revert relentlessly to the urgent problems of here and now in the final three stanzas:

> To-day the deliberate increase in the chances of death,
> The conscious acceptance of guilt in the necessary
> murder;

To-day the expending of powers
On the flat ephemeral pamphlet and the boring
   meeting.

To-day the makeshift consolations: the shared
   cigarette,
The cards in the candlelit barn, and the scraping
   concert,
The masculine jokes; to-day the
Fumbled and unsatisfactory embrace before hurting.

The stars are dead. The animals will not look.
We are left alone with our day, and the time is
   short . . .

Although the poem offers a kind of projection of what a successful socialist revolution might accomplish, there is, too, the condemnation of an ideology whose ends justify the means ("the conscious acceptance of guilt in the necessary murder"). And there is
the derision implied about communist, bureaucratic procedures:
"To-day the expending of powers/On the flat ephemeral pamphlet
and the boring meeting." From the poem, Auden could not be
confused with a doctrinaire Marxist, but rather shows himself to
be disenchanted and aware of what the practical outcome of bureaucracy is. Also, Auden has soberly demythicized the idealism
of the present struggle in his projected, mundane, commonplace
future.

The poem's large rhetorical structure, contrasting past and future, necessity and political will, helps establish the poem's call to
action. There is frequent repetition of the refrain, "But to-day the
struggle." The words "yesterday" and "to-morrow" are also used
repetitively. Auden sets up rhetorical patterns; for example, he
begins abruptly "Yesterday all the past." There is no verb though
the meaning is vividly clear. This pattern recurs in each of the first
six stanzas: "Yesterday the assessment of insurance by cards . . .
Yesterday the abolition of fairies and giants," etc. Then, there is
the pattern established by "And the investigator peers through his
instruments," continuing with "And the poor in their fireless lodg-

ings . . . And the nations combine every cry," each critical of fascism.

Auden raised the discussion of the Spanish struggle to an objective level. The tone of the poem is impersonal. The language contains none of the slogans or cant so frequently used to exhort sympathy for the Republic. The poem is depersonalized in the same way that a philosophical analysis or report in the newspapers exists as an impersonal argument or as information:

> To-morrow, perhaps the future. The research on
> fatigue
> And the movements of packers; the gradual explor-
> ing of all the
> Octaves of radiation;
> To-morrow the enlarging of consciousness by diet
> and breathing.

The poet is outside these lines. There are no signs of Auden's emotional or physical involvement in the struggle, nor is there identification of the viewpoint of the poem—beyond its survey of conditions past, present, and future. Detachment makes the presentation more objective, but in excluding the personal element, Auden may have deprived the poem of the vital force needed to bring to life the rather lengthy rhetorical analysis, or, at least, Louis MacNeice might have concluded as much:

> His (poet's) object is not merely to record a fact but to record a fact plus and therefore modified by his own emotional reaction to it.[16]

Auden utilizes dialogue to make his points more dramatic. The best example is when Life/Spain speaks out, disclaiming creation and leadership: "I am not the mover," etc. (stanzas 12 through 14).

Auden's imagery suggests the essence and diversity of past and present societies. As man triumphed over ignorance and superstition or merely substituted new superstitions for old ones, he learned to use mechanized power, made discoveries about his origin, and gradually grew less dependent upon antiquity's "inviolate" example. He presents this panoramic view along with the values at stake and the possibilities for the future through a series of short, clipped images.

The logical development of the thought, advancing from yesterday through today to tomorrow, gives the poem clear definition and a firm structure. For example, Auden introduces the idea of struggle ("But to-day the struggle") to prepare for its actual demands in the final stanzas. The balance of the various aspects of the theme is careful. The intensity and high seriousness of the theme and its treatment are well sustained, and despite the fact that the poem is built entirely upon a series of choppy assertions, the rhythm moves smoothly. Auden has relied on long lines (and even longer sentences), packed with images and elevated diction. But he is also deft with conversational style:

> . . . I am not the mover;
> Not to-day; not to you. To you, I'm the
>
> "Yes-man, the bar-companion, the easily-duped;
> I am whatever you do. . . .

Through his regular peppering of assertions, verbs in the present tense, and condensed wording, Auden has achieved for the poem a sense of immediacy and urgency.

The poem states an argument in favor of the Loyalist cause, but it is not an oversimplification or a romantic idealization of the war. On the contrary, the less pleasant demands of the struggle are clearly shown in the last three stanzas. But somehow "To-day the deliberate increase in the chances of death" is unconvincing. It is a ponderous and abstract way to express death in wartime. Add to this the unemotional tone of the entire piece and the reader can conclude that Auden was not involved in the war or the cause in a profoundly emotional way and that the poem was written far from the battlefield. However, the notion that Auden was clinically detached, diagnosing the ills of society, is not limited to this poem. His antiromantic and scientific attitude predominates in most of his poetry before as well as after *Spain*.

Auden seems never to have been seriously troubled by the temptation to confuse art and propaganda. His poetic view, expressed in the Introduction to *The Poet's Tongue*,[17] is almost a statement of the central thesis of *Spain:*

> Poetry is not concerned with telling people what to do, but with extending our knowledge of good and evil, perhaps making the necessity for action more urgent and its nature more clear, but only leading us to the point where it is possible for us to make a rational and moral choice.

Spain represents a theoretical (not experiential) analysis of the values at stake in Spain, past, present, and future, with Spain the key to the direction history will follow. His consideration of Marxism, on the other hand, is practical ("boring meeting").

The audience he aimed at was that of the educated middle class with left-wing or revolutionary sympathies. Auden's relation to his reader is not one-to-one with a fellow human being, but as if he were presenting the reader with a verbal mirror to reflect some aspect of his human nature. Also, the elegant form of the poem would inhibit the reader's identification with it. However, Auden extracted from the occasion of the poem a universal significance. Although *Spain* is fundamentally political, it is also predominantly lyrical.

Auden disowned *Spain* years later, dismissing it as dishonest and having sacrificed doctrine for the sake of rhetoric. However, he was forever denigrating certain of his poems as unworthy or unripe.

Stephen Spender came from an educated and cultured family, with liberal views, of mixed German, Jewish, and English origins.[18] His father was a well-known journalist. Stephen was born in London on February 28, 1909. He was educated at the University College School and the University College, Oxford, where Auden was his slightly older friend and mentor. At Oxford he associated with Auden, Isherwood, Cecil Day Lewis, and MacNeice. He first attracted notice with *Poems* (1933); several pieces in this volume derive technically from Walt Whitman and D. H. Lawrence. Praising labor and denouncing capital, they are more political and more violent than most of the works of Spender's friends. Other poems in the volume concerning, for example, pylons ("those pillars/Bare like nude giant girls that have no secret"—from "The Pylons"), trains, and aerodromes, reveal Spender's lyric power. He was interested in contemporary material, and wrote about aspects, functions, and images of modern machinery:

> More beautiful and soft than any moth
> With burring furred antennae feeling its huge path
> Through dusk, the air-liner with shut-off engines
> Glides over suburbs and the sleeves set trailing tall
> To point the wind. Gently, broadly, she falls
> Scarcely disturbing charted currents of air.
> (first stanza of "The Land-
scape near an Aerodrome")

Vienna (1934), a long poem, celebrates the abortive revolution of Viennese socialists in 1934 against the Dollfuss government. In *The Destructive Element* (1936) Spender implied that the Russian government occasionally suppressed or opposed freedom and truth. In 1938 he published *Trial of a Judge*, an antifascist verse play in the manner of Auden.

At the suggestion of Harry Pollitt, Communist Party Secretary in London, Spender joined the Party, because it was the only group in England during the Spanish Civil War supporting the Loyalists. Spender accepted Pollitt's proposition on condition that he be permitted to state his reasons for joining in an article to appear in the *Daily Worker*. However, he rejected Pollitt's suggestion to go to Spain as a member of the International Brigade, maintaining that he was unqualified for soldiering, but that he would go in any "useful capacity."

He made three trips to Spain. His first visit grew out of an assignment from the *Daily Worker* to investigate the fate of the crew of a Russian ship which Italians had sunk in the Mediterranean.

The primary purpose of his second visit to Spain was to take a position as head of English broadcasting for the radio station of the Socialist Party in Valencia. When the position failed to materialize, he decided to remain in Spain. The experiences during the next few weeks provided most of the material for his Spanish War poetry and undermined his communist ties. Spender objected to party functionaries for enlisting men in the brigades without telling them they were communist-controlled and he resented their regimentation. This sentiment comes out somewhat in his poems "Ultima Ratio Regum" and "Two Armies."

Spender's third and final visit to Spain during the war occurred in July, 1937, when he joined a small band of British party writers at an International Congress in Madrid and Valencia. For ten days, intellectuals and writers from several European countries and Russia discussed their attitude toward the Spanish Civil War. The principal purpose of the Congress was to show the world that intellectuals supported the Spanish Republic. At the International Congress Spender came into contact with Rafael Alberti, Gide, Hemingway, Malraux, and Neruda, among many other distinguished writers. Manuel Altolaguirre became one of his best friends in Spain and served as catalyst for one of his war poems, "To a Spanish Poet."

In *Forward from Liberalism* (1937) he had maintained the individualism of the artist against Marxist demands, although he also revealed his commitment to communism. But after the German-Soviet pact of 1939, like most English leftists, he recognized the moral and intellectual failure of Marxism, and modified his political sympathies. He chronicled his repudiation of communism in his autobiographical *The God That Failed* (1950). He co-edited, with John Lehmann, an anthology occasioned by the Spanish Civil War, entitled *Poems for Spain* (1939).

Spender's subsequent volumes of poetry, *The Still Centre* (1939), *Ruins and Visions* (1942), and *Poems of Dedication* (1946), more self-centered than his earlier works, lack their conviction and power. Spender has also written critical essays, and published an analytical autobiography, *World Within World,* in 1951. In recent years he has been Professor of English at the University of Connecticut.

His *Collected Poems* (1928-1953), published in London in 1955, has eleven parts. The fourth, entitled "Poems about the Spanish Civil War (1936-1939)," contains ten poems from which I have chosen three for analysis: "Two Armies," "Ultima Ratio Regum," and "To a Spanish Poet." Of the three, only "Ultima" was included in his anthology *Poems for Spain.*

Spender's antiwar attitude was intensified by his visits to Spain and by his disenchantment with communism. Only occasionally in his poems does Spender allude to the themes of freedom and liberty, to the democratic nature of the war, or to the humanitarian feelings it evoked, all of which he had articulated at Loyalist rallies and in numerous articles published between 1936 and 1939, defending the legitimacy and morality of the Madrid government.

The depth of Spender's moral convictions antedated the Spanish Civil War and was sounded in an untitled poem beginning "I think continually of those who were truly great," in which the poet praises the unsung heroes and visionaries who never allowed "the traffic to smother/with noise and fog, the flowering of the Spirit":

> those who in their lives fought for life,
> who wore at their hearts the fire's centre.
> Born of the sun they traveled a short while toward
>   the sun,
> and left the vivid air signed with their honour.
>   (from "Preludes"—1930-1933)

He celebrated the heroism of the international volunteers, praised the meticulous care with which the Republic had handled Spain's art masterpieces, and confirmed the agony of Spain which Picasso had epitomized in *Guernica.* In writing alone, Spender did more than either Day Lewis or Auden to advance the Loyalist cause.

But Spender's philosophy of artistic creation was to maintain some separation between it and political commitment, and in his war poetry he excluded explicit political ideology. In this sense, Spender subordinated the war to his personal view and avoided mention of humane and political ideals of the period.

Spender included an apologia in *The Still Centre* (1939) to explain his restraint from a propagandistic stance or heroic vision:

As I have decidedly supported one side—the Republican—in that conflict, perhaps I should explain why I do not strike a more heroic note. My reason is that a poet can only write about what is true to his own experience, not about what he would like to be true to his experience.

Poetry does not state truth, it states the conditions within which something felt is true. Even while he is writing about the little portion of reality which is part of his experience, the poet may be conscious of a different reality outside.[19]

He preferred to treat this most political of wars in a personal, non-political, and traditional manner. Instead of fundamental ideals about freedom and liberty, his poems touch upon death, suffering, fear, and concern over the fate of the innocent and cowardly. His poems are the antithesis of poetry which fuses "public policy and poetry."

ULTIMA RATIO REGUM [20]

1 The guns spell money's ultimate reason
  In letters of lead on the Spring hillside.
  But the boy lying dead under the olive trees
  Was too young and too silly
5 To have been notable to their important eye.
  He was a better target for a kiss.

  When he lived, tall factory hooters never
   summoned him
  Nor did restaurant plate-glass doors revolve to
   wave him in
  His name never appeared in the papers.
10 The world maintained its traditional wall
  Round the dead with their gold sunk deep as
   a well,
  Whilst his life, intangible as a Stock Exchange
   rumour, drifted outside.

  Oh too lightly he threw down his cap
  One day when the breeze threw petals from the
   trees.

15   The unflowering wall sprouted with guns,
            Machine-gun anger quickly scythed the grasses;
            Flags and leaves fell from hands and branches;
            The tweed cap rotted in the nettles.

            Consider his life which was valueless
20   In terms of employment, hotel ledgers, news
                files.
            Consider. One bullet in ten thousand kills a
                man.
            Ask. Was so much expenditure justified
            On the death of one so young and so silly
            Lying under the olive trees, O world, O death?
                                    —Stephen Spender

Spender titled his poem with a Latin phrase meaning the last resort of kings, presumably the resort to arms or war. Its contemporary translation to "money's ultimate reason" suggests that behind the war were the interests of the wealthy and the powerful. If extended further, the metaphor of the title concerns itself with the mystique of a terrible experience which is the ultimate reality of modern life. The Spanish Civil War crystallized this feeling that the final reality of fascism, capitalism, and finally of Stalinism—was as tragic as the death of the boy in Spender's poem.

The plot line is very simple: obscure boy killed in battle, ultimately, perhaps, the victim of an economic system. While guns focused lethally on "the Spring hillside," an anonymous soldier was killed. The disparity between "Spring hill" and all considerations of war is huge, but at least the guns, lead, and money can be considered compatible. The boy, introduced by "but" to emphasize his contrariety to the situation in which he is found, was "too young and too silly" to have been worth killing. To the extent that they are lethal the guns take on importance. Spender's irony is sharp as he adds "He was a better target for a kiss." He was not only young, but harmless, and his fate under these olive trees, representative of Spain, was so unlikely.

To add to our sympathy for the boy, Spender gives us such details as: he had been too young to be employed; he had never been inside a fine restaurant, nor been written up in the newspaper. Spender implies that those with business success, with "gold sunk deep as a well," in the sense of being invested, were dead spiritually, if not physically, in contrast to our vital hero. (The idea of living dead people has often been considered by poets.) But while they were protected, he, being outside the mainstream, was vulnerable. The simile, "intangible as . . . rumour," suggests his vagueness and unimportance in their materialistic world. The "rumour" of the simile, although suitable to the comparison and meaningful, strikes me as being somewhat inconsistent with the other images of the poem.

In the third stanza, "lightly" has two implications, one physical and the other psychological. The day he made his decision was, in contrast to its repercussions, beautiful: "when the breeze threw petals from the trees." The repetition of "t" sounds adds to the delicacy of the phrase. The wall which would not have flowered in any other way "sprouted with guns," as if it were a natural development. Meanwhile, nature itself was being destroyed by the fighting: "machine-gun anger quickly scythed the grasses." "Flags and leaves fell from hands and branches" as humans and trees were destroyed simultaneously and confusedly. As time passed, "The tweed cap" of civilian life "rotted in the nettles."

In the last stanza, Spender asks the reader to consider the boy's life as "valueless" in ordinary economic terms and obscure by accepted social standards. The poem is bitter and ironic as Spender compares the unformed boy's trivial life with the enormous expenditure required to destroy him: "One bullet in ten thousand kills a man." It is ironic that that one bullet found him. The poem ends with Spender's rhetorical question to the reader: "Was so much expenditure justified/On the death of one so young and so silly/Lying under the olive trees, O world, O death?" His repetition of "so young and so silly" makes a final appeal for an outraged sense of justice. The enormity of the fact of this boy's death, played down by language, statement, and (ironic) tone, is nevertheless effectively communicated.

The last phrase contains a compound apostrophe, which Spender personifies into listening creatures, "O world, O death." Perhaps he is not so much directing his question to "world" and "death" as crying out to them. He couches his last statement in an interrogative form, because he wishes to point out ironically the absurdity of what happened.

The first stanza gives a close-up of the battle and the dead boy and introduces the essential fact of his death. The middle two stanzas describe some of the background information on the boy and what happened to him; the second stanza stresses his unimportance in the world of important people, and the third stanza presents the casual effect of the character of his death. The last stanza analyzes why it happened and asserts the pointlessness of it all. The title, exaltedly in Latin, further emphasizes the remoteness of the course of events from this innocent, kissable boy.

The vocabulary is popular and the images are, at times, rural: "scythed . . . grasses," "tweed cap." The metaphors are predictable: money and gold to represent the business interests supporting the cost of the war; factory, restaurant, hotel to represent the social system; olive trees and spring hill-side to indicate Spain; guns and lead, the fallen tweed cap, the mowing down of grass, flags, and leaves, and the boy's death to show aspects of the war. Ironically, Spender uses investment terminology of gain and loss to express what happened to this young soldier: "money's ultimate reason," "gold sunk deep as a well," "valueless," "was so much expenditure justified." Such terms are a far cry from his uncomplicated life. There are no clues to the identity of the boy; he is just another innocent victim. We are not told which war or when, although "olive trees" clearly suggest Spain and the poem appears in his "Poems about the Spanish Civil War—1936-1939." On the contrary, Spender presents it as a personal tragedy. It is a rhetorical and subjective poem depending mostly on Spender's attitude. The abstraction of the poem suggests that the poet was not physically involved in the war.

The tone of the poem is important. Not much happens quantitatively, but Spender sustains a relentless mood of irony.

TWO ARMIES [21]

1   Deep in the winter plain, two armies
       Dig their machinery, to destroy each other.
       Men freeze and hunger. No one is given leave
       On either side, except the dead, and wounded.

5   These have their leave; while new battalions wait
        On time at last to bring them violent peace.

        All have become so nervous and so cold
        That each man hates the cause and distant words
        That brought him here, more terribly than bullets.
10   Once a boy hummed a popular marching song,
        Once a novice hand flapped their salute;
        The voice was choked, the lifted hand fell,
        Shot through the wrist by those of his own side.

        From their numb harvest, all would flee, except
15   For discipline drilled once in an iron school
        Which holds them at the point of the revolver.
        Yet when they sleep, the images of home
        Ride wishing horses of escape
        Which herd the plain in a mass unspoken poem.

20   Finally, they cease to hate: for although hate
        Bursts from the air and whips the earth with hail
        Or shoots it up in fountains to marvel at,
        And although hundreds fall, who can connect
        The inexhaustible anger of the guns
25   With the dumb patience of those tormented
            animals?

        Clean silence drops at night, when a little walk
        Divides the sleeping armies, each
        Huddled in linen woven by remote hands.
        When the machines are stilled, a common suffering
30   Whitens the air with breath and makes both one
        As though these enemies slept in each other's arms.

        Only the lucid friend to aerial raiders
        The brilliant pilot moon, stares down
        Upon this plain she makes a shining bone
35   Cut by the shadows of many thousand bones.
        Where amber clouds scatter on No-Man's-Land
        She regards death and time throw up
        The furious words and minerals which destroy.
                                    —Stephen Spender

Written in an even more somber tone than "Ultima Ratio Regum," though similarly ironic, "Two Armies" is a sobering poem about two opposing armies during wartime. It breaks down romantic illusions. It is not just against the Spanish Civil War but against all war; the same general condemnation of war was present in "Ultima Ratio Regum."

There is an unusual number of monosyllabic words in the poem, which accelerate the beat. It is simply expressed, clear, and direct, but its war dissent is hardly simplistic.

To analyze the poem systematically: it takes place in winter. The two armies are there "to destroy each other," "destroy" having strong emotional connotations. The discomfort of war is stressed, "men freeze and hunger." Ironically, Spender notes: "No one is given leave/. . . except the dead, and wounded." He adds, bitterly, that new battalions will replace them, providing "violent peace" for recently-removed souls.

In stanza two the men are still uncomfortable and tense. Curiously and unfairly, those who caused and planned the war are not the same as those who fight it. Those distant manipulators with their political propaganda have become anathema. The victims sound so innocent: one who "hummed a marching song" and another who saluted. Being shot by happenstance by those of his side (politically) is one of the hazards of war. There is, perhaps, another explanation. Spender has objected to the ruthless methods communists used to maintain superiority and to force men to stay in the line, among which firing on a "comrade" was not unknown. The poem may refer to deliberate firing upon a fellow-soldier who wished to desert.

In stanza three the metaphor for war is "numb harvest," numb both psychologically because war is an ordeal, and physically because the weather is cold. This so-called harvest produces not crops, except in the minds of the perverted, but discomfort, suffering, and death. The soldiers do not run and go AWOL, because they are trained and guarded by severe taskmasters. Only during sleep do they give vent to their real desires for escape—which, in their waking moments, remain "a mass unspoken poem." Finally, they become senseless of their hate for their enemy as well as for the cause in which they must fight. They are "tormented animals" and their numbness and servility (as opposed to the tyranny of their leaders and discipline) reveal themselves in a "dumb patience."

At night nothing less ethereal than silence and sleep separates the enemy armies. They seem small and dependent, "huddled in linen woven by remote hands." The affectionate concern of others for them is far removed.

Stanza five describes enemy forces resting at night only a few yards apart:

> When the machines are stilled, a common suffering
> Whitens the air with breath and makes both one
> As though these enemies slept in each other's arms.

Wartime enemies are practically indistinguishable in their "common suffering." The exigencies of war act as a kind of neutralizing agent, or common enemy, and create a bond between combatants on both sides. These men "cease to hate" and like "tormented animals" practice a "dumb patience" while waiting for the fighting to end. This is the sadness which men at war share.

The final stanza introduces the moon as illuminator and spectator. She (the moon) is personified as watching while "death and time," those ubiquitous, omnipotent forces, emit "the furious words and minerals which destroy." Here we have repetition of the word, "destroy," used with the same strong effect as in the second line except that it reverberates in its final position. We may assume that minerals in the right combination comprise the "machinery" of destruction used in war. And the poem ends on that note.

Spender is antiromantic on the subject of war and sees none of its heroism. Here again (as in "Ultima Ratio Regum") the armies and individuals are anonymous. His points are all negative. His sense of the irretrievable loss during war is universal, rather than limited to a specific war. He has deep pity for the victims of war, the weak and unheroic, and sympathizes here with the dispirited volunteers. Spender considers the ironic notion that it is a struggle they would gladly abandon if they could. His concern for innocent and common people extends to a feeling for all men who become involved in a war without realizing all the implications and contingencies, and who would get out of it if they possibly could. The defeatist sentiments are probably thinly veiled references to what Spender considered the communist strangle hold on the Republican army, although they are applicable to any war.

TO A SPANISH POET [22]
(To Manuel Altolaguirre)

1   You stared out of the window on the emptiness
Of a world exploding;
Stones and rubble thrown upwards in a fountain
Blown to one side by the wind.
5   Every sensation except being alone
Drained out of your mind.
There was no fixed object for the eye to fix on.
You became a child again
Who sees for the first time how the worst things
     happen.

10   Then, stupidly, the stucco pigeon
On the gable roof that was your ceiling,
Parabolized before the window
Uttering (you told me later!) a loud coo.
Alone to your listening self, you told the joke.
15   Everything in the room broke.
But you remained whole,
Your own image unbroken in your glass soul.

Having heard this all from you, I see now
—White astonishment haloing irises
20   Which still retain in their centres
Black laughter of black eyes.
Laughter reverberant through stories
Of an aristocrat lost in the hills near Malaga
Where he had got out of his carriage
25   And, for a whole week, followed, on foot, a
     partridge.

Stories of that general, broken-hearted
Because he'd failed to breed a green-eyed bull.

But reading the news, my imagination breeds
The penny-dreadful fear that you are dead.

30   Well, what of this journalistic dread?

Perhaps it is we—the living—who are dead
We of a world that revolves and dissolves
While we set the steadfast corpse under the earth's
    lid.
The eyes push irises above the grave
35   Reaching to the stars, which draw down nearer,
Staring through a rectangle of night like black
    glass,
Beyond these daylight comedies of falling plaster.

Your heart looks through the breaking ribs—
Oiled axle through revolving spokes.
40   Unbroken blood of the swift wheel,
You stare through centrifugal bones
Of the revolving and dissolving world.
                                        —Stephen Spender

This third poem by Spender is more objective than the other
two in the sense that it deals with its subject more specifically. It
is localized in its dedication to the Spanish poet Manuel Altolaguirre, to whom the "you" of the poem refers.

In the first stanza Altolaguirre is looking out his window during
wartime. The metaphor which compares his sensitivity to that of
a child "Who sees for the first time how the worst things happen"
is apt. War is exaggeratedly dreadful and as remote to the unini-
tiated as evil is to the innocent.

In stanza two the stucco pigeon that fell from the roof uttered
"a loud coo." Spender injects parenthetically that the Spanish poet
had told him so, lending support to the validity of the anecdote.[23]
His soul of glass suggests the fragility of life and of all things in
such an environment, though he had managed to survive that
particular holocaust. Prior to the massive bombings of World

War II, the attacks on Spanish cities were the largest and deadliest the world had yet seen.

Spender claims to have described the situation as the Spaniard had explained it to him, and then proceeds to describe the man himself:

> —White astonishment haloing irises
> Which still retain in their centres
> Black laughter of black eyes.

The laughter originates from several more anecdotes allegedly told in his presence: one concerns "an aristocrat lost in the hills near Malaga" during an unlikely mission in pursuit of a partridge. The other mocks a general, saddened by his failure to breed a green-eyed bull. Both of these absurd quests appear grotesque amid the real trials and contingencies of war.

Spender now reverts to the present, the three prior stanzas having referred to the past. This two-line stanza followed by a single line stanza adds a certain immediacy to the poem. Spender has been reading newspapers, most likely tabloids. These would have dramatized events and cost about a penny each in the 1930s. Their sensationalism would exploit the dangers of the war scene and remind Spender of the likelihood of his friend's death.

It is at this point that Spender becomes more philosophical: "Well, what of this journalistic dread?"—journalistic in the sense that it resulted from a newspaper.

In the penultimate stanza, the notion that it is the living who are dead recalls those living dead, laden with money, in "Ultima Ratio Regum." He qualifies the death by characterizing a disintegrating world, reminiscent of Yeats' prediction in "The Second Coming." The imagery in this stanza is extended and complex. Spender suggests our responsibility for the present crisis: "we set the steadfast corpse under the earth's lid." The world resurrects to the level of its irises. "Irises" offers a double entendre, being the colored portion of the eye surrounding the pupil, as well as the name of a plant and flower. The stars gaze through the "rectangle of night like black glass" to meet the staring eyes. "Rectangle" suggests the shape of a coffin and, otherwise, seems an unlikely choice for the description of night. There is something sinister in characterizing the holocaust of war as "daylight comedies of falling plaster." Perhaps the hope lies in the possible recovery of a world not completely underground. Its "steadfast corpse" indicates durability.

The final stanza is rather anatomical. The heart is literally encased beneath the ribs. It is Altolaguirre's heart that "looks through the breaking ribs." Spender envisions this as "oiled axle through revolving spokes." "Unbroken" in reference to blood seems a mixed image since blood is liquid and not to be broken. It likely implies that the flow of blood is uninterrupted. The wheel is analogous to the rib cage and comprised of the axle and spokes. Again Altolaguirre is staring. In the first line of the poem he stares through a window, and this time through his ribs, "centrifugal bones." "The revolving and dissolving world" is an expansion upon the body/wheel imagery and a further indication of Spender's penchant for machine terminology. The poem appeals mostly to the sense of sight.

The incident on which the poem was based was not particularly significant to Altolaguirre, who had played it down ("I have been too ashamed to tell about the air raid"—p. 263 of *World Within World*). But the story captured Spender's imagination or, at least, appealed to him as a vehicle through which to honor his friend, about whom he obviously cared (". . . my imagination breeds/ The penny-dreadful fear that you are dead").

Muriel Rukeyser was born in New York City in 1913, at the beginning of World War I.[24] She entered Vassar College in the fall of 1930, and before she left in 1932 had written what has been called a "painfully mature" poem, "Effort at Speech Between Two People." In December of 1932 she became literary editor of the *Student Review,* a left-wing publication aimed toward undergraduate consumption.

She was urban-oriented, aware of what was happening, liberal, revolutionary (in spirit), strong minded, and Jewish. She associated with no group of radical poets like that of Auden, Lewis, Spender, and others in England. Her poetic interests and moods, often highly subjective, extended to social, political, and scientific themes. Besides being a poet of the proletariat, she has been a journalist, translator, prose writer (biographies, short stories, children's books, essays), and teacher.

In the spring of 1935, she became associate editor of *New Theatre* magazine, leaving this post the following summer. That same year her first volume of poetry, *Theory of Flight*, was chosen for the Yale Series of Younger Poets, an annual contest sponsored by Yale University Press. The poetry shows her power of expression, strong technique, and rebellious nature. Some critics accused her of "striving for effect" but they were agreed that the twenty-one-year-old had real inventiveness and wisdom to speak her politics "like a poet." [25] In *Theory of Flight*, she portrayed youth as rebelling against the older generation and its tradition. The meaning may be obscure, but the language is unadorned and often simplified to the rhythm of actual speech:

> One day we voted on whether he was Hamlet
> or whether he was himself and yesterday
> I cast the deciding vote to renounce our mouths.
> > (from II. "The Committee-
> > Room," *Theory of Flight*)

The style is swift, abrupt, and syncopated, in keeping with the disrupted world of the thirties and its technological progress:

> Master in the plane shouts "Contact"   :
> master on the ground: "Contact!"
> > he looks up :   "Now?" whispering :   "Now."
> > "Yes," she says.   "Do."
> > Say yes, people.
> > Say yes.
> > YES
> > > (ending of "Theory of
> > > Flight," *Theory of Flight*)

The force and intensity of flight (of an airplane) symbolizes the energy of all powerful machines. The impression of the work is emotional and affirmative.

Rukeyser, who had undergone the disappointments and tortured doubts of the 1930s, including the Depression, had succeeded in enlarging her strength of purpose and the scope of her poetry. Having glimpsed the collapsed prosperity of the Depression generation, she enlisted in the cultural movement of the Left.

Life and Letters Today, the London magazine, sent her in the fall of 1936 to Spain to cover the first People's Olympiad, proposed as an anti-Nazi celebration of workers' sports clubs of Europe and America and an active retort to Hitler's Olympics. She arrived by train with a group of antifascist Olympic participants at the outbreak of the Spanish Civil War, and was evacuated on July 25, 1936. Of her Spanish visit, she later wrote: "I crossed the frontier into Spain on the first day of the war, and stayed long enough to see Catalonia win its own war and make peace, a peace that could not be held." [26] Before her return to the States, she worked with the Spanish Medical Bureau. She, later, described the Spanish Loyalists as being "weaponless against what must have seemed like the thunder and steel of the whole world." [27]

After Spain, she explored U.S. Highway 1 from Maine southward. The title of her second book of poems, *U.S. 1,* was derived from the federal highway that runs from Maine to Florida. Its first section, "Book of the Dead," appeared in the late spring of 1938. It was originally conceived as part of a long, poetical evaluation of the Atlantic Coast, from Maine to Key West. Having been criticized for too much intensity, emotionality, and even melodrama, here she tended to objectify her feelings.

U.S. 1 reveals her assimilation of such influences as Hart Crane and W. H. Auden. Her diction is condensed, and her presentation of factual data somewhat dramatic.

A Turning Wind, her third volume, revealed further progress in her intentness and originality. Written between her twenty-third and twenty-fifth years, the book indicates continuing growth and complexity. From the simple form of declaration in the common phrases of urban speech of her earlier poetry, she developed a gnarled, intellectual, almost private observation. In her earlier verse, the poetic images were few and simple; in her later works, images became those of a psychologist or a surrealist—ubiquitous, charged with meaning, and increasingly complicated. Some critics complained of the complexities of *A Turning Wind:* abrupt changes of tense and action, overcrowded lines, fragmentary phrases and half-sentences, inexactness of pronominal references, too swiftly juxtaposed images, and allusive symbols. They criticized her "baffling style" and the uncertainties of her "metaphysical soul-searching," stressing that communication is essential for the social poet. However, Rukeyser's poetry clearly shows strength of conviction and power of communication.

There are five long poems at the end of the volume, offering a kind of metaphysical soul-searching of a painter, a poet, a mathematician, a musician, and an agitator.

Rukeyser finished *A Turning Wind* on September 1, 1939, at a time when world peace was a far-off possibility. She said of the poems that they projected "some of the valid sources of power which have come down to us." [28]

Instinctively pacifistic, she was against everything in any organization which represented the brutal life of enforced regimentation and national slavery. She was against war, conscription, and the forcing of others into war. "M-Day's Child is Fair of Face" (from *A Turning Wind*) contains the particular theme of the menaced child within a broader denunciation of military horror in general:

> M-Day's child is fair of face,
> Drill-day's child is full of grace,
> Gun-day's child is breastless and blind,
> Shell-day's child is out of its mind,
> Bomb-day's child will always be dumb,
> Cannon-day's child can never quite come,
> but the child that's born on the Battle-day
> is blithe and bonny and rotted away.

Her attitude was antiwar, but she knew what she had to fight; she was unconditionally pledged to oppose Hitlerism and preserve civil liberties. She remembered the poet Lorca, who could have been murdered by both sides—who figuratively was, since neither could protect him.

In the midst of desperate remedies and clamoring negatives, she affirmed the life of people and the life of poetry—the life of the spirit which makes possible the creative life which was at once an answer to the problem of living slavery and to the wish for quick escape, comforting death. She asserted:

> that climax when the brain acknowledges the world,
> all values extended into the blood awake.
> > (from "Reading Time: 1 minute 26
> > seconds," *A Turning Wind,* p. 43)

Having been criticized for the objectification of social data in the poem *U.S. 1,* she made the symbols in *A Turning Wind* strong and evocative, when, for example, expressing the concept of death:

> This was their art: a wall daubed like a face,
> a penis or finger dipped in a red pigment.
> > (from "Third Elegy. The Fear of
> > Form," *A Turning Wind,* p. 24)

It became evident in the late Thirties that the "revolution" was a lost cause. While the movement slackened and its influence diminished, its partisans were thrown into even greater despair by the spectacle of an appeasement policy on the part of great nations that violated every tenet of progress. In the face of this, Rukeyser achieved perhaps her finest sequence of poems—the five elegies that begin the volume *A Turning Wind.* These poems showed an authority superior to all that she had done before. She had come to terms with tragedy:

> Rejecting the subtle and contemplative minds
> as being too thin in the bone; and the gross thighs
> and unevocative hands fail also. But the poet
> and his wife, those who say Survive, remain;
> and those two who were with me on the ship
> leading me to the sum of the years, in Spain.
>
> When you have left the river you will hear the war.
> In the mountains, with tourists, in the insanest groves
> the sound of kill, the precious face of peace.
> And the sad frightened child, continual minor,
> returns, nearer whole circle, O and nearer

all that was loved, the lake, the naked river,
what must be crossed and cut out of your heart,
what must be stood beside and straightly seen.
                                    (from "First Elegy. Rotten
                            Lake," *A Turning Wind,* p. 16)

The Soul and Body of John Brown was published in 1941. A
biography of the scientist Willard Gibbs was published a year
later. *Beast in View* came out in 1944, and *The Green Wave,* a
year later. This last work represented a change toward imperson-
ality. She presented herself and love affairs in unusually abstract
terms:

The motive of all of it was loneliness,
All the panic encounters and despair
Were bred in fear of the lost night, apart,
Outlined by pain, alone. Promiscuous
As mercy. Fear-led and led again to fear
At evening toward the cave where part fire, part
Pity lived in that voluptuousness
To end one and begin another loneliness.
                                    (from "The motive of all
                            of it," *The Green Wave,* 1948)

In 1949 came *Orpheus.* If the *Elegies* (1957) stresses outrage,
Orpheus affirms possibility:

To live and begin again.
The body alive and offering,
whole, up and alive,
and to all men, man and woman,
and to all the unborn,
the mouth shall sing
music past wounding
and the song begin:
. . . sing/creation not yet come.
                            (ending of *Orpheus*)

This is an allegory of poetic love; the poet is a prototype of humanity. The death of Orpheus is creative in effect, for from this death comes the birth of the god.

The Life of Poetry (1949) is an essay speaking for the interrelations of poetry and other disciplines, including science, and for the linkings of imagination. *Body of Waking* (1949) includes the long poem, "Suite for Lord Timothy Dexter," a ballad celebrating the life and fortune of a famous New England eccentric. It also includes translations from the Spanish of Octavio Paz. Translations of his poems were published further in *Selected Poems of Octavio Paz* and in *Sun Stone*. The poems in *Elegies* (1957) are general and cosmic in their reference, brooding upon the confusion and bitterness of human fate, attempting finally to arrive at some affirmation of hope within despair. Other of her writings include *Selected Poems* (1951) and *One Life* (1957), a biography, dealing with the American conflict as seen in the life of Wendell Willkie. That same year she also published a biography of Houdini.

In 1960 *The Speed of Darkness* was published, followed the next year by three works: *Colors of the Day* (a play), *The Speaking Tree*, and *Poems Selected and New*. *Waterlily Fire* came out in 1962. Rukeyser collaborated with Leif Sjoberg in translating poems of Gunnar Ekelöf. *The Orgy,* a voyage of discovery by a few people on the west coast of Ireland, was published in 1965. She has also written children's books: *Come Back, Paul* (1955), and *I Go Out* (1961).

I have chosen for analysis the following three poems in which Rukeyser alludes to the Spanish Civil War: "Mediterranean," published in *New Masses* magazine in 1937, celebrated her timely arrival in Barcelona; "Third Elegy. The Fear of Form"; and "Nuns in the Wind," the last two published in *A Turning Wind* (1939).

MEDITERRANEAN [29]

On the evening of July 25, 1936, five days after the outbreak of the Spanish Civil War, the Americans with the antifascist Olympic games were evacuated from Barcelona at the order of the Catalonian government. In a small Spanish boat, the

Ciudad di Ibiza, which the Belgians had chartered, they and
a group of five hundred, including the Hungarian and Belgian
teams as well as the American, sailed overnight to Sete, the
first port in France. The only men who remained were those
who had volunteered in the loyalist forces: the core of the
future International Brigades.

I

1   At the end of July, exile. We watched the
         gangplank go
     cutting the boat away, indicating: sea.
     Barcelona, the sun, the fire-bright harbor, war.
     Five days.

5   Here at the rail, foreign and refugee,
     we saw the city, remembered that zero of attack,
     chase in the groves, snares through the olive hills,
     rebel defeat: leaders, two regiments,
     broadcasts of victory, tango, surrender.
10   The truckride to the city, barricades,
     bricks pried at corners, rifle-shot in street,
     car-burning, bombs, blank warnings, fists up, guns
     busy sniping, the torn walls, towers of smoke.
     And order making, committees taking charge,
         foreigners
15   commanded out by boat.

     I saw the city, sunwhite flew on glass,
     trucewhite from window, the personal lighting
         found
     eyes on the dock, sunset-lit faces of singers,
     eyes, goodbye into exile. Saw where Columbus rides
20   black-pillared: discovery, turn back, explore
     a new-found Spain, coast-province, city-harbor.
     Saw our parades ended, the last marchers on board
     listed by nation.

     I saw first of those faces going home into war
25   the brave man, Otto Boch, the German exile,
         knowing

he quieted tourists during machine-gun battle,
he kept his life straight as a single issue—
left at that dock we left, his gazing Breughel face,
square forehead and eyes, strong square breast
    fading,
30   the narrow runner's hips diminishing dark.
I see this man, dock, war, a latent image.

The boat *Ciudad di Ibiza,* built for two hundred,
loaded with five hundred, manned by loyal sailors,
chartered by Belgians when consulates were
    helpless,
35   through a garden of gunboats, margin of the port,
entered: Mediterranean.

II

Frontier of Europe, the tideless sea, a field of power
touching desirable coasts, rocking in time
    conquests,
fertile, the moving water maintains its boundaries,
40   layer on layer, Troy-seven civilized worlds,
Egypt, Greece, Rome, jewel Jerusalem,
giant feudal Spain, giant England, this last war.

The boat pulled into evening, underglaze blue
flared instant fire, blackened towards Africa.
45   Over the city alternate light occurred;
                                        and pale
in the pale sky emerging stars.
No city now, a besieged line of light
masking the darkness where the country lay,
but we knew guns
50   bright through mimosa
singe of powder
and reconnoitering plane
flying anonymous
scanning the Pyrenees
55   tall black above the Catalonian sea.

Boat of escape, dark on the water, hastening, safe,
holding non-combatants, the athlete, the child,
the printer, the boy from Antwerp, the black boxer,
lawyer and Communist.
60   The games had not been held.

A week of games, theater and festival;
world anti-fascist week. Pistol starts race.
Machine-gun marks the war. Answered unarmed,
charged the Embarcadero, met those guns.
65   And charging through the province, joined that
          army.
Boys from the hills, the unmatched guns,
the clumsy armored cars.
Drilled in the bullring. Radio cries:
To Saragossa! And this boat.

70   Escape, dark on the water, an overloaded ship.
Crowded the deck. Spoke little. Down to dinner.
Quiet on sea: no guns.
The printer said, In Paris there is time,
but where's its place now; where is poetry?

75   This is the sea of war; the first frontier
blank on the maps, blank sea; Minoan boats
maybe achieved this shore;
mountains whose slope divides
one race, old insurrections, Narbo, now
80   moves at the colored beach
destroyer, wardog. "Do not burn the church,
companeros, it is beautiful. Besides,
it brings tourists." They smashed only the image
madness and persecution.
85   Exterminating wish; they forced the door,
lifted the rifle, broke the garden window,
removed only the drawings: cross and wrath.
Whenever we think of these, the poem is,
that week, the beginning, exile
90   remembered in continual poetry.

Voyage and exile, a midnight cold return,
dark to our left mountains begin the sky.
There, pointed the Belgian, I heard a pulse of war,
sharp guns while I ate grapes in the Pyrenees.

95   Alone, walking to Spain, the five o'clock of war.
In those cliffs run the sashed and sandaled men,
capture the car, arrest the priest, kill captain,
fight our war.
The poem is the fact, memory falls
100   under and seething lifts and will not pass.

Here is home-country, who fights our war.
Street-meeting speaker to us:
                              ". . . came for games,
        you stay for victory; foreign? your job is:
        go tell your countries what you saw in Spain."
105   The dark unguarded army left all night.
M. de Paiche said, "We can learn from Spain."
The face on the dock that turned to find the war.

III

Seething, and falling black, a sea of stars,
black marked with virile silver. Peace all night,
110   over that land, planes
death-lists—a frantic bandage
the rubber tires burning—monuments,
sandbag, overturned wagon, barricade
girl's hand with gun—food failing, water failing
115   the epidemic threat
the date in a diary—a blank page opposite
no entry—
however, met
the visible enemy heroes: madness, infatuation
120   the cache in the crypt, the breadline shelled,
the yachtclub arsenal, the foreign check.
History racing from an assumed name, peace,
a time used to perfect weapons.

If we had not seen fighting
125 if we had not looked there
the plane flew low
the plaster ripped by shot
the peasant's house
if we had stayed in our world
130 between the table and the desk
between the town and the suburb
slow disintegration
male and female
If we had lived in our cities
135 sixty years might not prove
the power this week
the overthrown past
tourist and refugee
Emeric in the bow speaking his life
140 and the night on this ship
and the night over Spain
quick recognition
male and female

And the war in peace, the war in war, the peace,
145 the face on the dock
the faces in those hills.

IV

Near the end now, morning. Sleepers cover the
decks,
cabins full, corridors full of sleep. But the light
vitreous, crosses water; analyzed darkness
150 crosshatched in silver, passes up the shore,
touching limestone massif, deserted tableland,
bends with the down-warp of the coastal plain.

The colored sun stands on the route to Spain,
builds on the waves a series of mirrors
155 and on the scorched land rises hot.
Coasts change their names as the boat goes to

France, Costa Brava softens to Cote Vermeil,
Spain's a horizon ghost behind the shapeless sea.

Blue praising black, a wind above the waves
160   moves pursuing a jewel, this hieroglyph
boat passing under the sun to lose it on the
attractive sea, habitable and old.
A barber sun, razing three races; met
from the north with a neurotic eagerness.

165   They rush to the solar attraction; local daybreak
        finds
them on the red earth of the colored cliffs; the
        little islands
tempt worshipers, gulf-purple, pointed bay;
we crowd the deck,
welcome the islands with a sense of loss.

V

170   The wheel in the water, green, behind my head.
Turns with its light-spokes. Deep. And the
        drowning eyes
find under the water figures near
in their true picture, moving true,
the picture of that war enlarging clarified
175   as the boat perseveres away, always enlarging,
to become clear.

Boat of escape, your water-photograph.
I see this man, dock, war, a latent image.
And at my back speaking the black boxer,
180   telling his education: porter, fighter, no school,
no travel but this, the trade union sent a team.
I saw Europe break apart
and artifice or martyr's will
cannot anneal this war, nor make
185   the loud triumphant future start
shouting from its tragic heart.

Deep in the water the Spanish shadows turn,
assume their brightness past a cruel lens,
quick vision of loss. The pastoral lighting takes
190   the boat, deck, passengers, the pumice cliffs,
the winedark sweatshirt at my shoulder.
Cover away the fighting cities
but still your death-afflicted eyes
must hold the print of flowering guns,
195   bombs whose insanity craves size,
the lethal breath, the iron prize.

The clouds upon the water-barrier pass,
the boat may turn to land; these shapes endure,
rise up into our eyes, to bind
200   us back; an accident of time
set it upon us, exile burns it in.
Once the fanatic image shown,
enemy to enemy,
past and historic peace wear thin;
205   hypocrite sovereignties go down
before this war the age must win.

VI

The sea produced that town: Sète, which the boat
   turns to,
at peace. Its breakwater, casino, vermouth factory,
   beach.
They searched us for weapons. No currency went
   out.
210   The sign of war was the search for cameras,
pesetas and photographs go back to Spain,
the money for the army. Otto is fighting now, the
   lawyer said.
No highlight hero. Love's not a trick of light.
But.—The town lay outside, peace, France.
215   And in the harbor the Russian boat Schachter;
sharp paint-smell, the bruise-colored shadow swung
under its side. Signaling to our decks

        sailors with fists up, greeting us, asking news,
        making the harbor real.
                        Barcelona.
220   Slow-motion splash. Anchor. Small from the beach
        the boy paddles to meet us, legs hidden in canoe,
        curve of his blade that drips.
        Now gangplank falls to dock.
                      Barcelona
        everywhere, Spain everywhere, the cry of planes for
          Spain.
225   The picture at our eyes, past memory, poems,
        to carry and spread and daily justify.
        The single issue, the live man standing tall,
        on the hill, the dock, the city, all the war.
        Exile and refugee, we land, we take
230   nothing negotiable out of the new world;
        we believe, we remember, we saw.
        Mediterranean gave
        image and peace, tideless for memory.

        For that beginning
235   make of us each
        a continent and inner sea
        Atlantis buried outside
        to be won.

"Mediterranean," divided into six sections of free verse, considers the Spanish Civil War from a rather special point of view. It is presented in the first person and autobiographically. As the prose narrative preceding the poem explains, Rukeyser was evacuated from Barcelona and Spain along with other Americans connected with the antifascist Olympic games by order of the Catalonian government. The poem vivifies that departure. Barcelona was five days into the war. Rukeyser reviews the excitement and other emotions of those first chaotic days: ". . . barricades,/ bricks pried at corners, rifle-shot in street,/ car-burning, bombs, blank warnings, fists up, guns/busy sniping, the torn walls, towers of smoke." The first part ends with the boarding by 500 escaping foreigners onto a boat built to contain 200 passengers, *Ciudad di Ibiza*. Ironically, it was not the consulates who were able to arrange and execute the departure, but the Belgians. The poet speaks feelingly of Otto Boch: "I see this man, dock, war, a latent image." The poet looks upon the recent past nostalgically.

The second section describes the Mediterranean by reviewing its past. She provides information about the circumstances of the ordered departure, the passengers, and the "world anti-fascist week," which had been canceled:

> . . . of escape, dark on the water, hastening, safe,
> holding non-combatants, the athlete, the child,
> the printer, the boy from Antwerp, the black boxer,
> lawyer and Communist.
> The games had not been held.

In contrast to a pistol shot which announces the beginning of a race, machine-gun fire attended the war. With gunfire in the distance, those to leave the country were advised: "go tell your countries what you saw in Spain."

Part III again evokes the fighting. The five days had been world-shaking: "the power this week/the overthrown past/ tourist and refugee."

The ship, having left Barcelona around midnight, the scene the following morning was: "Sleepers cover the decks,/cabins full, corridors full of sleep." The Costa Brava becomes the Cote Vermeil: "Spain's a horizon ghost behind the shapeless sea." As they approach some little islands, emotions are ambivalent: "welcome the islands with a sense of loss." As distance from Spain increases, the war can be focused more clearly.

In Part VI the boat is ready to dock at the peaceful French city of Sete. The passengers are searched for cameras, pesetas, and photographs—to be confiscated and sent back to Spain. With nostalgic memories of Spain, they go forth, taking with them nothing that might prove useful to the Republic:

> For that beginning
> make of us each

> a continent and inner sea
> Atlantis buried outside
> to be won.

Atlantis, the mythical island or continent located in the Atlantic Ocean, west of Gibraltar, was purported to have sunk. A free Spain, the Republic of the Loyalists, was something to be sought, won, and prized. The lines are reminiscent of Donne's "no man is an island unto itself," with very similar implications.

Rukeyser is sensitive to the lighting of the sea and harbor under both sun and moonlight. She notices the light reflected off people as well:

> I saw the city, sunwhite flew on glass,
> trucewhite from window, the personal lighting found
> eyes on the dock, sunset-lit faces of singers,
> eyes, goodbye into exile.

She also notices the smoke above the city.

She emphasizes with metaphors the contrast between her safe retreat to the Pyrenees and the war below: "I heard a pulse of war,/ sharp guns while I ate grapes in the Pyrenees."

Part II begins with a description of stars. In Part IV the lighting again is paramount in her observation:

> But the light
> vitreous, crosses water; analyzed darkness
> crosshatched in silver, passes up the shore,
> touching limestone massif, deserted tableland,
> bends with the down-warp of the coastal plain.

Sights and sounds converge in poetic expression of her Spanish experience. The colored sun stands on the route to Spain, builds on the waves a series of mirrors, and rises on the scorched land.

She frequently brings in color: "Blue praising black, a wind . . ." and "local daybreak finds/them on the red earth of the colored cliffs."

In the final stanza of the poem, Atlantis is the metaphor for Spain, offering a remote repository of hope.

Grammatically, there is a frequent absence of verbs. An example of her telegraphic style occurs in Part III:

> . . . Peace all night,
> over that land, planes
> death-lists—a frantic bandage
> the rubber tires burning—monuments,
> sandbag, overturned wagon, barricade
> girl's hand with gun—food failing, water failing,
> the epidemic threat
> the data in a diary—a blank page opposite
> no entry—

Such sounds as those of broadcasts, music, rifle shots, bombs, and guns sniping abound. The machine-gun fire of war replaces the pistol shot initiating peacetime races. In Part II, "I heard a pulse of war." Later, as the anchor is thrown overboard, there is a "slow-motion splash." And, as they disembark, there is the "cry of planes for Spain," a plea repeated in her "Third Elegy."

The unpreparedness of the Loyalists for war is stressed in the following imagery:

> Boys from the hills, the unmatched guns,
> the clumsy armored cars.
> Drilled in the bullring.

In wartime, poetry does not have top priority, and the poet asks: "Where is poetry?"

The tone of the poet is revealed somewhat in her calling herself an "exile and refugee." She had identified with the struggle and cause during her brief stay. The inclination of the Republic toward liberal reform would have matched her own. She was moved and felt somewhat guilty about eating grapes in the Pyrenees, simultaneously with the war below. Her description of Sete, "its break-water casino, vermouth factory, beach," also suggests her guilty conscience. She does not delude herself about its being an easy "escape." She was emotionally and philosophically, if not physically, involved: "we believe, we remember, we saw."

THIRD ELEGY. THE FEAR OF FORM [30]

Tyranny of method! The outrageous smile
seals the museums, pours a mob skidding
up to the formal staircase, stopped, mouths open.
And do they stare? They do.
At what? A sunset?

Blackness, obscurity, bravado were the three colors;
wit-play, movement, and wartime the three moments;
formal groups, fire, facility, the three hounds.

This was their art: a wall daubed like a face,
a penis or finger dipped in a red pigment.
The sentimental frown gave them their praise,
prized the wry color, the twisted definition,
and said, "You are right to copy."

But the car full of Communists put out hands and
    guns,
blew 1—2—3 on the horn before the
surrealist house, a spiral in Cataluña.

New combinations: set out materials now,
combine them again! the existence is the test.
What do you want? Lincoln blacking his lessons
in charcoal on an Indiana shovel?
or the dilettante, the impresario's beautiful skull
choosing the tulip crimson satin, the yellow satin
as the ballet dances its tenth time to the mirror?
Or the general's nephew, epaulets from birth,
run down the concourse, shouting Planes for Spain?

New methods, the staring circle given again
force, a phoenix of power, another Ancient
sits in his circle, while the plaster model
of an equation slowly rotates beneath him,
and all his golden compass leans.
Create an anti-sentimental : Sing!

"For children's art is not asylum art,
"there are these formal plays in living, for
"the equal triangle does not spell youth,
"the cube nor age, the sphere nor ever soul.
"Asylum art is never children's art.
"They cut the bones down, but the line remained.
"They cut the line for good, and reached the point
"blazing at the bottom of its night."

*

A man is walking, wearing the world, swearing
saying You damn fools come out into the open.
Whose dislocated wish? Whose terrors whine?
I'll fuse him straight.
The usable present starts my calendar.
Chorus of bootblacks, printers, collectors of shit.
Your witwork works, your artwork shatters, die.
Hammer up your abstractions. Divide, O zoo.
—He's a queer bird, a hero, a kangaroo.
What is he going to do?

He calls Rise out of cities, you memorable ghosts
scraps of an age whose choice is seen
to lie between evils. Dazzle-paint the rest,
it burns my eyes with its acetylene.
Look through the wounds, mystic and human fly,
you spiritual unicorn, you clew of eyes.

Ghosts to approach the blood in fifteen cities.
Did you walk through the walls of the Comtesse de
    Noailles?
Was there a horror in Chicago?
Or ocean? Or ditches at the road. Or France,
while bearing guarding shadowing painting in Paris,
Picasso like an ass Picasso like a dragon Picasso like a
romantic movement
and immediately after, stations of swastikas
Prague and a thousand boys swing circles clean
girls by the thousand curve their arms together

geometries of wire
the barbed, starred
Heil

Will you have capitals with their tarnished countesses
their varnished cemetery life
vanished Picassos
or clean acceptable Copenhagen
or by God a pure high monument
white yellow and red
up against Minnesota?

Does the sea permit its dead to wear jewels?

Flame, fusion, defiance are your three guards,
the sphere, the circle, the cluster your three guides,
the bare, the blond and the bland are your three
    goads.

Adam, Godfinger, only these contacts function:
light and the high accompanied design,
contact of points   the fusion say of sex
the atombuster too along these laws.
Put in a sphere, here, at the focal joint,
he said, put it in. The moment is arrangement.
Currents washed through it, spun, blew white,
fused.   For!   the sphere!   proving!

This was the nightmare of a room alone,
the posture of grave figure, finger on other head,
he puts the finger of power on him,
optic of grandiose delusion.
All you adjacent and contagious points,
make room for fusion; fall,
you monuments, snow on your heads,
your power, your pockets, your dead parts.

Standing at midnight corners under corner-lamps
we wear the coat and the shadow of the coat.
The mind sailing over a scene lets light arrive
conspicuous sunrise, the knotted smoke rising,

the world with all its signatures visible.
Play of materials in balance,
carrying the strain of a new process.
Of the white root, the nature of the base,
contacts, making an index.
And do they stare? They do.
Our needs, our violences.
At what? Contortion of body and spirit.
To fuse it straight.

—Muriel Rukeyser

"Third Elegy. The Fear of Form" is the third in a series of five elegies found in *A Turning Wind* (1939), probably modeled on Rilke's *Duino Elegies*. It is an elegy in the sense that it commemorates the war dead, presumably the Spanish Civil War dead in 1939, and in the broader sense of being a lyric-contemplative poem of deeply serious cast. Its title states that there is something to be feared in form. The form in question is symbolically represented as that of artworks but suggests further the state or shape of the world as the poet sees it. The art symbolizes reality, and the real world of 1939, as Rukeyser sees it, is dehumanized and horrible. As we are abruptly informed, the method of going about making the form is authoritarian and overbearing ("Tyranny of method!"). It suggests the attitude of dictators or storm troopers. The contemporary (1939) vista is presented symbolically as nightmare horror in a museum of art.

Rukeyser gives ironic emphasis to the fact that the viewers are not exposed to an ordinary sunset, but to: "Blackness, obscurity, bravado . . ./witplay, movement, and wartime . . ./formal groups, fire, facility," alliterations being common to the stanza. Each aspect of its "art" is expressed by a trinity of words. The spectators are impressionistically described in a state of flow and shock. The "outrageous smile" would belong, perhaps, to the guide of this exhibition; his expression is grossly inappropriate because there should be no pleasure amid the wreckage of war.

The art itself is strongly expressed: "a penis or finger dipped in a red pigment," the coloring matter being the blood of war. Again the "sentimental frown" refers to the tour leader's face which spouts praise for the show and encourages the artistically-inclined to imitate the works ("you are right to copy"). This has to be cynical and bitter. The poet elsewhere urges creativity: "new combinations," "new methods," "create an anti-sentimental : Sing!" And the poem itself is a living example of the destruction of traditional form in poetry and an assertion of individualism.

The art is genuine. One picture shows communists shooting their way through Cataluña. Like the poem, the house in the painting is transformed into a spiral surrealistically. The poem is most experimental (revolutionary for its time) in technique.

The poet or narrator asks what subject matter one might want if not this. The sentimentality of "Lincoln blacking his lessons in charcoal on an Indiana shovel"? That would be edifying but irrelevant. An even more superficial subject is suggested: "the dilettante, the impresario's beautiful skull," and others. These examples remind us of the aristocrat chasing a partridge and the general trying to breed a green-eyed bull in Spender's "To a Spanish Poet." They are far removed from the present tragedy and the tone of presentation is disdainful. The imagery is superficial and unreal with the showy, cheap satin in bright colors and the ballet arranged before a mirror. Even the shouts for "Planes for Spain" ring hollow when we learn that the shouter is running, hardly a dignified, serious, or effective framework for his request, and that he has gained his high position through nepotism.

What are needed are "new combinations," "new methods." "Anti-sentimental" plays upon its similarity to "anti-Semitism," a concept not foreign to the perpetrators of the Spanish Civil War. The song in quotes speaks grotesquely of the art at hand: asylum art in contrast to children's art. The art is appropriately antisentimental; the extremity of the subject matter could not be dealt with otherwise. The new methods are dehumanized, abstract, and geometrical: "They cut the bone down, but the line remained."

The theme is life and death. The death imagery is often black: "Blackness, obscurity," while the imagery of life refers to art and suggests flux and change.

The second part begins with a man, burdened by the world, but who has some perspective. The world is a shambles but he is ready to begin again with what is left: "The usable present starts my calendar." The so-called artists of the holocaust are defamed: "Chorus of bootblacks, printers, collectors of shit" and cursed ("die"). A jingle follows:

> Divide, O zoo.
> —He's a queer bird, a hero, a kangaroo.
> What is he going to do?

They are like wild animals and represent a kind of zoo in their colossal and diverse inhumanity. On the other hand, he is a type of savior, a hero. The vision out of which he commands the ghosts to rise is warlike in its facets: chaos ("clew"), destruction ("scraps"), "evils," "burns my eyes with its acetylene," and "wounds." The blood pervades a wide area ("the blood in fifteen cities"). The ghosts of those who died in the war are told "to approach" the destruction and to explain where they have been and what they have seen.

There is a predominantly "o" sound in this consideration of ghosts. Picasso, a staunch upholder of the Republic, is included. The Nazi "swastikas" and large numbers of disciplined youngsters crowd the forceful scene of war:

> geometries of wire
> the barbed, starred
> Heil.

The capitals of the world endure while their inhabitants are "tarnished," surely an ironic euphemism for what can happen. On the other hand, cemeteries are crowded and "varnished."

The irrelevance of the question, "Does the sea permit its dead to wear jewels?" is striking. A materialistic concern about the dead can only be bitter. Again we have triads of words:

> Flame, fusion, defiance are your three guards,
> the sphere, the circle, the cluster your three guides,
> the bare, the blond and the bland are your three
>   goads.

There is alliteration in each of these lines and the last words alliterate also. There is force in the laconic style.

The concepts are again abstract considerations of design: contacts, function, points, fusion, and arrangement. There is an analogy of these concepts to sex: "the fusion say of sex":

> Put in a sphere, here, at the focal joint,
> he said, put it in. The moment is arrangement.
> Currents washed through it, spun, blew white,
> fused. For! the sphere! proving!

The "say" is an attempt to be casual about something which obviously preoccupies Rukeyser. The masculine command in this sexual act proves his assertiveness, authority, force, and strength. These characteristics are those of activists in any sense and are not unrelated to wartime. Fusion at certain points suggests art work as well.

The last stanza describes destruction:

> . . . fall,
> you monuments, snow on your heads,
> your power, your pockets, your dead parts.

The viewers of this destruction ("Our needs, our violence./ . . . contortion of body and spirit") try to make some sense out of it all ("To fuse it straight") The poet wants the relation of life (sex, art) to be clear and out in the open. She is for art that faces issues honestly. Realizing the meaningless violence—the death that pervades the world—we need to confront the antihuman terror. Her title is, therefore, ironic, since she wishes us *not* to fear form.

This is a thoughtful poem that frequently asks questions and demands rereadings. The dominant symbol is that of a kind of tour (journey) through the landscape of a museum, the subject matter of whose art results from the realities of war and the present state of ruin in the world. Life and death mingle in this highly serious poem. The poem represents, through the pretense of viewing paintings on the subject, a negative, depressing situation.

This surrealist poem is a conscious denial of objective reality (a kind of nihilism) through Rukeyser's extreme individualism. It is as if the poet were looking with contempt upon the exterior world, refusing to follow the contours of objects and the succession of events. Logical language proves inadequate to express alienation of sensations. As a result, there is disorder in the poem and the referents of the symbols are not always limited and clear. Rukeyser has deliberately destroyed traditional form in the poem. She is urging against "the fear of form." Form is a living, organic, dynamic principle, not a set of conventions or static achievements.

The poem is preoccupied with life and death and there is an effort to distort our focus upon the dehumanized figures involved. The poet blends the concrete with the abstract. The conciseness of the language lends itself to the emptiness and ruin of the landscape. It is a pessimistic poem, oriented toward the past, not the future.

The pervasive blood over the landscape recalls Hernández' "Recoged esta voz"; Hernández was twenty-seven and Rukeyser was twenty-six when they wrote their respective poems.

NUNS IN THE WIND [31]

As I came out of the New York Public Library
you said your influence on my style would be noticed
and from now on there would be happy poems.
              It was at that moment
the street was assaulted by a covey of nuns
going directly toward the physics textbooks.
Tragic fiascos shadowed that whole spring.
The children sang streetfuls, and I thought:
O to be the King in the carol
kissed and at peace; but recalling Costa Brava
the little blossoms in the mimosa tree
and later, the orange cliff, after they sent me out,
I knew there was no peace.
              You smiled, saying: Take it easy.

That was the year of the five-day fall of cities.
> First day, no writers. Second, no telephones.
> Third, no venereal diseases. Fourth, no income
> tax. And on the fifth, at noon.

The nuns blocked the intersections, reading.
I used to go walking in the triangle of park,
seeing that locked face, the coarse enemy skin,
the eyes with all the virtues of a good child,
but no child was there, even when I thought, Child!
The 4 a.m. cop could never understand.
You said, not smiling, You are the future for me,
but you were the present and immediate moment
and I am empty-armed without, until to me is given
two lights to carry: my life and the light of my death.

If the wind would rise, those black throbbing umbrellas
fly downstreet, the flapping robes unfolding,
my dream would be over, poisons cannot linger
when the wind rises. . . .

All that year, the classical declaration of war was lacking.
There was a lot of lechery and disorder.
And I am queen on that island.

Well, I said suddenly in the tall and abstract room,
time to wake up.
Now make believe you can help yourself alone.
And there it was, the busy crosstown noontime
crossing, peopled with nuns.
> Now, bragging now,
the flatfoot slambang victory,
> thanks to a trick of wind
will you see faces blow, and though their bodies
by God's grace will never blow,
cities shake in the wind, the year's over,
calendars tear, and their clothes blow. O yes!

> —Muriel Rukeyser

Rukeyser has looked at the Spanish Civil War in the way a North American poet can, and perhaps must—from a distance. What she has done in "Nuns in the Wind" is to combine memories of her personal life with civilian impressions about the war, and her free-verse poem is complex in symbolism. The scene opens at the New York Public Library. Curiously, the nuns "assault" the street before their visit to the library to secure physics books. Nuns travel in groups, "covey of nuns," and are a kind of dark manifestation associated with the church and alien to the life of the speaker (poet). Rukeyser can find escape in a library. Also, love and religion might help her create a dream world, but, nevertheless, she yearns for peace—her own and the world's—while absorbed by the dreadful reality of war: "O to be the King in the carol/kissed and at peace"; this King would be Jesus Christ, and her wish is wistful. This is wartime, and its contrast to peacetime is striking:

> but recalling Costa Brava
> the little blossoms in the mimosa tree
> and later, the orange cliff, after they sent me out,
> I knew there was no peace.

She had seen the difference in Spain at the time of her evacuation (1936) as well as later in New York, where she encountered "that locked face, the coarse enemy skin."

She is clearly against war. Her metaphor for the disruptive influence of war is understatedly sarcastic:

> That was the year of the five-day fall of cities.
> > First day, no writers. Second, no telephones.
> > Third, no venereal diseases. Fourth, no income
> > tax. And on the fifth, at noon.
> The nuns blocked the intersection, reading.

The "five-day fall of cities" refers to Spain, particularly. The abrupt shift to the nuns blends the not-so-remote war and the library experience. Reading may seem doubly impractical in the context of traffic and wartime, but they did succeed in interfering with the activity around them. Besides, it is physics that they choose to study—not anything emotional or idealistic. The nuns are both definite and vague and manage to block the speaker's desire. This is analogous to the balking of life by war. In a sense, the speaker's pleasure and happiness are part of this complex image. And they are being stymied by the accidental presence of nuns. It is a sort of nightmare vision.

The poet's male companion and lover had claimed he would have a happy influence upon her and her poetry, but the pessimistic times would not permit his effect to last. War pervades all as does the wind. Her lover could think in terms of their future, but Rukeyser was skeptical and, as it turned out, more realistic. There was only the here and the now and, in fact, she is without him and alone in the immediate present of (the writing of) the poem.

"All that year, the classical declaration of war was lacking," because although Germany and Italy were involved in the Spanish Civil War, no formal announcement was given.

The poet's sex life has been amplified by the war tension—perhaps through promiscuity, lack of inhibition, and experimentation:

> There was a lot of lechery and disorder.
> And I am queen on that island.

This queen is quite a switch from the previous King. The lack of classical declaration is related to the sense of disorder in her own life. Her being "queen on that island" on a personal level suggests further the disorder in the world. She reminds herself to awaken from the dream-like escape of sex.

The end of the poem with its wind imagery presents the revolutionary potential of the time. It has been a nightmarish vision which the wind could affect. The wind, transforming everything, could make a difference. Rukeyser names the poem after the vague nuns who are studious and gregarious. If the nuns could brag over a victory, they may represent the religious power that rooted Franco so firmly. The curious affirmation at the end of "O yes!" is surely another example of sarcasm. As time passes, the wind affects everything except (the bodies of) these sturdy nuns who are staunchly protected by God and whose repressed bodies are not alive and would not be moved. But, still, there may be hope symbolized through the wind. The wind suggests, also, the passage of time which may help: "cities shake in the wind, the year's over,/ calendars tear, and their clothes blow. O yes!"

Of the five English-writing poets under consideration, four supported the Republican side (to varying degrees), while one (Campbell) was firmly aligned with Franco, Roman Catholicism, and the Nationalists. We would expect foreign poets to have a more international perspective on the war than Spanish and Latin-American poets. At the same time, a dimension of intimate experience open to Spaniards would not likely impress foreigners. Campbell had a romantic love affair with the Spain of his choice during the Spanish Civil War. He eulogized the Nationalists and defamed the Republicans. He took this extreme stand for the propagandistic purpose of converting his readers to the fascist/Franco camp and of gloating over their victory. He also used the opportunity to harangue about his own personal, poetic, and prophetic prowess, while chastising such poets as Spender and Auden and the social basis of their point of view. His involvement in the struggle probably came about more because of a wish to defend himself and the Catholic faith, and to castigate his literary enemies, than from his desire to propound the merits of fascism (especially since he later fought against the fascists in World War II). He saw the situation in absolute terms of Right and Wrong and expressed his view with confidence. While Campbell criticized the Republican side for falsehoods ("For them the Lie, false Lenin's 'powerful arm,' "—p. 82), *Flowering Rifle* would seem to be full of his own deliberate distortions and untruths. Campbell's style is grandiose with vigorous and flamboyant rhetoric in keeping with his exaggerated thinking. In view of the fascist victory (at least by the 1939 publication date), it is not surprising to find his epic written in an attitude of optimism and exuberance.

Of the poets discussed, Neruda, Felipe, MacDiarmid, and Campbell would appear to have the greatest egos, with Rukeyser a close second. Like Neruda, Felipe, and MacDiarmid, Campbell wrote in a stentorian voice. He, too, saw his role as poet-prophet, but although their egos seem sturdy, Campbell's arrogance looms;

he pontificates. All poets writing about the Spanish Civil War were partisan, but Campbell presents the most absolute value judgments. While Neruda calls the Nationalists derogatory names like "jackals," Felipe, considering his partiality for the Republican side, is remarkably objective. Campbell is most vehement in downgrading the side he opposed. Neruda's "Almería" is a bitter attack but the facts alluded to, although dramatized, are valid.[32] Also, unlike *Flowering Rifle,* "Almería" has intrinsic artistic merit. Neruda uses the artistic means at his command as a poet, which Campbell does not. Neruda's motivation is political too, but he applies a poet's graphic ability by making visual, auditory images come to life. Campbell does not.

Campbell expressed no feelings that were subtle (in the sense that Vallejo could), only extravagant ones. Most of Campbell's shouting seems to verge on hysteria, while Felipe's polemic is rational. It could be argued that the poem was not meant to be subtle, but to elicit an ideological response on a nonreflective basis. Who, then, would his audience have been?—the lowest common denominator of prejudice.

While Hernández is recruiting in his poem, Campbell is pamphleteering and haranguing at the pettiest, name-calling level. He uses the typical clichés of fascist propaganda; for example, Jews are avaricious and equated with communists. He employs the language of propaganda in a verbal, political, cartoon context. He labels people. He evokes no visual or auditive response—only an emotional, instant reaction to Jews and communists, among others. In the manner of cartoonists and caricaturists, he capitalizes stereotypes, exaggerates, and deforms.

Vallejo and Hernández identify with the common people. Campbell prides himself with having shared the common life of Spain, but there seems to be no feeling of shared experience. He is anti-intellectual but somehow much more intellectual than a peasant. Perhaps this same objection could be brought against Vallejo, but Vallejo expressed a great sense of and feeling for humanity, while Campbell is even contemptuous of humanitarianism.

Campbell is very defensive, and his relation with the rest of the literary world at the time is so negative that he may be considered to be outside his contemporaneous literary current, rejecting the whole English literary Establishment.

The appeal or interest of *Flowering Rifle* would be very limited outside the context of the Spanish Civil War. The poem is difficult to understand and follow, since he wrote from an extremely personal perspective and relied upon his own particular hang-ups to focus his attack. Nor does the aesthetic quality of the poem save it from oblivion. Only as an historical curiosity is the poem fascinating, if not grotesque.

Like Campbell, MacDiarmid has a weak sense of architectonics and form. He has written far too much (for a polemical poem), quoted too much, and discriminated too little. Both expend their energy in tearing down, but MacDiarmid depends more upon reason (especially in Part III of *The Battle Continues*) to lead us to a forward-looking challenge. Campbell, on the other hand, relies upon diatribe without offering any constructive message. Besides, one can follow a logical argument in MacDiarmid's poem which is absent in Campbell's. Because of this, *The Battle Continues* has more shape and is easier to follow and analyze.

MacDiarmid has the positive outlook of a true believer in an ideology. He has faith in communism and democracy. Neruda and Vallejo were also communists, and for communists and Scottish Nationalists Spain offered a giant metaphor. MacDiarmid's idealism derives, in part, from the fact that he was so far removed from the scene of the battle and, in part, from his being convinced of the right (and wrong) of the battle. MacDiarmid glorifies the International Brigades (as Neruda had) and the Spanish Republicans.

Both Scots and Spaniards are noted for their individuality. It is this fierce individuality that made it impossible to organize their forces—of which factions Felipe was critical—and which would have appealed to MacDiarmid. MacDiarmid is first, last, and always a Scotsman. As a Scottish nationalist, he saw the lack of support for the Republic as a sacrifice of "morality" in favor of political self-interest.

At the same time MacDiarmid has a strong, enduring interest in justice for the common people. The Spanish Civil War appealed to his humanitarian instincts because he believes in man—whatever the nationality. He speaks of other tragedies of the nature of Spain's. Having never gone to Spain during or before the war, his involvement was necessarily limited. Also the catalyst for his poem (at a publication distance of twenty years!) was Campbell's poem, although its inspiration derives from the war itself. While the poem is very sincere and was written by someone who knows how to harbor hatred, for MacDiarmid it might have been any other war. Not so for Hernández, Felipe, Neruda, and Vallejo. For the Spaniards and Latins it was personal; it was an assault upon their very being. For MacDiarmid it was ideological and humanitarian, although the stakes are a continued preoccupation ("the battle continues") and source of anguish. Those who were closer to the events would perhaps be more passionately committed, but, as in the case of someone who goes from passionate involvement to bitter reflection, MacDiarmid has reached that later stage. In a way, MacDiarmid was addressing himself to a double defeat: to the irrevocable defeat of the Republican cause in Spain at that time; and to the loss of the living memory of the struggle for those to whom this period has become meaningless history.

His perspective on the war is international and very knowledgeable. He seems to understand its complexities in an objective way, while at the same time to feel its emotional impact.

Auden and Spender were very different from Campbell in background, tastes, values, interpretations of the Spanish Civil War, poetic talent, and touch. Whereas Campbell expended considerable poetic energy blaspheming Auden and his so-called group, Auden remained emotionally detached. While *Flowering Rifle* lacks economy and form, "Spain" is concise and orderly, and its thesis is clear and cogent.

Of the poets considered, Auden is the least present in his poem and the most impersonal. *Spain* surveys rather than participates in the battle. It is also true that, among Hernández, Felipe, Neruda, Vallejo, and Campbell, Auden was the least familiar with Spain at firsthand. Felipe was objective, too, but was an integral part of "La insignia" in the role of poet/prophet. Auden's poem is somewhat prophetic, but the narrator of the third-person presentation is lacking—which adds a certain abstraction to the poem.

Auden does not impose his identity, or that of any other persona, upon his poem. Being outside his lines gives him an air of authority. His imagery is not especially emotional, but reveals scientific-technological leanings. Neruda wrote political poems; "Llegada a Madrid de la Brigada Internacional" showed awareness of the international brigades, and "Almería" showed awareness of the class struggle. Felipe, too, had written of the participation of foreign powers in the war. Such considerations were not present in Auden's poem, although a vision of the class struggle is shown indirectly in Spender's "Ultima Ratio Regum."

Both Felipe and Auden relied upon logical argument. Auden has a detached, objective, and impersonal view as perhaps only a non-Spaniard and noncombatant could. Since he was in Spain for so short a time (three months) and was involved so superficially, his poetic effort was not infringed upon by the demands of participation. Not overly concerned about the fate of Spain, he gave it nominal support. He wrote only one Spanish Civil War poem, and it was also his last poem to include communism significantly. That Auden could thereafter neglect Spain poetically and later denounce his poem suggests that he remained unscathed psychologically or otherwise by that upheaval. His detachment eventually led him to withdraw from politics altogether.

His attitude about death was not that of a combatant: "To-day the deliberate increase in the chances of death." Anyone who had actually seen people shot would have been less glib and less detached about the occurrence.

Although *Spain* is more about war politics than the personal emotion of the poet, Auden offers insights that are universal and avoids mere political propaganda (unlike Campbell). Auden's poem transcends the immediate issues of the war to consider the fundamental values at stake. His perspective is broad enough to permit a deep understanding. When he speaks of "the conscious acceptance of guilt in the necessary murder," he is conscious of something beyond the Spanish Civil War. Besides, *Spain* is an accomplished, visionary poem—one of the best in the English language about the war. Auden successfully separates his poem from political propaganda.

In Auden's poem we do not find the suffering and personal

involvement of Vallejo and Hernández, nor the emotional outrage of Neruda, Campbell, and even Felipe (in his attack against the British). But, like the level-headed Felipe (with the aforementioned qualification), Auden was objective. Auden succeeded in appealing more to the intellectual conscience than to the heart of his readers—which was his intention.

In his derision of the bureaucratic procedures (presumably, those of communism), Auden approaches the objective skepticism of Felipe, who symbolized the divisions on the Republican side by the use of the metaphor of multiple insignias. Such objectivity suggests that the motivation for these poems was not primarily partisan. Also the rhetorical analysis of *Spain* is like that of Felipe's poem. Auden attempted in *Spain* to present a theoretical as well as practical application of the hypothesis of Marxism.

The consciousness of a larger perspective from which to view the war is reasonably a non-Spanish ability. Auden, for example, could look at it in the context of an ideological, modern, new age. Of the poets writing in Spanish, Felipe comes closest in sophistication and perspective to Auden.

The abstraction of such a poem as "Ultima Ratio Regum" suggests Spender's lack of involvement in the war, that is, in the fighting itself. It reflects Spender's left-wing politics, but Spender believed that personal experience and private emotion were the real basis of poetry, and for that reason direct reference to his politics seldom occurred in his verse. "Two Armies" reveals Spender's traditional (in the manner of Thomas Hardy, for example) attitude against war. Of the three poems by Spender, "To a Spanish Poet" is the least abstract and most personal. In this poem Spender considers that, even if his friend is dead, perhaps it is the living who are most dead, rationalizing about an unhappy state of affairs. These three poems are a form of protest against the Spanish Civil War. They are antiromantic but, at the same time, emotional. Spender is full of pity for the victims of war: for the weak and unheroic. He is obsessed with the incalculable loss felt by all humanity. He is concerned with man in relation to his fellow man and believes in the love of one man for another.

Spender wrote two kinds of war poems: those that depict the impact of war upon his sensibility and are defeatist, like "Ultima

Ratio Regum," "Two Armies," "The Room Above the Square," and "Thoughts During an Air Raid"; and those that render wartime events objectively, with a few oblique references to the struggle's tragic implications, for example, "Fall of a City," "At Castellon," and "To a Spanish Poet." "Port Bou" combines both kinds, as the poet is a first-person spectator at a definite time and place on the periphery of the war.

Spender has a fine poetic ear and often employs subtle combinations of sound effects. For that reason as well as for the truth of his insights into human nature and genuine emotion, his poems reach beyond the Spanish Civil War.

Rukeyser's language is provocative and strong, but she is not always a perfectionist about language (in the sense that T. S. Eliot was). Her poems are sometimes rhetorical and sometimes untidy (especially the earlier ones). She has a rich nature, with strong convictions and feelings; her liberal attitudes have been consistent throughout the years.

Her antiwar vigor is shown in "M-Day's Child" via the shocking nature of an innocent child's destruction by war. Her language is much stronger but her perspective is similar to that of Spender in "Ultima Ratio Regum." "M-Day's Child" is as bitter as Neruda's "Almería," but she is looking beyond the Spanish Civil War to the oncoming World War II and to all war.

Like Neruda in "Explico algunas cosas," Rukeyser sees children as vulnerable. But, while Neruda's wrath is vindictively turned against the enemy (the Nationalists), Rukeyser's is more universally applied to all warmongers, whatever their politics. At least, there are no direct references in "M-Day's Child" except to a generalized war situation.

She can be as nihilistic as Neruda, and her nightmarish vision in "Third Elegy" compares with some of the landscapes inundated by blood evoked by Hernández. But Hernández could look optimistically (perhaps romantically) to the future, while Rukeyser makes no favorable affirmations. Her first Spanish Civil War poem, "Mediterranean," was written about her 1936 experience and left some room for hope. It is largely narrative, with lyric expressions of changing impressions. It is straightforward (journalistic), perceptive, sensitive (to implications in the objective events as well as to sensory data), and poetic. "M-Day's Child" is devastating and completely negative. It is condensed and strongly expressed. Its being included in a 1939 collection of poems helps account for its expression of disillusionment. The "Third Elegy" makes no hopeful predictions. The picture is honestly reported as bad. But her technique here is impressionistic and highly symbolic.

Rukeyser's philosophical and political inclinations were always liberal, and she would have rooted for the Republicans in any case, but her physical presence at that time was a coincidence. As a result, she was able to write "Mediterranean." Her strong antiwar stand in "M-Day's Child" is vaguely focused, making her criticism universally applicable. "Third Elegy" makes vague reference to Spain and the war, but its surrealistic presentation further blurs assignation. The main purpose of surrealist poetry is not to communicate ideas. It presents disordered images and impressions, not well-defined concepts. It seems to me that a Spaniard deeply involved in the cause of the Spanish Civil War would not choose to put a smoke screen in front of his message. Vallejo's poem "Pequeño responso a un héroe de la República" has surrealist elements but its framework is unmistakably clear.

Rukeyser's perspective is more general than that of Hernández, Felipe, Neruda, and Vallejo, and she does not prove through her poems that she understands the politics of the war as does Felipe. Rukeyser is very serious, honest, and intense, but her focus is not purely Spanish. What she is is a humanitarian (most like Spender) with strong convictions, poetic talent, liberal views, and an accidental arrival in Spain at the outbreak of the war. Although Campbell and MacDiarmid are more extreme in their viewpoints, she shares something of their emotional nature and exposes herself (at times) as they do. Her preoccupation with sex, for example, is evident in her poems. Neruda, Vallejo, and Hernández could write about sex but not in their Spanish Civil War poems. A similar example would be that of Campbell. In denouncing him, MacDiarmid picks up his fatuous masculinity, because Campbell so often flaunted his manhood in *Flowering Rifle*. This concern with extraneous and most personal aspects was much more frequent in the poems of those poets not deeply involved in Spain and its war.

Notes

1. Muriel Rukeyser, "Mediterranean," *New Masses,* XXIV (Sept. 14, 1937), 18-20.

2. Sources for biographical information on Campbell were the following works: David Wright, "Roy Campbell," *Writers and Their Work,* No. 137 (London: Longmans, Green & Co., 1961); *Encyclopaedia Britannica: Micropaedia* (Chicago: Encyclopaedia Britannica, Inc., 1974), II, 490; Hugh D. Ford, *A Poets' War: British Poets and the Spanish Civil War* (Philadelphia: University of Pennsylvania Press, 1965), pp. 177-201; and Esteban Pujals, *España y la guerra de 1936 en la poesía de Roy Campbell* (Madrid: Ateneo, 1959).

3. Roy Campbell, *Flowering Rifle: A Poem from the Battlefield of Spain,* Part II (London: Longmans, Green & Co., 1939), p. 41.

4. Ford, *A Poets' War,* p. 178.

5. Robert Graves, "A Life Bang Full of Kicks and Shocks," *N.Y. Times Book Review* (Jan. 5, 1958), p. 6.

6. My analysis of *Flowering Rifle* is largely derivative from an original and excellent interpretation by Doug Ford, "Roy Campbell, the Voice of the Insurgents," *A Poets' War,* Ch. 7, pp. 177-201. Here, for example, I have expanded upon Professor Ford's breakdown of Campbell's glaring exaggerations and distortions.

7. Information about MacDiarmid came from the following sources: Kenneth Buthlay: "Hugh MacDiarmid (C. M. Grieve)," *Writers and Critics Series,* eds. A. Norman Jeffares, David Daiches, and C. P. Snow (Edinburgh and London: Oliver and Boyd, 1964); David Daiches, "MacDiarmid and Scottish Poetry," *Poetry Magazine,* vol. 72, no. 4 (July 1948); K. D. Duval and Sydney Goodsir, eds., *Hugh MacDiarmid: a festschrift* (Edinburgh: Duval, 1962); *Encyclopaedia Britannica: Micropaedia,* VI, 437; Hugh MacDiarmid, *The Battle Continues* (Edinburgh: Castle Wynd Printers Limited, 1957); and MacDiarmid, *Lucky Poet—A Self-Study* (London: Methuen & Co., Ltd., 1943).

8. *Lucky Poet,* pp. 8-9.

9. "Talking with Five Thousand People in Edinburgh," *Poetry—Scotland,* 2nd collection, p. 50.

10. Hugh MacDiarmid, *Stony Limits and Other Poems* (London: V. Gollance, Ltd., 1934), p. 53.

11. "Hugh MacDiarmid: The Poet at Seventy," *Glasgow Herald,* 11 August 1962.

12. I referred to the following works while researching Auden's background: Joseph Warren Beach, *The Making of the Auden Canon* (Minneapolis: University of Minnesota Press, 1957); John Blair, *The Poetic Art of W. H. Auden* (Princeton: Princeton University Press, 1965); *Colliers Encyclopedia* (New York: Collier Publishing Co., 1965), III, 211-12; *Encyclopedia Britannica:* Micropaedia, I, 642; John Fuller, *A Reader's Guide to W. H. Auden* (New York: Farrar, Straus & Giroux, 1970); Herbert Greenberg, *Quest for the Necessary: W. H. Auden and the Dilemma of Divided Consciousness* (Cambridge, Mass.: Harvard University Press, 1968); Justin Replogle, *Auden's Poetry* (Seattle: University of Washington Press, 1969); Francis Scarfe, "W. H. Auden," *Contemporary British Poets* series (Monaco: The Lyrebird Press, 1949); Monroe K. Spears, ed., *Auden: A Collection of Critical Essays (Twentieth Century Series)* (Englewood Cliffs, N.J.: Prentice-Hall, 1964); and Spears, *The Poetry of W. H. Auden: The Disenchanted Island* (New York: Oxford University Press, 1963).

13. Stephen Spender, "W. H. Auden and His Poetry," *Twentieth Century Views* (Englewood Cliffs, N.J.: Prentice-Hall, 1964), p. 27.

14. The later version of the poem, with slight revisions, was also contained in *The Collected Poetry of W. H. Auden* (New York: Random House, 1945) on pp. 181 ff. as "Spain 1937"; the text I chose for my analysis was that of the first edition in 1937.

15. Spender, "W. H. Auden and His Poetry," p. 32.

16. Louis MacNeice, *Modern Poetry* (Oxford: Oxford University Press, 1938), p. 197.

17. *The Poet's Tongue* is an anthology of poems edited by Auden in collaboration with John Garrett (London: Bell, 1935). The quotation appears on p. ix.

18. Sources for biographical information on Spender were: biography by William Y. Tindall, *Collier's Encyclopedia;* Ford's *A Poets' War;* and *World Within World: the Autobiography of Stephen Spender* (London: Hamilton, 1951).

19. *The Still Centre* (London: Faber and Faber, Ltd., 1939), p. 10.

20. Stephen Spender, "Poems about the Spanish Civil War (1936-1939)," *Collected Poems 1928-1953* (London: Faber and Faber, Ltd., 1965), p. 99.

21. Spender, *Collected Poems 1928-1953*, pp. 97-98.

22. Spender, *Collected Poems 1928-1953*, pp. 108-09.

23. Spender wrote of the air raid which Altolaguirre recounted to him in his autobiography *World Within World* (1951), pp. 262-63. Their original meeting and something of their friendship ("one of my best friends in Spain") is related on p. 231.

24. Information about Rukeyser was culled from the following sources: B. Alsterlund, biographical sketch, *Wilson Library Bulletin,* no. 15 (Oct. 1940), 110; J. M. Brinnin, "Social Poet and the Problem of Communication," *Poetry,* no. 61 (Jan. 1943), 554-75; T. Parkinson, "Some Recent Pacific Coast Poetry," *Pac. Spec.,* IV, no. 3 (1950), 300-02; Muriel Rukeyser, autobiographical essay, "Under forty," *Contemporary Jewish Rec.,* no. 7 (Feb. 1944), 4-9; and L. Untermeyer, "Language of Muriel Rukeyser," *Sat. R. Lit.,* no. 22 (Aug. 10, 1940), 11-13.

25. Stephen Vincent Benet, Foreword, *Theory of Flight* (New Haven: Yale University Press, 1935).

26. From autobiographical essay, *Contemporary Jewish Record,* p. 7.

27. From *Contemporary Jewish Record,* p. 8.

28. From the Author's Note which precedes *A Turning Wind* (New York: The Viking Press, 1939).

29. Muriel Rukeyser, "Mediterranean," *New Masses,* XXIV, New York, Sept. 14, 1937, pp. 18-20.

30. Muriel Rukeyser, *A Turning Wind,* pp. 24-28.

31. Rukeyser, *A Turning Wind,* pp. 55-56.

32. My standard for factuality is based upon my understanding of two histories of the war, one by Hugh Thomas, the other by Gabriel Jackson.

CHAPTER IV

Concentration on Poets in German, French, Russian, and Italian

The extraordinary reaction in poetry to the Spanish Civil War was not limited just to the Spanish and English languages. The contribution of continental European poets in German, French, Russian, and Italian attests to the literary and human history resulting from that war. The poems by foreigners to Spain proved that the Spaniards were not alone in their opposition. Despite the discrepancies among these poets, there exists a profound common denominator: upon dealing with a Spanish theme, they Europeanize and universalize it. An interest solely in Spain would not have motivated this literature. What happened in that war was that it aroused the most vivid themes of that epoch, to which few writers could feel foreign. The war helped awaken their social consciences. In the literature of the war in Spain were planted the great themes of the twentieth century: the value of liberty and the sense of democracy; the criticism of fascist and Nazi totalitarianism as an enemy of democracy and liberty; the criticism of

205

the society of capitalism and the search for a humanitarian socialism; the protest against the disillusionment provoked by communism; and, also, the desire to establish better equality among the
social classes, by means of distribution of wealth, in order to
extend to all the benefits of modern civilization. Somewhere
among these values a great quantity and quality of writers found
an identity.

Among the major powers, it was only in the Soviet Union that
popular feeling and government policy coincided in favoring the
cause of the Republic. The dictators of Italy and Germany were
committed on the side of the Nationalists.

The conflict in Spain, which had started as a military insurrection against an established regime, soon degenerated into a labora-
tory experiment where fascists and communists tested out themselves and each other. Italian and German ground and air detach-
ments were rushed to General Franco's Nationalist side while
Soviet planes and generals under assumed names fought for the
Republic. The Luftwaffe tried out tactics and the Russians tried
out aircraft. Communist leadership assumed a strong voice in the
government while outright fascism succeeded the rebels' conventional military rule. The democratic powers opted out of the
struggle.

As many as 40,000 foreigners fought in the International Brigades, though the Brigades never exceeded 18,000 at any time.
Most of them were volunteers, a fraction of them being mercenaries, who fought in five brigades, numbered 11 through 15,
whose strength varied between 2000 or 3000 to 10,000 to 15,000
men. The majority of Internationals acted as fellow travelers,
regarding the communists as the most efficient organizers of the
antifascist resistance in Europe.

The poets from Germany, France, Russia, and Italy were interested in antifascist revolutionary movements in general and some
fought in their own country, Spain, or elsewhere, either prior to,
during, or subsequent to the Spanish Civil War, for greater freedom and humanitarian reforms.

Johannes Robert Becher was born in Munich in 1891 and died
in Berlin in 1958. The son of a magistrate, he early broke with

the *bürgerliche klasse* of his origin, like many of his generation. He became a poet, dramatist, critic, editor, and political activist. As a government official he was among the most important advocates of revolutionary social reform in Germany during the 1920s.

Becher studied medicine, literature, and philosophy, and, in 1918, at a time when the Russian Revolution was an inspiration to many German leftist intellectuals, he joined the German Communist Party (KPD). He shared Brecht's faith in and action for the Party. Becher was already an established commentator on the social and artistic scene and a leader of the movement to transform German society through a revolution of the proletariat. Involved in the Expressionist school that dominated German writing in the period 1910-1920, he wrote romantic, emotionally complex poetry that mirrored both his personal turmoil and his visions of a new social order. His earliest verse *Der Ringende* (1911) and his novel *Erde* (1912) prefigure the collision in his Expressionist verse of religious and (in broadest sense) political emotions.

Becher's work shows a clear development: from religiously motivated antibourgeois aggression (with its emotional disorder), to communist *Kulturpolitik* and doctrinaire popular verse. His verse of the former phase was later recanted by him in favor of his later work.

Though elected to the German Reichstag in 1933, he was forced into exile with the advent of Nazi power and went to Moscow. Like Brecht again, Becher wrote in exile. In Moscow he edited a German language newspaper (1935-1945). Life in Moscow disillusioned him about Joseph Stalin's communism but not about the ideology.

The class struggle, the Spanish Civil War, life in the Soviet Union, and exile in general gain in emotional impact by the factualness of their presentation in his poems. Banned from Germany, he rediscovered through his poetry the land, the villages and the cities, the people, its history and its culture; the old fatherland became a "gescholossene Realitat" which the poet interwove with a decade of experience in Russia. Love of homeland and gratitude for the country of his refuge were, along with class and party loyalty, activating elements of Becher's poetry.

Returning to Germany in 1945, he was made President of the

Association for the Democratic Rebirth of Germany (*Kultur-bund*). In 1954 he returned to Berlin and subsequently became a leading figure in the literary life of the German Democratic Republic, and was appointed East German Minister of Culture.

Many of his works are political and of a revolutionary tone: *Verbruderung* (1916), *Paean gegen die Zeit* (1918), *Ewig im Aufruhr* (1920), *Am Grabe Lenins* (1925), *Arbeiter, Bauern, Soldaten* (1925), and *Der Glucksucher und die sieben Lasten* (1938). Of the three poems included for analysis, "General Mola" is from *Ausgewahlte Dichtung aus der Zeit der Verbannung, 1933-1945*, while "Barcelona" and "Fliehende Mutter" are from *Gedichte 1936-1941*.

BARCELONA [1]

1   Unsere Stadt, am Meere hochgebaut,
       Und das Meer hat lichtvoll sie durchblaut,
       Und das Meer schaut träumend zu ihr her,
       Denn dort, wo sie steht, war einst das Meer—

5   Weite Stadt der Säulen und der Hallen.
       Seht, es glänzt wie Muscheln und Korallen,
       Und versunkene Glocken tönen nah,
       Santa Anna, Santa Monica . . .

       Freundenklänge und ein Lied voll Klagen
10   Hast du fernhin bis zu uns getragen.
       Barcelona! Oh, dein Name hat
       Uns verzaubert. In uns lag die Stadt.

       Bargen dich wie einen heiligen Schatz.
       Deine Plätze nahmen in uns Platz
15   Und in meinem Herzen kreuzten sich
       Deine Strassen und belebten mich.

       Wir—wir haben uns mit dir empört,
       Und die ganze Welt hat dich gehört,
       Als du sprachst mit Volkes Stimme—deine
20   Stimme machte stark und fest die meine.

Mir auch stand der Himmel grausam offen,
Und ich sah, du sankst, zu Tod getroffen,
Und ich richtete in mir ein Feuer
Gegen jene feigen Ungeheuer . . .

25 Barcelona, Trümmer. Blutige Pfützen.
Henker in den roten Baskenmutzen.
Fremder Söldnerknecht als Mordgeselle.
Francos Fahne auf der Zitadelle.

Schlechter Rat spricht tückisch auf mich ein:
30 "Schweige still und lass dein Fragen sein!"
Nein, ich werde nach der Wahrheit fragen,
Muss ich mir doch selbst die Wahrheit sagen.

Wie geschah es? Wie war's möglich, dass—
Frag ich, frage ohne Unterlass,
35 Und ich fürcht auch diese Wahrheit nicht:
Scheiterhaufen, Folter, Blutgericht.

Was niemals gelang der Übermacht,
Hat Verrat, hat der Verrat vollbracht,
Und ich frag in London und Paris,
40 Wer ist's, der die Feste fallen liess? . . .

Barcelona. Opferreiche Stadt.
Stadt, die auch für mich geblutet hat.
Unsere Gräber aber öffnen sich.
Barcelona—das bist du und ich—

45 Und das Meer schaut träumend zu dir her,
Denn dort, wo du stehst, war einst das Meer,
Und das Meer hat lichtvoll dich durchblaut;
Unsere Stadt, am Meer hochgebaut!
                    —Johannes R. Becher

Barcelona, the capital of Catalonia, played a strategic role in the Spanish Civil War. A port on the Mediterranean, Barcelona was built as a fortress and its original site was walled, as Becher suggests.

There were a few days of civil war within the city in early 1937.

Ever since July 18, 1936, Barcelona had been the mecca of unorthodox revolutionary groups. French Proudhonians, English utopian socialists, Italian and Balkan anarchists, Russian menshevik intellectuals—all saw in the Catalan revolution the beginnings of a non-Stalinist, "pure" revolution. The communists did not have the prestige in Barcelona that they had in Madrid. Becher's disillusionment with Stalinist communism may have attracted him to the plight of Barcelona.

At the request of Prime Minister Negrin, France (under Leon Blum) opened its border and long-held Russian supplies began rapidly to pass to Barcelona. Mussolini replied to the French with a series of mass bombing raids on the city of Barcelona, beginning on the full-moon night of March 16, 1938. The military damage accomplished was very minor, but coming after twenty months of war, and striking at a slowly starving city, the raids contributed to the steadily sinking morale of the general population. As in the cases of Madrid and Guernica, the Western powers protested the fate of this civilian population in wartime.

On January 22, 1939, General Yajui's troops began to occupy the city of Barcelona, virtually without firing a shot. The battle had already been fought within the city. One-half million refugees from Catalonia began trudging toward the French border. Both Tíkhonov and Eluard consider this exodus and its aftermath in their poems. The majority of the population, and most of the municipal officials, passively awaited the arrival of the Nationalists. The Moors entered vacated apartments and looted heavily. By January 26 the occupation of Barcelona was accomplished.

Becher identifies with the natives, "unsere Stadt," and the city has appealed greatly to his sensibilities. Becher knew the lovely city well and describes it perceptively. Much of the description of the city is lyrical and contains rhymed couplets. He describes the city and angrily despairs over its ruin. He considers its wreckage and defeat a betrayal by all those powers who might have helped and didn't. The cry for help from Barcelona, a metaphor for the pride and potential of all of Republican Spain, was neglected by such capitals as London and Paris. It takes an international perspective (of a foreigner to Spain) to put the blame clearly outside of Spain.

There is repetition of lines: 45 and 3; 46 and 4; 47 and 2; and line 48, in echoing line 1, allows the poem to end neatly with the same line with which it began.

GENERAL MOLA [2]
Aus dem spanischen Bürgerkrieg

1   Wenn er so dasass, ohne aufzuschauen,
    Ein Urteil nach dem andern unterschrieb:
    Nichts Menschliches sass da—ein hagres Grauen,
    Daran allein der Rock noch menschlich blieb.

5   Als könnte er auch weinen oder lachen,
    So menschlich war der Rock, aus feinem Tuch,
    Von Menschenhand gemacht, wie der Versuch,
    Ein Menschenbild aus einem Rock zu
        machen . . .

    Als eines Tags ein Flugzeug unbekannt
10   Abstürzte im Gebirge und verbrannte,
    Aus nichts war eine Herkunft ablesbar:

    Bis man ein Stück von einem Rocke fand,
    Woran man ihn, den General erkannte—
    Das einzige, was menschlich an ihm war.
                —Johannes R. Becher

General Emilio Mola Vidal was the last Director General of Security under the monarchy. Early in 1932 it looked as though the government would retire him to the reserve; however, he appeared to be one of the more loyal to the governmnt of the senior generals. In the spring of 1936 he was moved from command of the Moroccan army to that of the Pamplona military district. Mola's new assignment was a stroke of luck for the plotters against the Republic. While the General was no monarchist, he had developed a violent hatred for Azaña because of the latter's military reforms. And now he was military commander in the heart of the Carlist country, the one portion of Spain where the conspirators could count on a degree of public support.

One of the original junta of military men to rise against the Republic, in the months of August and September 1936, Mola shared the military power of the Nationalists with Queipo de Llano and Franco. He was a shrewd man of great intelligence and energy. Among his peers he had a reputation as a policeman rather than as a soldier and, generally speaking, authoritarians of both the Right and the Left have never wished to hand over supreme power to the head of the police.

To indicate his character, as commander of the North (Navarre-Castille), Mola once told assembled mayors of Navarre that he would not hesitate to shoot anyone caught sheltering "Reds" for any reason whatever. As commander of "four columns" marching on Madrid, Mola claimed to have a "fifth column" of partisans waiting within the city. Also, in March of 1937, General Mola concentrated roughly 40,000 troops in Guipuzcoa and Alava with Navarrese and Moroccans in the lead and Italians in reserve.

Flying to Burgos on June 3, 1937, General Mola crashed on the hill of Buitrago. Inevitably, a question mark surrounds the manner of Mola's death. Was there, perhaps, a time bomb in the airplane? Certainly there were many who might have desired the death of Mola—Franco among them.

Very sarcastic and bitterly denunciatory, Becher views General Mola. He is seen as a scarecrow without humanness or humanity. Becher offers the poetic conceit of two highly dissimilar objects, General Mola, portrayed as a nonsubstantive, complete nonentity, and his richly made and bedecked military jacket. The man himself was nothing—only an authoritarian robot-like military-political figure, responsible for many decisions and many deaths, leading up to and during the war. The jacket, in contrast, is much closer to being human than the man.

Mola was killed without fanfare, in an anonymous plane in an obscure region. Even in death he was unrecognizable. He was identified only through a piece of his jacket—not even the whole jacket —all that was left of this anonymous, insignificant "thing." Becher here sharply ridicules and indicts everything that Mola stood for. The poem indicates a degree of hatred also seen, for example, in Neruda's "Almería."

The sonnet has aspects of both Petrarchan and Shakespearian

sonnets. It has the blank verse of the Shakespearian and the octave and sestet of the Petrarchan. Besides, there is the generalization about the man in the octave and the specific comment about him in the sestet, common to Petrarchan sonnets. Its tone is highly ironic, full of hate and contempt for General Mola.

Becher tells of a fascist general in Spain who in a machine-like fashion had signed one death sentence after another and who, when he crashed in a plane in the mountains, could not be identified until "man ein Stück von einem Rocke fand,/Woran man ihn, den General erkannte—/Das einzige, was menschlich an ihm war."

FLIEHENDE MUTTER [3]

1   "Ich weiss ja nicht, ob ich willkommen bin
In Ihrem Land . . . Ich bin so weit vertrieben . . .
In diesem Bündel? . . . Waffen? . . . 's ist darin
Was Liebes, Herr . . . Sonst ist mir nichts
    geblieben . . .

5   Das kam nun so . . . Das Dorf war lang schon leer,
Die Männer fort im Krieg . . . nur Kinder,
    Frauen . . .
Da kam ein Donnern, Herr, vom Ebro her . . .
Wir liefen auf das Feld um auszuschauen . . .

Kein Stückchen Brot. Nichts—viele Tage lang . . .
10   Und da, da kamen sie . . . So schnell von oben . . .
Und einer, der sich tief herunterschwang . . .
Kein Schrein . . . Ich hab mein Kindlein
    aufgehoben—

Und plötzlich war die Strasse nicht mehr da.
War eine Schlucht. War Eis. Ein Felsen meinte
15   Es gut mit mir . . . Sie kamen wieder nah . . .
Der Felsen barg mich. Auch der Felsen weinte . . .

Ich weiss ja nicht, bin ich noch irgendwo?! . . .
Darf ich es jetzt in Ihre Erde betten? . . .

Verzeihen Sie, mein Herr . . . Das kam nun so . . .
20   Man muss die Toten . . . auch die Toten
          retten . . ."

—Johannes R. Becher

Since Becher has also written a poem commemorating Barcelona, it is likely that he had the general exodus from Catalonia
in mind. The emigrants would cross the French border to seek
escape from the intolerable present conditions and the darkly foreshadowed future in Spain. Away from home, they would be dis-
oriented aliens, having lost, perhaps, everything, including loved
ones.

On July 24, 1938, the Republicans crossed the Ebro heading
southward. The Nationalists opened the dams along the Pyrenean
tributaries of the Ebro, flooding the area. Meanwhile, General
Franco rushed reinforcements to the area with the result that
by August 1 the Republican advance had been stopped just short
of the towns of Gandesa and Villalba de los Arcos. Nationalist
artillery kept the Republican troops pinned to the ground during
daylight hours and destroyed all land communication. It was a
losing battle and, when they saw the writing on the wall, many
began to evacuate across the French border. The "fliehende mutter" would have been among these.

This mother who, as she says, had lost everything else was carrying her dead baby: "auch die Toten retten," hoping to bury him
away from the battlefield, having kept him with her as long as
possible. He had died without cries, shot down by airplane fire,
within hearing distance of the Battle of the Ebro.

The ellipses suggest the groping in the woman's mind concerning what happened and where she is going. The weeping of the
boulder suggests the flow of blood from the wounded, dying, and
dead. In fragmented glimpses Becher presents a brief, narrative,
suggesting the utter rootlessness, defenselessness, and desperation
of this solitary woman who carries her treasure-tragedy along with
her. No home. No family. No solace. No future. Nothing but
being alive with a tortured memory. And, even in her nothing-
ness, she must supplicate, in asking permission to bury her trea-
sured dead.

Of the generation of French poets who came to maturity between the two world wars, Eluard is one of the few whose work has enduring value. Paul Eluard, the pseudonym of Eugene Grindel, was born in Saint-Denis, Paris in 1895. After fighting a lung disease in his youth, for which he spent two years in a Swiss sanatorium, and being gassed during World War I, Eluard turned to Dadaism as to a bitter refuge against the absurdity of wars and of a literature which had stooped to carrying nationalistic propaganda.

He lived almost exclusively in Paris and frequented avant-garde literary and artistic groups. In 1919 he met the poets André Breton, Philippe Soupault, and Louis Aragon, with whom he participated in the foundation of surrealism, and remained in close association with them until 1938.

Many of his early poems were formless and obscure, and nearly always attempt to translate into verse his vision of a world beyond reality. Much of his best-loved poetry was written in the 1920s but he continued to publish a good deal of verse throughout his lifetime. At its best his work has a direct tone and a concrete simplicity.

In 1926 he joined the Communist Party, which he abandoned in 1933. The Spanish Civil War and the crisis of Munich made him, along with his friend Picasso, approach communism again. He rejoined the Party in 1942.

His works emerge from his life experiences: World Wars I and II, the Spanish Civil War (he visited Spain during that war), German occupation, Resistance, struggles of the Communist Party, the women he loved, daily tide of events, encounters, friendships, and dreams.

He wrote some political poetry for the communist movement which is not among his best. His best verses are lyrical and have the clarity of classical French poetry. After the Spanish Civil War, he abandoned surrealist experimentation as being too rigidly doctrinaire. In reaction to the war he simplified his verse, aiming for broad understanding, very much what Neruda and Vallejo had done for the same reason. His late work reflects his political militance and a deepening of his underlying attitudes: rejection of tyranny and search for happiness. During World War II, he was one of the Resistance writers. He died in 1952.

Among his volumes of verse are: *Le Devoir et l'inquietude* (1917), *Poèmes pour la paix* (1918), *Mourir de ne pas mourir* (1924), *Capitale de la douleur* (1926), *Defense de savoir* (1928), *La Vie immediate* (1932), *Les Yeux fertiles* (1936), *Cours naturel* (1938), *Chanson complete* (1939), *Le Livre ouvert* (1940), *Poesie et verite* (1942), *Le Malheurs des immortels* (1945), *Au Rendezvous allemand* (1945), *Poesie ininterrompue* (1946), *Poèmes politiques* (1948), and *Le Phoenix: Poesie ininterrompue* (2ᵉ edition, 1953).

Of the poems chosen for analysis, two are from *Cours naturel*, published in 1938; the other two, one of which is very brief, were published in *Poèmes politiques*, 1948.

NOVEMBRE 1936 [4]

1   Regardez travailler les bâtisseurs de ruines
        Ils sont riches patients ordonnés noirs et bêtes
        Mais ils font de leur mieux pour être seuls sur
           terre
        Ils sont au bord de l'homme et le comblent
           d'ordures
5   Ils plient au ras du sol des palais sans cervelle.

        On s'habitue à tout
        Sauf à ces oiseaux de plomb
        Sauf à leur haine de ce qui brille
        Sauf à leur céder la place.

10   Parlez du ciel le ciel se vide
        L'automne nous importe peu
        Nos maîtres ont tapé du pied
        Nous avons oublié l'automne
        Et nous oublierons nos maîtres.

15   Ville en baisse océan fait d'une goutte d'eau
           sauvée
        D'un seul diamant cultivé au grand jour

Madrid ville habituelle à ceux qui ont souffert
De cet épouvantable bien qui nie être en
   exemple
Qui ont souffert
20   De la misère indispensable à l'éclat de ce bien.

Que la bouche remonte vers sa vérité
Souffle rare sourire comme une chaîne brisée
Que l'homme délivré de son passé absurde
Dresse devant son frère un visage semblable
25   Et donne à la raison des ailes vagabondes.

—Paul Eluard

LA VICTOIRE DE GUERNICA [5]

1

1   Beau monde des masures
De la mine et des champs

2

Visages bons au feu visages bons au froid
Aux refus à la nuit aux injures aux coups

3

5   Visages bons à tout
Voici le vide qui vous fixe
Votre mort va servir d'exemple

4

La mort coeur renversé

5

Ils vous ont fait payer le pain
10   Le ciel la terre l'eau le sommeil
Et la misère
De votre vie

6

Ils disaient désirer la bonne intelligence
Ils rationnaient les forts jugeaient les fous

15   Faisaient l'aumône partageaient un sou en
       deux
    Ils saluaient les cadavres
    Ils s'accablaient de politesses

7

Ils persévèrent ils exagèrent ils ne sont pas
    de notre monde

8

Les femmes les enfants ont le même trésor
20   De feuilles vertes de printemps et de lait pur
    Et de durée
    Dans leurs yeux purs

9

Les femmes les enfants ont le même trésor
    Dans les yeux
25   Les hommes le défendent comme ils peuvent

10

Les femmes les enfants ont les mêmes roses
       rouges
    Dans les yeux
    Chacun montre son sang

11

La peur et le courage de vivre et de mourir
30   La mort si difficile et si facile

12

Hommes pour qui ce trésor fut chanté
Hommes pour qui ce trésor fut gâché

13

Hommes réels pour qui le désespoir
Alimente le feu dévorant de l'espoir
35   Ouvrons ensemble le dernier bourgeon de
       l'avenir

14
Parias la mort la terre et la hideur
De nos ennemis ont la couleur
Monotone de notre nuit
Nous en aurons raison.

—Paul Eluard

"Novembre 1936" and "La Victoire de Guernica" have in common that they reflect Eluard's outrage over the injustice and inhumanity of the attacks on Madrid and Guernica. Both poems are obscure, reflecting surrealist tendencies in their visions outside reality, but also suggesting the brutal truth of what happened to these two places.

In November of 1936 Madrid was, indeed, under siege. General Mola commanded 25,000 troops and attempted to terrorize the city into surrender by indiscriminate bombing. There were air raids every day, and on November 17 the Nationalists made a supreme effort at bombardment. Two thousand shells an hour landed in the center of Madrid, which had no air-raid shelters and almost no antiaircraft artillery. Although approximately five hundred persons were killed that night, Madrid Republicans held their own so that from late November 1936 until the end of the Civil War, the areas of the city held by Nationalists and Republicans remained about the same.

The poem evokes the ferocious resistance of Madrid in the autumn of 1936. The enemies are "bâtisseurs de ruines." They overwhelm Madrid by their creation of garbage, but the capital ("ville habituelle à ceux qui ont souffert") is strongly determined not to give an inch ("Sauf à leur céder la place"). The hope of liberty and equality lives despite the terrifying impact of the land and air attacks.

This same hope inspires the poet in "La Victoire de Guernica." The bombardment of the ancient capital of the Basque country becomes under his pen a "victoire" for the men who endured it because they were conscious of their power and their despair: "Alimente le feu dévorant de l'espoir." The harassed people, enduring so many military reversals affecting their existence, have learned to know their masters and have determined to face up to the future and fight:

> Parias la mort la terre et la hideur
> De nos ennemis ont la couleur
> Monotone de notre nuit
> Nous en aurons raison.

In these poems of 1938 Eluard's poetry has become more accessible through simplified expression. The lines are, in general, short, having been reduced to the essential. But, for that same reason, the style is telegraphic, leaving out transitions that would clarify obscure ideas.

"La Victoire de Guernica" suggests its meaning through a fragmentary series of brief images from the unexpected perspective of Guernica's having been a victory. Guernica, a small town in the Basque province of Vizcaya, had a population of 7000. On April 26, 1937, a Monday (and, therefore, like all Mondays in Guernica, a market day), the small farmers from nearby were bringing into the main square the fruits of the week's toil. At this time Guernica lay about eighteen miles from the front. At half-past four in the afternoon, a single peal of church bells announced an air raid. There had been some raids in the area before, but Guernica had not been bombed. At twenty minutes to five, German Heinkels (flown by Condor aviators) began to appear, first bombing the town and then machine-gunning its streets. The Heinkels were followed by Junkers 52. People began running from the town; they were machine-gunned. Incendiary bombs, weighing up to one thousand pounds, and also high explosives, were dropped by waves of aircraft arriving every twenty minutes until a quarter to eight. The center of the town was, by that time, destroyed and burning. 1654 people were dead; 889 wounded. These facts have been attested to by eye witnesses. This became one of history's most famous premeditated experiments in terror. It symbolized the Nationalist intention to destroy Basque autonomy, and Hitler made it possible.

In no way would Eluard view this disaster area as "beau monde." The people massacred were civilians, among them women and children. "La mort si difficile et si facile" suggests the suddenness and swiftness of their tragic finality. If one were to extract victory from such a debacle, it would be in the dedicated purpose of the lives of those who remain: "Nous en aurons raisons."

Eluard paints a picture so horrible and unjust that the final exhortation ("Nous en aurons raison") has to be true if civilization is to survive. The wish is desperate and romantic, perhaps more despairing than idealistic, but strongly felt and strongly expressed. Eluard, illustrating the affinity between Frenchmen and Spaniards, closely identifies with the Spanish tragedy in general, and with Guernica and Madrid in particular.

EN ESPAGNE [6]

S'il y a en Espagne un arbre teint da sang
C'est l'arbre de la liberté

S'il y a en Espagne une bouche bavarde
Elle parle de liberté

S'il y a en Espagne un verre de vin pur
C'est le peuple qui le boira.

—Paul Eluard

ESPAGNE [7]

1   Les plus beaux yeux du monde
           Se sont mis à chanter
           Qu'ils veulent voir plus loin
           Que les murs des prisons
5   Plus loin que leurs paupières
           Meurtries par le chagrin

           Les barreaux de la cage
           Chantent la liberté
           Un air qui prend le large
10   Sur les routes humaines

Sous un soleil furieux
Un grand soleil d'orage

Vie perdue retrouvée
Nuit et jour de la vie
15   Exilés prisonniers
Vous nourrissez dans l'ombre
Un feu qui porte l'aube
La fraîcheur la rosée

La victoire

20   Et le plaisir de la victoire.
—Paul Eluard

In 1948, in his *Poèmes politiques,* Eluard resumed his theme of Spain. "En Espagne" is a strong, brief poem. Anaphora, repetitions, simple words, density collaborate to express the ardent desire of Eluard for the liberty of the Spanish people. The vision being after the war, the tree stained with blood suggests the fighting and bloodshed that should have earned Spain its liberty. Eluard further implies that if there is anything in Spain worth talking about, it is liberty. And, finally, if there is to be wine drunk (so typically Spanish) and toasts made, the wine will be pure (because Spanish) and it is the people who will drink it. The masses of the people, then, are still for liberty and, therefore, opposed to Franco and everything his succession to power represents.

"Espagne" does not refer directly to the Spanish Civil War but to Spanish resistance to the French regime afterwards. The exiles and prisoners become in "Espagne" "les plus beaux yeux du monde" (Spaniards frequently have large, striking, brown eyes) that sing of their obsession with light and freedom. Despite their confinement (in relocation centers behind barbed wire or, actually, in prisons, they haven't lost their courage. Meanwhile the air ("Chantent la liberté") escapes and these prisoners will end by triumphing. The long phrases of this poem are produced by run-on lines and, separated by one or two lines which mark time, allowing for reflection, they present a look of firm marching toward a definite goal: victory. These exiles, already having lost their homeland, want their freedom.

Eluard's viewpoint as a Frenchman had naturally been attracted to the situation and condition of the Spaniards in France.

Like other surrealists, Eluard was fundamentally an optimist; he was confident that ways could be found or devised to alter man's fate and to accomplish miracles challenging the misery of the world. But, like all men, he knew moments of dejection. These ups and downs are reflected in his poems both during and after his surrealist period.

Eluard was a poet with a moral conscience who repudiated poetry of complacent self-contemplation, which bemoaned the writer's solitude. He also abhorred all that was ornamental and rhetorical in poetry; he wished to be understood even by common people, for which purpose he chose simple language and evocative imagery.

Nikoláy Semyónovich Tíkhonov was born in St. Petersburg (now Leningrad) in 1896. Born into a lower-middle-class family, he attended a commercial high school and received a rather poor formal education. He fought in a hussar regiment during World War I, later joining the Red Army and participating in the Revolution and Civil War in Russia from 1918-1922. Having helped to defend Leningrad from the Whites, he later (still in the early 1920s) settled there.

Spirited and fond of adventure, in the 1920s and 1930s, he traveled in the outlying parts of the Soviet Union, Asia, and Europe, and tried several occupations, acting among them, before he turned to literature, which to him then meant poetry. His first collection of poems appeared in 1922. Other books of verse, as well as of prose, followed, and of translations, chiefly of Georgian poetry. In the early 1920s he belonged to the Serapion Brothers, a literary group who in the midst of the Russian Revolution were bold enough to champion political neutrality. Tíkhonov confessed publicly to a weakness for anarchy. This fraternity of writers admired the romanticism of the German writer E. T. A. Hoffmann and was strongly influenced by Gumilev, who glorified courage, virility, and loyalty in his terse poems of civil war and revolution.

In his first two collections of poetry *Orda* (1922) and *Braga* (1923), Tíkhonov sought to express the sensations of his years of war and adventure. He extolled the revolutionary romanticism of civil war and individual acts of bravery. In these and other early poems, the influence of Acmeism (a literary doctrine that advocated concrete, individualistic realism, stressing clarity, emotional intensity, and verbal freshness) is evidenced by his use of concrete images, pictorial detail, and semantic precision. These poems also showed the influence of Gumilev and of the English romantics, especially in Tíkhonov's predilection for the ballad. Tíkhonov had a positive attitude toward the 1917 Revolution, which he saw as a release of tremendous energy and as an event from which to learn and exhibit courage.

In the mid-1920s under the influence of the poets Velemir Khlebnikov and Boris Pasternak, Tíkhonov experimented in his poetry. He traveled to the East and to Central Asia, gaining new materials, tones, and colors for poetic use.

By the early 1930s Tíkhonov began to concern himself in his poetry more and more with broad social issues. His prose works, however, continued to be romantic in style and in spirit, as in his short stories of marvels and mysteries. He changed his mind about anarchy and became a staunch supporter of the Soviet regime and an ardent patriot. He stressed in his writings during World War II the same ideals of duty and courage he had in his earlier writings.

From 1944 until the purge in the field of the arts which took place in the summer of 1946, Tíkhonov held the important post of chairman of the board of the Union of Soviet Writers. Tíkhonov's literary and political work (he served as cultural ambassador on several occasions and also wrote propaganda) earned him the Order of Lenin. During World War II he wrote many patriotic poems, one of which won him the Stalin Prize, and essays, including *Leningrad Tales* (1943), a series of stories in which he celebrated the heroism of the seige of Leningrad. He won Stalin Prizes in 1942, 1949, and 1952.

During the late 1950s Tíkhonov alienated many other Soviet writers because of his part in a critical campaign against Pasternak.

In his poetic career, Tíkhonov, after 1922, left the misty symbolism of the Cosmists Movement and developed toward greater concretization and toward realism, romantic and otherwise. Tíkhonov had an intensely private vision of the world. He was a poet of the Russian Revolution whose devotion to the cause went beyond idealized allegiance. His highly individualistic, lyrical verse found its inspiration in the cause of communism. His ballads on the Russian Civil War were both romantic and realistic. Their lyrical tone was that of heroic romanticism. For his poems he preferred sharp, definite outlines and bright colors.

Tíkhonov, although Pasternak's principal rival for top honors in Soviet poetry, possessed neither the sheer poetic power nor the originality of Pasternak. On the other hand, his poems are relatively free of the difficult language and complicated handling of themes that prevented Pasternak's poems from winning wide popularity.

It is difficult to place Tíkhonov in any particular poetic school, for from his early narrative verse tales (*Orda* and *Braga*) to his later ballads on civil war themes and his recent poems, he has consistently and independently developed his art largely as a medium for treating romantic themes of revolution in a clear, realistic manner. At times, Tíkhonov seems more like a novelist in verse. His simple, unrestrained realism has influenced later Russian poets.

Among his poems are "David" (1919), "Orda" (1922), "Ballada o sinem pakete" (1922), "Ballada o gvozdyakh" (1919-1922), "Braga" (1923), "Litsom k litsu," "Doroga," "Shakhmaty" (1920s). Among his collections of verse are: *Poeski geroya* (1927), *Yurga* (1926-1930), *Stikhi o kakhetii* (1935), the last two concerning contemporary life in Turkmenia and in Georgia. His collection *Tien' drouga* (1936) was based on his Western impressions and contains a passionate condemnation of fascism, declaring the poet's loyalty to the antifascist forces. The poems in this grouping present impressionistic perspectives of the upheavals wrought in Western Europe by World War I, as well as premonitions of the coming of new battles. *Chudesnaya trevoga* was written from 1937 to 1940 and *Gori* from 1938 to 1940. Among his patriotic verse and poems are "Kirov s nami" (1941), "Leningrad prinimaet bay" and "Ognenny god" (both in 1942). Among his verse cycles are: "Stikhi o Yugoslavii" (1947), "Gruzinskaya vesna" (1949), "Dva potoka" (1951), and "Na vtorom vsemirnom kongresse storonnikov mira"

(1951). He wrote the poem "Mys dondra" in 1960. *Mayskoe utro* (1961) is a collection of verse and stories.

Although Tíkhonov did not fight in Spain or even go to Spain, he had fought in Russia in a popular revolution and could identify intellectually with such a movement in Spain. Besides, he was a communist at the time of the war and still is. The three poems for analysis are: "Ispantsi otstupili za Pirenyiei," "Govorit fashist," and "Govorit antifashist." The first is in the section of Tíkhonov's collected poems titled "Gorï" (1938-1940). The other two appear under the heading "Numancia" (1938).

И С П А Н Ц Ы
О Т С Т У П И Л И   З А   П И Р Е Н Е И [8]

1   Не могу прикоснуться к перу,
       Словно полны чернила заклятий,
       А в глухом иностранном бору
       Лишь о войнах выстукивал дятел.

5   Только видятся женщины мне
       Среди зимней дороги скалистой,
       Только дети, упавшие в снег,
       Только рощ обгоревшие листья.

       И о пепельных, полных седин,
10   Так пронизанных порохом рощах,
       И о людях, молящих воды
       За колючею проволкой ночью, —

       Что ни скажешь о жизни такой,
       Все не так, и не то, и все мало, —
15   Все уж сказано детской рукой,
       Из-под снега торчащей на скалах.
       —Níkolay Semyónovich Tíkhonov

In this neatly arranged lyrical poem, Tíkhonov evokes the aftermath of the Spanish Civil War. It is very powerful, the final disturbing image being a child's hand projecting from the snow. Over the hushed terrain, devastated, destroyed, ruined a woodpecker hammers as if via the Morse code. Women and children, among others unmentioned by Tíkhonov, have trekked from Catalonia, across the Pyrenees, to France in search of refuge. Their march was long, harassing, and brutal, sometimes terminating in death. There is also a glimpse of those who reached their destination and were interned behind barbed wire fences. They are now thirsty beggars in this hapless solution to the problem of the large influx into France. The poet admits his inadequacy to the task of writing down such a scene; however, unlike that of Braccialarghe, Tíkhonov's modesty belies his skillful, poignant poem. Tíkhonov claims that the vision he wishes to evoke has already been far more eloquently expressed by the isolated hand of the dead child and other remnants of the war—which does give one pause for thought.

The poem appeals to the emotions, expressing compassion for the suffering of the women and children, the most innocent victims of war. It also makes a strong visual appeal. This might have been an antiwar poem about any war except for the title which clearly depicts the final retreat from Spain beyond the Pyrenees and the barbed wire which denotes the French internment camps thereafter.

Говорит Фашист:[9]

1   Вот говорят: фашистская держава
      Не знает человеческого права,
      Что мы глядим на вещи слишком просто,
      Что любим мы лишь тишину погоста.

5   Сейчас я объясню вам, отчего:
      Народ — дитя, мы — фюреры его.
      Ребенка вы, чтоб вырос он титаном,
      С младенчества кормите барабаном.

      Парадов факелом слепите по ночам,
10   Привейте вкус к воинственным речам.
      Довольно книг — в костер обложек глянец!
      Вокруг костра устраивайте танец,
      Какой плясал в медвежьей шкуре предок,
      И песню затяните напоследок,
15   Что всей земли народов вы грозней
      И призваны господствовать над ней.

      Но так как ваш народ не до конца
      Покорен воле фюрера-отца
      И хочет жить, трудиться, веселиться,
20   И предками не хочет он гордиться,
      И с ним вы не справляетесь добром, —
      Вооружитесь добрым топором.

И вот, когда по мере власти роста
Во всей стране величие погоста,
25 И введены военные харчи,
И есть приказ: работай и молчи! —
Тогда, чтоб не нагрянула разруха,
Возьмитесь вы за воспитанье духа:

Верните женщин кухне и перине,
30 Утехой воинов будут пусть отныне.
Усильте рев газетных батарей:
Виной всех бед марксист или еврей,
И что подчас они одно и то же —
Пускай наш гром скорей их уничтожит!
35 Нас вовсе сжали жалкие соседи,
В военной мы нуждаемся победе!

Твердите всем: обижены судьбою,
Отныне приступаем мы к разбою!
Чтобы за вами выла вся страна:
40 «Война! Война! Да здравствует война!»

Да здравствует война всегда и всюду,
И городов пылающие груды,
И вопли женщин, и оружья грохот,
Победы гул и побежденных ропот.
45 Покой и труд — марксистская гримаса,
Все расы — прах, есть только наша раса!

Так в пепел все — над пеплом знамя наше,
Пусть вражьи черепа идут на чаши.
Дохнем из них дыхание вина —
50 И все до дна: да здравствует война!
　　　　—Níkolay Semyónovich Tíkhonov

Tíkhonov wrote a Prefatory Note to the two poems, "Govorit fashist" and "Govorit antifashist," among others, explaining that the play *Numancia* by Cervantes depicts an episode of the battle between ancient Rome and Spain. The tragic details of the attack on the city of Numancia by the Romans show us the unceasing struggle for freedom of the Spanish people, their courage and contempt for death. The Roman world became aware of the Spaniards' sacrificial acceptance of death through the defense of their ally, the city of Saguntum, against the Carthaginians, and by the long fight of their enemy, the Celtiberian stronghold of Numancia, climaxed by the destruction of the city and the collective suicide of its inhabitants—who thus deprived Scipio of his victory over them. The bravery and love of liberty of Spain's ancestors compares with the heroism of the defenders of Republican Spain, 1936-1939.

In Cervantes' tragedy, comprised of four days' journeys, he introduced an intermezzo in verse. In the scene were presented allegorical figures: Spain, War, the River Duero, Hunger, and Glory (this listing is Tíkhonov's and differs somewhat from Cervantes' original). These allegorical figures deliver speeches about Spain during the time of Cervantes, and each figure speaks according to his viewpoint. The heroic tragedy, *Numancia,* was performed with great effect during the Spanish Civil War as an antifascist play.

Tíkhonov translated the intermezzo to *Numancia* and added new figures, the Fascist and the Antifascist, each speaking from his particular role's philosophy. He also changed the River Duero to the River Ebro.

"Dovorit fashist" is politically motivated and offers hard line Party rhetoric. The true fascist, according to Tíkhonov's scathing view, wishes to subjugate the world, while destroying it at the same time:

> Tak v pyépyel vsye—nad pyéplom známya náshe,
> Pust'vrázhyi chyeryepá idut na cháshi.
> Dokhnyóm iz nikh dĭkhániye viná—
> I vsyo do gna: da zdrávstvuyet voyná!

It is a completely military, anticultural viewpoint: "Dovól'no knyig—v kostyór oblózhek glyányets!" Women would be objects, exploited in the kitchen and bedroom. The enemy is the familiar .Marxist-Jewish scapegoat. The defensive claim is that the fascists have been oppressed by miserable neighbors, thus explaining their self-righteous prerogative to dominate and seize everyone and everything.

The devastation they will cause is a source of pride and is vividly depicted by violent, audio-visual-olfactory images of lines 41 through 50.

It is a patronizing perspective in which: "Naród—dityá, mĭ—fyúreri yevó." The masses are to be trained from childhood by military drums, martial speeches, torch parades, bonfires, songs, the specter of the war mentality pervading.

This is a highly ironic poem, with an exaggerated depiction of the fascist stand. The vocabulary is strong and energetic, as are the images. Death imagery is a motif. There is a pun on the word "pogosta" in line 4. Silence would prevail in a cemetery, but also, implicitly, there would be many graves. Again he speaks of enemy skulls and of complete ruination.

Considering the content, the traditionally pleasant rhyme scheme (aabb) is striking. The vocabulary is adapted to the theme and the poem and its implications are very strong, providing a merciless, violent attack upon fascism.

Its general condemnation rather than specific one against fascism in Spain (although the Spanish tie-in was clearly stated in Tíkhonov's Prefatory Note) suggests Tíkhonov's ideological aversion to fascism wherever it occurs, and lack of particular identity with Spain.

Говорит Антифашист:[10]

1	Чтоб надо мной стояла ночь и день
	Тюремщика вихляющая тень,
	Чтоб каждой мысли вольное движенье
	Немедленно бралось под подозренье,
5	Чтобы страницы мной любимых книг
	Костер фашистский уничтожил вмиг,
	Чтоб вместо слов простых и человечных
	Рев фюреров я слышал бесконечный,
	Чтобы всю жизнь под диких песен вой
10	Шагал с лопатой в лагерь трудовой,
	Чтобы, презренной жизнью дорожа,
	К народам пленным шел я в сторожа,
	Участвовал в разбойничьих походах,
	Чтобы убийц я славил в рабских одах,
15	Чтоб стал, как труп, безмолвен и, как труп,
	Гнил заживо между заводских труб,
	Одной войне дымящих славословье,
	Моих друзей обрызганное кровью,
	Чтоб я забыл, что есть на свете разум.
20	Косясь на мир налитым злобой глазом,—

Нет! Будет мир стоять неколебим!
Он помнит все, что пережито им:
Пожары, казни, бедствия, сраженья,
Века позора, рабства, униженья,
25 Где б ни свистел кнутами новый Рим —
Мы ничего ему не отдадим!

Ни наших нив, шумящих морем хлеба,
Ни наших гор, вонзивших пики в небо,
Ни наших рек, струящихся в тиши,
30 Ни начатых народами работ,
Ни городов, где улиц гул веселый,
Ни тех полей, где расцветают села;
И соловей не должен умереть,
О нашей славе будет он греметь,
35 И ястреба, что над холмов горбами,
Пускай парят простыми ястребами,
И ни тропинки розовой, весенней,
И ни морей, что нету многопенней,
И ни костра, чей вьется рыжий дым
40 В лесу осеннем, — мы не отдадим.
Не отдадим улыбок наших смелых,
Ни парусов на лодках наших белых,
Ни воздуха, которым дышим мы,
Ни блеска дня, ни теплой ночи тьмы,
45 Последней ветви яблони румяной,
Луча зари над спящею поляной,
Ни гордости самим собою быть,
Ни права завоеванной судьбы.
Фашизм найдет лишь гибель впереди —
50 Мы ничего ему не отдадим!

Пусть северный иль южный встанет Рим —
Смертельно с ним в бою поговорим!
—Níkolay Semyónovich Tíkhonov

This poem, written from an antifascist viewpoint, begins in the first person as a German (or Russian) soldier ponders his conscription into an army under a führer (or führers) against his will. He feels himself and even his innermost thoughts imprisoned and judged. Fascism destroyed a culture that he loved and he worked in a labor camp where he was forced to listen to nothing but the loudest incantations of the führer and indoctrination songs.

He has been forced to serve as a soldier with those whom he despised, and forced to repeat poems glorifying soldiers who were no more than pirates. He worked in factories, serving the war effort, and could not speak up without risk of his life. His friends were dying from overwork in these factories, and he was numbed into forgetting that there might be a reasonable world somewhere outside and beyond.

This antifascist hates what he has seen and protests against what he has had to do. The first stanza offers a lament for what has happened and what is happening. In the second part he is awakened out of his stupor and doubting into a strong assertion of his convictions. Rome's imperialism is equated with that of Nazi-fascism. The stanza ends with his declaration never to surrender what freedom offers and what fascism would, most assuredly, destroy.

The third stanza lists magnificently, beautifully, and lyrically what it is he is unwilling to part with and surrender to Nazi-fascism. And it is a lovely vision of peacetime, nature, and what is best in the world.

Finally, he shouts that whether Northern or Southern Rome (Germany, that is) rises up, he and his antifascist, fellow-soldiers will meet them in a battle to the death. It expresses a stand as well as a threat. There is a point beyond which men will not submit even if it costs them their lives.

The poem reveals its message in a stentorian voice. It is a strongly-felt, strongly-stated, didactic poem preaching antifascism, condemning Nazi-fascism. Although rhetorical, the words are not empty; the verse expresses a militancy, hostility, and vitality that must derive from an energetic, absolutely dedicated antifascist.

Giorgio Braccialarghe was the son of a better-known writer than himself, Comunardo Braccialarghe (who wrote under the pseudonym Folco Testena). Despite Giorgio's obscurity, he had the distinction of having fought in the Spanish Civil War as vice-commander of the Garibaldi Battalion, composed of idealistic young Italians, numbering 3350, and of having written at least four poems about the war. Two of the poems eulogize his International Brigade; and the other two, also, speak directly from his war experience. He signed his poems, collected in an anthology of International Brigade poetry, *Romancero de los voluntarios de la libertad,* published in Madrid in 1937, only with his last name. It was only in his father's biography in *Dizionario bio-grafico degli italiani* that Giorgio is not only mentioned, but definitely connected with the Spanish Civil War. After the war, he continued to fight against Nazi-fascism in Europe, where he was arrested and imprisoned on Ventotene, an island in the Gulf of Naples. His ultimate fate remains unknown.

TERRA DI SPAGNA . . .[11]

1   Terra di Spagna quando annotta. Freme
per gli uliveti e sopra l'arsa terra
la nuova voce di chi più non teme
l'immane vergogna della guerra.

5   Per quelli che verranno un'altra sorte
la voce canta, e noi che l'ascoltiamo
in essa la consegna ritroviamo:
Non v'è resurrezione senza morte.

       Terra di Spagna quando annotta. Voi
10   col sublime linguaggio degli eroi
questa consegna tramandaste a noi
ed ai venturi che verran da noi.

       Voi moriste, o compagni, ma la morte
v'illuminò la vita. Noi vivremo
15   perchè la vita illumini la morte
di chi prescelse il sacrificio estremo.
                   —Giorgio Braccialarghe

This is a very idealistic, lyrical poem written with youthful vigor and faith by a soldier-poet who desperately wants and needs to believe that the many deaths in his own battalion have not been in vain. In order to carry on one must believe that the sacrifice has meaning, purpose, and possibilities beyond itself ("resurrezione," "illuminò la vita").

The voice that roars above the subdued landscape of nighttime Spain ("per gli uliveti e sopra l'arsa terra") comes from those

heroes (with whom the poet closely identifies) who have died—
who are beyond fear—but are still present in spirit. The voice
commands that those still left in the fight know that death for
their cause has positive value with great rewards. Such a philosophy offers consolation, hope, courage, and faith in the difficult
trials of war that lie ahead. Braccialarghe meant to inspire his
fellow-men in a continuing struggle. He considers the language
of these dead heroes "sublime." Braccialarghe addressed his poem
to his fellow soldiers with simple and repetitious praise.

Reminiscent of "Notti di Spagna" when the lull at nighttime
makes such thoughts possible, "Terra di Spagna . . ." glorifies
death in this battle to achieve some meaning from life. It is
through death in such a struggle that life might have some meaning in the future. Identification with the aims of the war, as well
as hope and faith, align this soldier-poet with the Hispanic poets
we have discussed.

NOTTI DI SPAGNA [12]

1
    V'è tanta biacca nel cielo
    che sembra che una sposa
    abbia dimenticato il suo velo
    appeso ad una rosa.

5
    E il velo sventoli nella campagna
    come un filtro pieno d'incantamento
    che lasci passare
    il chiarore lunare
    tra i fremiti del vento.

10
    Notti di Spagna,
    cantando le raganelle
    lungo i fossati
    tra i prati.

    V'è un bisbiglio assonnato
15
    come se le belle
    ascoltassero i segreti
    dei loro innamorati.

Notti di Spagna,
mantelli di pace gettati
20   sui martoriati giorni
ritorni di calma
sussurri indefinite
rumori azzittiti.

Le seninelle immobili nell'ombra;
25   sembrano statue sperse
nei sentieri d'un parco.

Notti di Spagna
nelle trincee serpeggiano
ingenue confidenze
30   qualcuno parla della fidanzata
qualcuno narra l'ultima avanzata.

E nei brevi silenzi
che punteggiano le frasi
voci lontane
35   di compagni scomparsi
sussurrano parole strane.

Intanto, nella notte stellata
risuona qualche fucilata.
—Giorgio Braccialarghe

As a soldier Braccialarghe would have known the dreamlike nights of Spain, as well as the days of desperate, determined destruction. He looks at the dark sky with its clouds and moon and sees them metaphorically in terms of a bride's veil hanging upon a rose. The nights are so quiet that the toads can be heard. The trenches, ironically, are located in meadows which were once peaceful and beautiful. The silence is, for the poet, like the atmosphere when lovers whisper secrets.

The peaceful nights belie the horror-filled days that have preceded and will follow. Even the sentry on guard, ready to shoot at a moment's notice, seems like a statue in a peacetime park. Again, because of the stillness, innocent conversations about loved ones or past battles are heard in the trenches.

It seems, between sounds, when the hush is total, that even the strange, remote dialogue of dead comrades can be heard, as in "Terra di Spagna . . . ." Meanwhile, from time to time, in the night full of stars, a gunshot shatters the calm, reverberates, and reminds us of what the situation really is.

This is a laconic poem that leaves out more than it includes. Full of brief glimpses and sounds in the night, the poem offers a romantic and oblique perspective during the respite between battles. It is what is suggested, but not mentioned, that makes an impact. The gunshot in the final line provokes sober, somber reflection from the reader. This is a lyrical, eulogistic poem whose mood is nostalgic for peacetime behavior, attitudes, and environment.

AI FRATELLI LONTANI . . .[13]

1 Stanotte voglio cantare per voi
 senza rima né metro.
 Povere parole balbettate
 come quando dopo aver pianto tanto,
5 uno ricerca chi sparì per sempre.
 E gli parla. E non sa cosa dice
 né che vorrebbe dire.
 Voglio parlarvi, O fratelli lontani
 come quando m'eravate vicini
10 e sembravate titani.
 Titani nella lotta, fanciulli nella pace.
 Non posso pensare che qualcuno giace
 sbiancato, in un bianco letto
 col suo sembiante di giovinetto
15 che non vuol morire.
 Non posso pensare che non debba venire
 il giorno della resurrezione
 per il nostro battaglione.

Il terzo: il più forte!

20 Primo all' attacco e primo alla vittoria.

Scriveva le pagine più belle della storia

tra una canzone e l'altra.

Colonna gagliarda di gagliardi eroi.

Poco meno di mille,

25 mille anime in ognuno.

Avanti, avanti, avanti.

Sopportando fatiche e digiuno

sonno e sete ma avanti

come tanti giganti

30 che s'alimentano d'ideali

e che non chiedono che ali

per il volo trionfale

verso la meta finale.

Poco meno di mille,

35 ma quanta, quanta fede!

Sui colli martoriati del Jarama

nei boschi dell'Alcarria

tutto un inno di gloria

scritto col vostro sangue

40 immortalato dal vostro sacrificio.

—Madrid intanto

sopportava il lugubre canto

dei cannoni nemici.

E su nella Viscaglia

45 l'eterna canaglia

distruggeva ogni cosa.—

Che importa? Nei lettini

degli ospedali da campo

sorgeva una rosa

50 di sangue, sorgeva un sorriso

nel vostro viso di giovani eroi

Avevate fiducia in noi.

In noi che restando alla lotta

occupavamo, fieri, il vostro posto

55   o scomparsi di ieri
            o destinati a vivere domani.
            Domani, quando dai campi liberati
            dalle officine redente
            s'eleverà solennemente in coro
60   l'inno della pace e del lavoro.
                              —Giorgio Braccialarghe

Similar to "Fratelli dell'Internazionale," "Ai fratelli lontani . . ." deals with the International Brigade. Randolfo Pacciardi, an Italian Republican émigré (never a communist) had approached the Spanish government and had gotten its approval for his idea of forming an Italian Legion in Spain, independent of political parties, to be recruited at first in Paris out of Italian political exiles.

The first groups of International Brigades arrived in Spain in October of 1936. They were nearly all Frenchmen, with some Polish and German exiles from Paris. There were also some White Russians. These were shortly joined by many of the foreign volunteers who had fought in Aragon and in the Tagus valley, including the German Thaelmann Centuria, the Italian Gastone-Sozzi Centuria, and the French Paris Battalion.

The Garibaldi Battalion was formed in November of 1936 as the Italian trainees took over the village of Madrigueras. On November 12 the new XIIth International Brigade, comprised of the Thaelmann, André Marty, and Garibaldi Battalions of Germans, French, and Italians, was sent to the sector of the front at the Madrid-Valencia highway. Braccialarghe's calling his battalion the third is, therefore, confusing.

Pacciardi, who proved himself from the start an outstanding leader, led the Garibaldi Battalion. Giorgio Braccialarghe was a vice-commander.

When the Brigade first entered battle, commands were confused because of the language problem in giving orders. Besides, having marched almost nine miles that day, the Brigade was tired before it started to fight. Artillery support was inadequate, and certain companies got lost. Fighting went on for the rest of the day, but the object of the attack, the hill in the geographical center of Spain known as Cerro de los Angeles, remained impregnable. The Brigade then withdrew and was transferred to the Madrid front. The Brigade was also later involved in the attack against Huesca on the Aragon front, in an attempt to draw Nationalist fire away from Bilbao.

It can be assumed that Braccialarghe was painfully aware that the fighting of the Brigade was very rough going and that a third of the Brigade died in action in Spain.

"Ai fratelli lontani . . ." is full of the clichés of war and peace and of enemies and allies. It glorifies the memory of those soldiers who are now far away in Death. He explains his technique: no rhyme, no meter. And he addresses himself directly to the war dead.

Although Braccialarghe is a part of the military force, he has not lost his humanity. He feels obliged to write, wishing to express what he has inside himself. Yet he recognizes his poetic limitations. Like Hernández, he is a young idealist who fights and writes poems on behalf of his convictions.

He yearns to believe in the resurrection of the war dead. Again, as in "Fratelli dell'Internazionale," the soldiers through their deeds, figuratively, write beautiful pages of history. From lines 19 to 22, he speaks of the soldiers and the poems they have within them. Their idealism, youth, hope, bravery, hardships, and final sacrifice are eloquent. Braccialarghe numbers the battalion at a thousand and mentions various locations of their battles: Jarama, Alcarria, Viscaglia. He uses the rose, a common metaphor, here as in "Notti di Spagna." Turning to those still left to fight, he means to urge them on by reminding them of their obligation to their dead brothers. He dreams of liberty and imagines the future, after victory is achieved: "della pace e del lavoro." The poem is nostalgic in tone as it romanticizes the soldiers, the war, and the future.

The poem begins lyrically and becomes epic and martial toward the end as it lists some of the battlegrounds. Of lyrical origin in its desire for peace, it is a political poem, socialistic in its notion of brotherhood.

FRATELLI DELL'INTERNAZIONALE [14]

1
I primi sei mesi di lotta sono passati: avanti, fratelli dell'Internazionale.

2
La vittoria ancora non è stata raggiunta: avanti, fratelli dell'Internazionale.

3
A palmo, a palmo, e con al fianco il sacrificio che è bello, e con il ricordo dei nostri caduti nel cuore: avanti, fratelli dell'Internazionale.

4
Voi siete i seminatori dei domani. Già l'alba si è affacciata nel cielo rosso della rivoluzione, già la terra di Spagna conosce la vostra seminagione: avanti, fratelli dell'Internazionale.

5
La lotta dell'oggi reca le promesse di pace del domani, la sementa di ieri, i frutti dell'avvenire: avanti, fratelli dell'Internazionale.

6
Tra tutte le vostre canzoni manca quella della Spagna liberata. Voi ne sarete gli epici poeti, voi la creerete con le vostre gesta, giorno per giorno, ora per ora: avanti, fratelli dell'Internazionale.

7
Vi conosco uno per uno, ma se conoscessi uno solo di voi, vi conoscerei tutti. Per il patrimonio di fede, di disciplina e di volontà che vi rende uguali, per la semplicita che veste ogni vostra azione sublime.

8

Dopo sei mesi vi riconosco uno per uno. Siete
ancora gli stessi, ancora portate in voi il fermo
desiderio di vittoria che baciò la fronte chiara
dei nostri Caduti.

9

Avanti, fratelli dell'Internazionale. Per altre lotte,
per altri trionfi; uniti; per la Spagna accogliente,
nel suo grembo sanguinante, i destini del mondo:
invincibili.

10

Avanti, fratelli dell'Internazionale. Con voi la
giustizia, contro di voi la rabbia del falsi potenti.

11

Ognuno di voi che cade è una goccia d'olio nella
lampada votiva della Libertà. Ogni nemico che
abbattete e una maglia infranta della catena che
tiene avvinta l'Umanità.

12

Avanti, fratelli dell'Internazionale. Avanti, avanti,
avanti. Per il domani di Spagna. Per l'avvenire
di tutto il mondo. Avanti!

—Giorgio Braccialarghe

Braccialarghe presents his poem, "Fratelli dell'Internazionale,"
from a first-person-singular viewpoint and addresses it to the
Brigade in the second person plural: "Voi siete i seminatori dei
domani." He knows them "uno per uno," and identifies with
their cause of world freedom, at the same time that he has a perspective above them that a commander would have.

He dates the poem January 1937 in the first line. This early
in the war the outcome could still have been mistaken. Although
there have been heavy losses, he justifies the price of present glory
and future victory. The poem is reminiscent of those by Hernández, who glorified death in such a movement.

Until the Nationalist and Red Revolutionary (he sounds like a fellow traveler) side wins, Spain cannot be free. In this sense, it is a political poem. The side of the Republic is just; the enemy is "falsi." He knows not only whom they fight against, but what they fight for.

He honors the soldiers, calls them, figuratively, epic poets, glorifies their cause, and emphasizes the difficult epic struggle ahead. He considers that Spain herself, transformed into the metaphor of a bleeding bosom, awaits them.

The poem serves the purpose of a marching song, especially with its refrain, calling his fellow soldiers to arms, urging them forward toward final victory. It is youthfully optimistic, idealistic, encouraging, and inspirational. Their task is noble and will affect the whole world.

The poem is lyrical and has a limited vocabulary. It is energetic both in content and form. There is much repetition as well as internal and external rhyme, which takes advantage of the frequent vowel endings in Italian.

Since it was anthologized among poems by volunteers in a dangerous struggle, an anthology hastily put together without biographical information on the poets, dates, or even first names, the poems included were probably written hastily near the battlefield.

Braccialarghe has written straightforward, simple poems based on his firsthand experience of the war. He was young, idealistic, and caught up in a movement capable of changing the world for the better, as he saw it. His imagery relies on familiar symbols: blood, veil, and the rose, but has a vital simplicity. These poems are significant in terms of their time and place in the history of the war. Braccialarghe's vision is understandable in view of his youth and idealism, the year in which they were written (early 1937), the many efforts and sacrifices from himself and his countrymen in a cause to which, as a foreign volunteer, one had to be totally dedicated. The poems are subjective, appealing to emotions rather than to intellect, and humbly offered ("senza rima né metro./Povere parole balbettate").

Notes

1. Johannes R. Becher, *Gedichte 1936-1941* (Berlin: Aufbau-Verlag, 1966), pp. 411-12.

2. Becher, *Ausgewählte Dichtung aus der Zeit der Verbannung, 1933-1945* (Berlin: Aufbau-Verlag, 1945), pp. 119-20.

3. Becher, *Gedichte 1936-1941*, p. 413.

4. Paul Eluard, *Cours naturel* (Paris: Editions du Sagittaire, 1938), pp. 13-15.

5. Eluard, *Cours naturel*, pp. 48-52.

6. Eluard, *Poèmes politiques* (Paris: Gallimard, 1948), p. 31.

7. Eluard, *Poèmes politiques*, p. 35.

8. Níkolay Semyónovich Tíkhonov, *Izbránnye proizvédenija v dvuch tómach* (Moscow: State Publishing Co. of Literature of Art, 1955), p. 246.

9. Tíkhonov, *Izbránnye proizvédenija v dvuch tómach*, pp. 263-65.

10. Tíkhonov, *Izbránnye proizvédenija v dvuch tómach*, pp. 265-66.

11. "Nuestros héroes," *Romancero de los voluntarios de la libertad* (Madrid: Ediciones del Comisariado de las Brigadas Internacionales, 1937), p. 58.

12. "La hora de ensueños," *Romancero de los voluntarios de la libertad*, p. 61.

13. *Romancero de los voluntarios de la libertad*, pp. 70-72.

14. Section 5, "¡Adelante!," *Romancero de los voluntarios de la libertad*, pp. 88-89.

CHAPTER V

General Comparative Conclusions

All the poems discussed here have in common that they were written on the occasion of, or in memory of, the Spanish Civil War. Is there a valid basis for comparing and contrasting them? Limiting the selection of poems to those deriving from the broad impetus of a particular set of events allows us to concentrate on other variables. Many comparative factors affecting the poems were considered in Chapters II, III, and IV. It was shown, for example, that there are differences between the Spanish/Latin view of Spain and the war, and that of non-Spaniards. Countless other variables affected the war poetry: age of poet, environment, class, education, upbringing, personality, religion, political convictions, personal involvement (in war), knowledge and understanding (of war), moral conscience, objectivity, focus, style, talent, intellect, literary influences, purpose, when and where written (proximity to war). Each brought to the occasion of the war his own nature and uniqueness as a poet and as a human being.

The Spanish Civil War was contended on many levels. Men

244

were deeply moved to voluntary service, sacrifice, and death. Soldiers, civilians, peasants, aristocrats, politicians, businessmen, clergy, political activists, and many others took sides. Literary men, too. It was a truly ideological conflict and the issues were very clear. All literature about it is political to some extent. There were two writers' factions: one of the Left and one of the Right. There were no neutral writers. These poets were not all committed to the same ideals nor were their commitments equally strong. There were many forms their resistance took.

Although disapproving of extremism on both sides, most of the intellectuals were antifascist and sympathetic to the cause of the Republic. This is not surprising, since the socially conscious are traditionally on the Left. From both sides of the Atlantic, support came for Franco, especially from Roman Catholic writers.

While the war had multiple meanings outside Spain, to many Spaniards it was the latest episode in a long and tragic domestic conflict. The Spanish writers emphasized the internal strife of the country—the socioeconomic and political conditions that left the people dissatisfied and divided.

Foreign writers were often ignorant of the deadly struggle between the Spanish Right and the parties of the Left (anarchists, socialists, communists) which had precipitated the uprising. Foreign writers have been criticized for being narrow-minded about the total situation. They have been accused of propagandizing.

To the foreigners the war seemed less concerned with issues indigenous to Spain than with worldwide problems. When it became known that Italy and Germany had intervened on the side of the Nationalists and that Russia had begun to supply the Loyalists, little doubt remained that Spain had become the international battleground of opposing ideologies. Foreigners, then, tended to view the war as it happened (1936-1939) and in an international context.

Spaniards, on the other hand, looked back to the evolution of Spanish discord. They searched within Spain and its people for the deep roots of their misfortune and discontent. But Spanish writers, too, have their limitation. The Spanish could recall their history, knew the Spanish character as native, and concentrated on the origins of the conflict in Spain. But the war grew beyond

Spain. It developed beyond domestic strife and discontent. It assumed the proportions of big-power politics and modern warfare, so that "Spanish Civil War" became, decidedly, a misnomer.

Roy Campbell was violently pro-Franco. MacDiarmid was an ardent Scottish nationalist and saw the Spanish struggle in terms of his own people. The same is true of Tíkhonov, who looked at the struggle in relation to Russia; he would have been opposed to fascism wherever he found it, as would Braccialarghe. Auden, Becher, Eluard, MacDiarmid, Neruda, Spender, and Tíkhonov were, at one time or another, communists or, at least, fellow travelers. Members of the "Auden generation" tended to be fellow travelers partly for personal reasons to do with their background but mainly because they had already formed in their own minds sets of values which were not compatible with communist ideology. Spender and Rukeyser held general antiwar attitudes. Their diverse backgrounds and experience fostered divergent perspectives and some contradictory viewpoints. There are also parallels among their works: often they corroborate or supplement one another.

Believing wholly in an ideology (communism, Christianity, fascism, nationalism, or whatever) can give one a more confident, positive, and heroic outlook on events. The belief in a total enemy—such as is implied by religious or ideological conviction— encourages the idea of total commitment, whereas halfhearted belief can lead to questions, doubts, and soul-searching. When poets were moved enough or when they considered the message they wished to impart and the response they hoped to elicit important enough, there was always the possibility of oversimplifying or exaggerating reality. Besides, it is difficult under any circumstances to maintain objectivity, and especially so in a war as emotionally charged as this one. And, finally, objectivity is not a prerequisite of poems—the way it should be of journalism, for example.

Felipe understood the demands of his Republican cause and was deeply troubled by the divisions on his side as well as antagonistic toward powers that could have helped but, opportunistically, ignored the plight of the Republic. His religious faith, however, provided him with an idealistic hope which he embraced at the end of "La insignia." But it was a romantic notion much like Vallejo's. MacDiarmid was temporarily disillusioned but maintained hope through his faith in the final justice of communism and democracy. The note of disaffection with communism was apparent in Auden's *Spain* and Spender's "Two Armies" and "Ultima Ratio Regum." Auden criticized communist bureaucracy, Spender its duplicity. Campbell could be exultant and exuberant because he fiercely maintained that the side that had won he totally believed in. His religion, also, buoyed his spirits. Hernández fought for Spain poetically as if he were writing for his life. It was an all-out, idealistic commitment, partly attributable to his youth. Rukeyser and Spender were staunchly humanitarian and pacifistic, and critical disillusionment over the means and outcome (of war in general) crept into their poems. Becher, MacDiarmid, and Tíkhonov did not travel to Spain physically but supported the ideological cause of antifascism in Spain intellectually. They identified it as a struggle against tyranny.

Eventually the poets had to make a choice between poetry and physical participation in the events. Sometimes they did not have a choice (some poets were killed). Of all the poets who wrote about the war, a dozen or so volunteered to fight and all of them with the Loyalists (I think it's clear that fascism is not likely to inspire soldier/poets or poets at all). Sometimes they had to write under conditions inimical to poetry writing. There was apt to be a gap between conception and achievement of war poems. It is difficult, near a battlefield, to achieve the composure and concentration necessary for creating poetry. Hernández and Braccialarghe fought. The poet/soldiers had to snatch what moments they could from other, tyrannical duties. Vallejo was dead before the war was over.

Auden was able to separate his political poem from mere propaganda because of his disciplined sensibility and technique. Spender's intention was to separate his politics from his poetry, and therefore he expressed a personal reaction to the war, with ideology entering only as a vague backdrop. Rukeyser's poems had political overtones but were mainly, like Spender's, personal. Neruda was politically oriented and his poems were political, but in "Explico" he transformed the public tragedy into a personal one. Both MacDiarmid and Campbell wrote political poems, with little restraint of their propagandistic proselytizing; Tíkhonov would be of this school. Campbell squandered his energy in tearing down his enemies, while MacDiarmid spent much of his effort in destroying Campbell. Tíkhonov exaggerated the fascist and antifascist stands. Vallejo's political ideology, although an integral part of his thinking and being, was not brought out directly in his poems.

The Spanish Civil War was a vast and amorphous theme of which the poets could make what they wished. What matters in poetry on such a public subject is the vision which the poet has of it, his insight into its essential character, and its relevance to the human state. Perhaps the truth of human understanding can be found more in art than in politics. Personal emotion is perhaps a more enduring subject for poetry than war politics.

The poetic vision of these poets allowed them to know not only what they were fighting against, but also what they were fighting for. Broad patriotism, love of life, and faith in a better future combined with intense hatred, prompted by equally intense moral indignation.

There are things that cannot and should not be forgiven, things which it would be nothing but moral cowardice and callousness to forgive. It is with love—and hate—that some of these poems were written. Poems can help to overcome a moral crisis. The poems offered sympathy and encouragement as well as condemnation. Poems can be like ammunition to be used against an enemy that must be stopped.

The struggle for existence in the Spanish Civil War coincided, right from the start, with a gigantic struggle for fundamental human rights and decencies, united by a single purpose for whose achievement no effort, no sacrifice, seemed too great. Men were dying in order that future generations might lead a life worthy of human beings. That's why the war attracted so many idealists.

Some of the poems dealt with are more valid than others. My own bias is that the best war poems are not limited to war, but transcend it, leading to the deepest speculations about man. Good poems communicate experience, not propaganda. The most successful war poets are probably those who have no disposition to propagandize or to prophesy and write about their personal sensations in new ways or by adapting old ways. The best war poetry achieves a universality transcending the particular. It expresses the poet's attitude to something beyond the immediacy of war, encompassing a variety of interpenetrating meanings.

Which subjects other than the war did these poets consider in their poems? Auden wrote of human values and politics, and surveyed the past, present, and future in *Spain*. Vallejo considered death, love, man's aloneness, the arbitrariness of authority and fate, and the values at stake in Spain. The map of the peninsula of Spain played on the imagination of Hernández. He urged action, love, and even the sacrifice of one's life in his poems. Neruda and Rukeyser wrote of their personal lives as well as of the war, but Neruda's life was more integral to that of Spain ("Explico"). Neruda chose satire to express "Almería." He considered the effect of the war on his poetry in "Explico." Felipe, too, considered his role in view of the events. He emphasized unity, manhood, and justice. The poems of MacDiarmid and Campbell concerned multifarious aspects of their lives and philosophies while centering on the war. Braccialarghe concentrated on the perspective of a soldier and on the International Brigade to which he belonged.

Do the poems transcend politics and the immediate issues of war to consider the fundamental values of man? Auden's poem especially does. Felipe's comprehensive view allowed him to consider what ultimately counts. Neruda was concerned about the welfare of the Republicans. Vallejo and Hernández empathized with mankind. Rukeyser and Spender felt deeply for those who suffer in any war. Vallejo's feeling encompassed all of mankind. Spender, too, expressed the loss felt by all humanity. Neruda could see the tragedy both as personal ("Explico") and in broader ("Almería"), more panoramic ("Llegada") terms. There are international implications in the poems of Neruda ("Llegada"), Felipe, Hernández ("Recoged esta voz"), MacDiarmid, and Campbell. Auden's, Spender's, Rukeyser's considerations transcend the immediate war situation. Neruda and Eluard were outraged that a civilian population was ruthlessly attacked at Almería or anywhere. Eluard was concerned for the most innocent victims:

women and children; we see a similar focus in Tíkhonov's "Ispantsi otstupili za Pirenyiei."

What was the effect of the Spanish Civil War on their poetry? Once they had found a cause to communicate, Eluard, Neruda, and Vallejo changed from previously obscure styles to more clarity and simplicity. Neruda developed from subjectivism and multiple images to objectivity and fewer images. Vallejo left surrealism in favor of greater simplicity and realism ("Pequeño responso" is an exception). As for Vallejo, he was jolted into poetic creativity after a silence of fifteen years. Vallejo was depressed, while Neruda had energy for a sarcastic and militant stand ("Almería"). Eluard abandoned surrealism and simplified his verse, also. Becher ("General Mola") and Eluard ("La Victoire de Guernica") were caustic, while Tíkhonov ironically spouted his venom against fascism ("Govorit fashist"). Felipe became embittered, belligerent, and declamatory. The conditions of war create in many readers or listeners a state of mind which makes them more hungry for poetry and more responsive to it than ordinarily. Hernández met such a need; he was inspired and inspiring. Campbell and MacDiarmid gave free rein to their emotional, political, and talkative extremism. Auden maintained a measured calm, part of his essential nature and technique; Spender was more emotional. Rukeyser was bitterly against war in "M-Day's Child" and "Third Elegy." Braccialarghe was provoked into poetic expression by the war but admitted his inadequacy to the task. Tíkhonov, though far superior to Braccialarghe as a poet, also expressed that the war spoke much more eloquently for itself than any poem could.

How did the war, and their individual natures, affect the tones they assumed? A mature Vallejo, desperately disappointed, under-stated his poems (in tone). Neruda declaimed and asserted a strong, militant stand ("Almería"). Hernández and Braccialarghe, young, idealistic, and passionate, emotionally advocated martyrdom in the face of such a tragic future. Felipe was mature, objective, and knowledgeable in his rhetorical, dramatic analysis of the situation. He was also emotional and despairing, but offered a rather fanciful glimmer of hope at the end. Tíkhonov followed his Party line in "Govorit fashist" and "Govorit antifashist," assuming a pontifical tone, while "Ispantsi otstupili za Pirenyiei" is muted and lyrical.

Becher unmercifully and sarcastically attacked General Mola, while Eluard made a strong statement in "La Victoire de Guernica" through the use of sarcasm.

Campbell ranted and raved, flaunting his *machismo* and the absolute rightness of his causes while denouncing his foes. He defiantly proclaimed a new heroic age. MacDiarmid answered in kind, but with more of a relevant argument. Auden was detached and impersonal. Spender felt the tragedy personally and expressed it with measured emotionality. Rukeyser was strongly opinionated and passionate in her poems. Their natures accommodated, but did not change basically, to the perspectives from which they viewed the struggle and outcome. None of the tones in the war poetry was comic. Profound distaste and gravity do not lend themselves to comedy. You can't laugh about something unless you are detached and feel secure about it.

War, like love and justice, has had constant attention from poets and other writers. In a sense, all war literature is similar. War makes people come to grips with questions of values. The immediacy of death in war makes one question the value of life when weighed against such intangible stakes as freedom, justice, loyalty, honor, and courage. Scanning a threatening, hopeless present, León Felipe exhorted "Vamos a la muerte!" ("La insignia"). Not death for its own sake, but an heroic death in a fight against evil forces. For similar reasons, Hernández wrote "Cantando espero a la muerte" ("Vientos del pueblo me llevan"). It was to be a death that represented a brave fight and a refusal to submit to tyranny.

A difference in ways of looking at death in the war separated Hispanic poets, aligned with those poets who fought, from those who neither were Hispanic nor fought. Vallejo, Hernández, and Braccialarghe saw death itself as inevitable, while Auden, viewing death less directly, saw the inevitability of the "increase in the chances" of it. The Hispanic poets had faith in the fruitfulness of the sacrifice in bringing about a new life; this faith, perhaps desperate and romantic, was devoid of the bitterness apparent, for example, in Spender's "Ultima Ratio Regum" about the dead soldier on a Spanish field. Neruda employed bitter irony in "Almería," but it was not directed at war deaths. Among the Hispanic war poets, there were wrath, anger, imprecation as well as hope and pity, but rarely irony about the death. When Spender wrote "Consider. One bullet in ten thousand kills a man./Ask. Was so much expenditure justified/On the death of one so young and so silly . . . ," he expressed a bitter sense of the futility of the death of a boy. The Hispanic poets had more faith. The image of Spain, of its cities, of its people, dying and destroyed, but becoming the seed of a New Spain, appears time and again among Hispanic poems. They regarded the war dead not as dead but as a part of a living army, not as absent and finished but as sharing in the continuing struggle and in the future with the people with whom and for whom they had fought. The Hispanic poets abandoned themselves more to their fight and felt closer to the feelings of the people.

For Vallejo these men could be immortal, but not in the usual sense of immortality by fame and glory through people's memory, but immortal in being alive through the totality of their living comrades and of the ideals behind their cause. It would not, then, be survival in the traditional Christian sense of life after death of individual souls. Even in 1937, when the war was already lost, there was hope for a better future, if not immediately, then ultimately.

Overcoming death by resurrecting, after having died in battle, is not in the Hispanic poets of the 1936-1939 war a personal and individual survival. It was, on the contrary, a survival embodied in the prevailing ideals and cause in which the dead men believed and for which they accepted the need to sacrifice themselves, usefully and fruitfully. Even among pain, destruction, and death, the Hispanic and soldier/poets could be hopeful and joyful (Vallejo's "Masa" and "España, aparta de mí este cáliz"; Felipe's "La insignia"; Hernández' "Vientos del pueblo me llevan" and "Recoged esta voz"; Neruda's "Llegada a Madrid de la Brigada Internacional"; Braccialarghe's "Ai fratelli lontani . . ." and "Fratelli dell'Internazionale"). Spender and Rukeyser are more prone to personal despondency and despair.

If one might not (because Death rudely interrupts) enjoy a better future himself, at least, one's surviving comrades and one's children would, and a man could—through them—feel rewarded and justified. Vallejo ("España, aparta de mí este cáliz") and

Braccialarghe in his two poems about the Italian Brigade express this. For the Hispanic poet, then, the general, ultimate welfare took priority over personal salvation.

There is a difference between the treatment of death by combatants and noncombatants. Those who are not in constant contact with death might be deeply affected by it, glamorize it, or deal with it abstractly and remotely. They not only might express their grief freely but also might see in death much more than its immediate presence (for example, comradeship and glory). The average soldier is fatalistic, making speculation superfluous. It is useless to lament or do anything except remain silent and hide one's feelings. There is dignity in silence in the face of something about which there is nothing to say. Where death comes all the time, it hardly calls for special remark. The open expression of horror in the fairly abstract "M-Day's Child" suggests that Rukeyser's knowledge of combat was not firsthand. Spender's anonymous victim ("a better target for a kiss" than a bullet) in "Ultima Ratio Regum" suggests a similar distance from the fighting. Auden's poem, too, was far from the scene of battle: "All presented their lives." Braccialarghe, however, was able to reconcile himself to the abundant death surrounding him in battle by idealizing the cause, viewing the dead as martyrs, and thus justifying it.

Anyone who had actually seen children shot would have been less glib about the occurrence than Auden in *Spain* and less abstract than Spender in "Ultima Ratio Regum." The cold logic of Auden's phrases, "To-day the deliberate increase in the chances of death" and ". . . to-day the/Fumbled and unsatisfactory embrace before hurting" rings hollow. Attempts to grasp the war as a whole and to see it as a natural or cosmic process were made largely by men who were far from the front or, at least, took no active part in the fighting. They had the advantage of detachment and the freedom to look at things in a wide context without the distracting urgency of the battlefield. The perspective of MacDiarmid and Auden suggests this, as does Felipe's. Felipe's objectivity intimates a perspective of distance and maturity not available to Hernández, for example.

Living in his own isolated world of the trenches, the soldier may feel that the enemy is closer to him than many of his own countrymen, and especially than the invisible commanders who, from a remote security, order multitudes to a senseless death. Spender saw it this way and brought it out ironically in "Ultima Ratio Regum" and "Two Armies." Braccialarghe, looking around during the respite between battles, wrote from a soldier's perspective.

Those who stayed at home in England, America, Russia, or wherever and wrote were driven not by personal danger, but by abstract beliefs which probably meant a great deal to them. Their poems suffered from not being immediately engaged in the events of which they wrote. Their vision was generally unconfined by the borders of Spain. Tíkhonov saw the Spanish War in terms of the Russian Revolution and Civil War. Becher, too, saw it as another class struggle. They shared an intellectual affinity with the Republican side because of the ideology involved. Becher, MacDiarmid, and Tíkhonov were the only foreign poets (out of the thirteen discussed) not to have set foot on Spanish soil during the war years. Of the non-Spanish poets, only Braccialarghe actually fought and would later fight against Nazi-fascism in World War II. Among the Spanish poets, only Hernández was a soldier, but these poets had spent longer periods in Spain and were more intimately part of it. There is a desperation and understanding (especially in the poem by Felipe) and even an authenticity about the Spanish poems not to be found among the non-Spanish ones.

When poetry began to come from those who had a firsthand knowledge of battle and war, it took on a new character. It showed that war was not at all what romantic convention assumed (starting as far back as *The Iliad*), and it emphasized aspects of it which were commonplaces to fighting men but disturbing anomalies to those who stayed at home. It is from such moments that we can get the most revealing and most authentic poetry of war, based on a perceptive acquaintance with its real nature and an unpremeditated response to its unforeseen demands. It illustrates how wrong established notions of war may turn out to be when they are tested by hard facts. For the men who did the fighting, or knew of it at close range, it was a war like any other: lice, betrayals, death, and all. Unpleasant aspects of the war were expressed by all these poets. Campbell's notions were the most glorified, but then he was the only poet on the winning side. The other poets put aside illusions, at least at times, to face the realities of war.

But those deeply involved were also able to transcend the reality they knew so well. Braccialarghe ("Ai fratelli lontani" and "Fratelli dell'Internazionale"), Eluard ("La Victoire de Guernica"), Felipe, Neruda ("Llegada"), and Vallejo ("Masa") expressed a hope that derived from desperation and, perhaps, from their religious backgrounds. Not one of them could have expected the Republic to win after 1937. Auden could write of a possible future because that future lay outside of Spain. MacDiarmid's notions of future success also lay beyond Spain. Felipe's and Vallejo's hopes were fantasies.

It is important to consider when, in relation to the war, the poems were written. During the first year, it was still possible to think that the Loyalists could win. By 1937 the battle was already uneven. Sommerfield wrote of exciting victories of 1936; Neruda spoke glowingly of the arrival of foreign volunteers in Madrid in 1936, while Alvah Bessie wrote of their evacuation in 1939. Campbell's poem was published after the Franco victory. None of the poems discussed was written early enough to be very hopeful about the Republic.

In difficult, chaotic times with strong opinions rampant, there are commonly poets so occupied with their theme or message that their mode of presentation is not of paramount concern to them. This would especially be true of young poets undeveloped poetically at the time of the crisis (e.g., Braccialarghe). Certainly, this is also true of Campbell and MacDiarmid, where quantity outweighs quality. Felipe, too, seems more interested in his views than in his aesthetics. Rukeyser would seem to be insistent about her ideas while sometimes hasty in expressing them. For them the urgent, immediate task was to transform their preoccupations or sorrow into poetry, and in some cases they had not the technique to make the most of their themes. Tíkhonov's "Ispantsi otstupili za Pirenyiei" is much more aesthetically conceived than his poems on fascism and antifascism. In the latter two he was more concerned with propaganda.

How did the war affect their imagery? The images, after all, are the logical products of the poet's vision of the war. Felipe's themes were justice, martyrdom, and unity (a form of patriotism). To achieve these goals, an insignia served both as the poem's title and as its unifying symbol. The proposed symbol to offset divisiveness would be cut out of blood in the form of a star. Another frequent symbol was that of Man—who believes in justice and the Republican cause. Whereas Felipe counted cadavers, representing the war dead, Hernández saw a landscape flooded with blood. Vallejo saw Spain through the metaphor of a dead combatant in "Masa" and a corpse sprouting poetry in "Pequeño responso." She was Mother Spain, an anthropomorphic figure, in "España, aparta de mí este cáliz." Neruda saw the dead as decaying garbage to be consumed by those who caused their murder in "Almería" and as blood in the streets in "Explico." As in Rukeyser's poems (and, to a lesser extent, in Felipe's), the wind was a pervasive force in the poems of Hernández. In "Vientos del pueblo me llevan" Hernández compared brave Spaniards to bulls, the antithesis of yoked oxen. In "Recoged esta voz" the imagery derives from the passion of the battlefield: bandages, bleeding, and blood. Vallejo's poems were included in his collection *España, aparta de mí este cáliz*. The encompassing image of this title is that of a cup or chalice representing suffering, anguish, and death. The request for its removal is as futile as Christ's in the Bible. The book of poetry which survived the destruction of the soldier's body in "Pequeño responso" may symbolize the art and culture of a Spanish people that will survive their limited mortality. Vallejo's mourners are joined in a brotherhood of perspiration rather than blood. In "Explico" Neruda contrasted the beautiful life prior to the war, symbolized by his house full of flowers, children, dogs, friends, with the image of blood: "Venid a ver la sangre por las calles." Does the anguish of the Spanish poets affect their images? Their morbid outlooks are revealed in their death imagery concretized, for example, through a predominance of blood. But the Catholic background of the Hispanic poets would make them fatalistic and resigned to death when it comes. Perhaps this allows them to consider death more openly than most people.

There is no comprehensive image to counterbalance the diffuseness of Campbell's poem. MacDiarmid set up some dichotomies that he sustained, for example, the light/life of communism versus the darkness/decay of Campbell.

Auden's imagery suggests the essence and variety of past, present, and future values and societies. The images reveal Auden's broad knowledge and intellect. Spender's images are drawn both from rural and technological spheres. In "Third Elegy" Rukeyser set up a tour/journey through the landscape of a museum's artworks, with sustained life and death (blood) imagery. In "Nuns in the Wind" the wind and nuns symbolize the war. It is a sophisticated poem whose imagery derives from an intellectual source.

Some of the poems were meant as agents of moral clarification with value judgments about the right and wrong of the situation (those of Auden, Becher, Campbell, Felipe, MacDiarmid, Neruda, Rukeyser, Spender, and Tíkhonov). The poems of Braccialarghe, Felipe, and Hernández offered calls to action and urged martyrdom. All but Campbell and Auden suffered and lamented. Campbell rejoiced. Auden calibrated the situation. Spender and Rukeyser denounced (all) war. Tíkhonov shouted the horrendous implications of fascism ("Govorit fashism"), which would be impossible to live under. Felipe's poetry was essentially didactic. Addressed to a specific audience, it was intended to teach the audience specific truths, both moral and practical.

For the most part the aesthetic quality of the selected poems in Spanish exceeds that of the poems in other languages. The poems written about the war are frequently more important to the corpus of an Hispanic poet's works than those of a non-Spanish poet in relation to his total poetic accomplishment. Not that my selection of other poets is unimpressive. There are major poets included here (Braccialarghe, most obscure, is an exception), but the contribution of non-Spanish poets in respect to the war was not often among their best or most important poetry.

The events of the Thirties are sufficiently remote to be "historic," but also offer parallels with contemporary political-moral issues—such issues as racism and manipulation of society by vast military and industrial interests. Too much government influence over political, social, moral, or aesthetic lives, and too much centralization of power within the head of the government, remind one of the dictatorships which many tried to avoid in the 1930s and 1940s. What happened in Spain could happen anywhere.

W. B. Yeats, T. S. Eliot, and Wyndham Lewis were Rightist

(though Eliot announced during the Spanish Civil War that he "preferred to remain isolated, and take no part in these collective activities"). Although Eliot did not write poems on the Spanish Civil War, he had an insight into the decadence of bourgeois Western civilization (e.g., in "The Love Song of J. Alfred Prufrock" and *The Waste Land*) but did not carry the situation further to revolution. For anyone with strong political convictions, Yeats was a reactionary.

In their youth many poets can be unpolitical, indeed antipolitical, and above all completely opposed to the idea that there is any connection between politics and literature. This was true of Auden, Day Lewis, MacNeice, and Spender, among others. Their generation inherited attitudes which were the aftermath of World War I. Important among these was a profound contempt for politics. The politicians were the cynical old men who had sent the young men into the trenches of the Eastern front (cf. Pound's "Hugh Selwyn Mauberley"). The rise of Hitler, rampant murders and vandalism, and suppression of liberal freedoms, forced the nonpolitical Thirties' generation into politics (delayed political consciousness would not be true in the Soviet Union). The slightly younger generation (e.g., John Cornford) had a different attitude, often more spontaneously passionate.

Ever since that grim July day in 1936 in Spain when modern ideological warfare began, the world has never been the same. The poets involved, also, were not to be the same. Some died; some went to prison or into exile. Some continued to write postwar poetry about Spain, but these were mostly Spanish poets in exile (since poems are apt to be spontaneous and emotional, most of the poems were written during the war years or shortly thereafter). Some poets radically changed their styles as a result or felt compelled into creativity. For some the Spanish Civil War has not ended.

The result was fascist victory followed by a global encounter in which the reluctant democrats and embarrassed communists managed to save themselves only by alliance against a, by then, vastly swollen Nazi danger. And, as Auden eloquently, but pessimistically, put it: "History to the defeated/May say Alas but cannot help nor pardon."

APPENDIX I

Survey of Spanish Civil War Poets Other Than Poets of Concentration

Among those poets who wrote in Spanish were: Rafael Alberti, Vicente Aleixandre, Dámaso Alonso, Manuel Altolaguirre ("Ultima muerte"), Felix Antonio, Antonio Aparicio, Luis Cernuda, Pedro Garfias, Jorge Guillén, Nicolás Guillén, José Herrera Petere, Antonio Machado, José Moreno Villa, Emilio Prados, Arturo Serrano Plaja, and Lorenzo Varela.

Rafael Alberti (b. 1902) wrote from Moscow, Paris, and Madrid about the International Brigades, about Madrid under siege, and finally sought exile in Argentina. Various of his collections contain Spanish Civil War poems: *De un momento a otro* (1937); *Poesías* (1940); and *Entre el clavel y la espada* (1941).

Vicente Aleixandre (b. 1898) had a collection of poems published in 1960, *Poesías completas*, which contained some Spanish Civil War poems. Manuel Altolaguirre (1905-1959) wrote a few poems on the subject in 1937.

In *Hijos de la ira*, published in 1944, Dámaso Alonso (b. 1898) mentioned nothing specific, but the poem, expressing anguish at human suffering, obviously resulted from the Spanish Civil War. Antonio Aparicio (b. 1912) wrote a few poems. Felix Antonio wrote a volume titled *Arriba las cruces*.

Luis Cernuda (1902-1963) left Spain after the war. He wrote "Elegía española" and "Elegía a la luna de España," included in the volume *La realidad y el deseo* (1936).

Pedro Garfias (1901-1967) went into exile in Mexico, having left Spain in 1939. His works *Poesía de la guerra* (1937) and *Héroes del Sur* (1938) deal with the war. Juan Gil-Albert wrote related poems in *Siete romances de guerra, Cancionero revolucionario internacional,* and *Candente horror.*

A relatively conservative group of poets who participated actively in the Spanish Civil War were: Leopoldo Panero (1909-1963), Luis Rosales (b. 1910), and Dionisio Ridruejo (1912-1975), who supported Franco. If a poet chose to remain in Spain after the war, he either had to support Franco, write subtly and ambiguously, or remain silent. Ridruejo later broke with Franco and went into exile.

Jorge Guillén (b. 1893) escaped to Massachusetts. He wrote *Guirnalda civil,* which was published in 1970. Nicolás Guillén (b. 1902), born in Cuba, went to Spain during the Spanish Civil War. Committed to social justice and human solidarity, he fought on the side of the Republic in the war. His *Cantos para soldados y sones para turistas* was published in 1937. *España, poema en cuatro angustias y una esperanza* (1937) expressed his admiration for Spain's history and despair at its imminent self-destruction. After the defeat of the Republic, he returned to Cuba.

José Herrera Petere (b. 1910) was a volunteer in the 5th regiment. His collections *Acero de Madrid* and *Guerra viva,* both published in 1938, contain some Spanish war poems.

Antonio Machado (1875-1939), born in Sevilla, died in exile. *Poesías completas* (1936) and *Poesías de guerra* (1961) contain Spanish Civil War poems.

José Moreno Villa (1887-1955) left Spain in 1937 on a cultural mission and, at the end of the war, sought refuge in Mexico. *Salon sin muros* (1936) and *Puerta severa* (1941) contain pertinent poems.

Blas de Otero (b. 1916) was born in Bilbao. A lyric poet he wrote about the war from a distance in time in *Pido la paz y la palabra* (1955) and *Que trata de España* (1965).

Emilio Prados (1899-1962) was born in Málaga. *Llanto subterráneo* (1936), *Llanto en la sangre* (1937), *Mínima muerte* (1939), and *Penumbras* (1942) contain relevant poems.

Pedro Salinas (1891-1951) included his war poems in *Poesías completas* (1955). After the war he went into exile, living in Baltimore.

Lorenzo Varela (b. 1917) emigrated to France after 1939 and then to South America (Buenos Aires). *Elegías españoles* (1941) has poems touching on the war.

Max Aub (1903-1972) mostly wrote prose, but composed the poem "Me acuerdo hoy de Aranjuez" in 1941 from the concentration camp at Djelfa, Algeria.

Many of these poets on the Republican side, grateful for international support, extolled the International Brigades: Rafael Alberti, Manuel Altolaguirre, Pedro Garfias, Juan Gil-Albert, José Herrera Petere, Juan Paredes, Perez Infante, Emilio Prados, Arturo Serrano Plaja, Lorenzo Varela. After 1939, all anti-Franco poets would have written in exile.

Among the poets who wrote in English were some who sacrificed their lives (and writing) for the physical struggle and died in Spain: Julian Bell, John Cornford ("Poem," "Full Moon at Tierz: Before the Storming of Huesca," and "Heart of Heartless World"), Christopher Caudwell, Ralph Fox, James Lardner, Sam Levinger. They were all volunteers in the International Brigades and wrote a few poems each. Some British communist poets were Caudwell, Charles Donnelly, Cornford, and Fox.

Edwin Rolfe (1909-1954), born in Philadelphia, had three volumes published: *To my Contemporaries* (1936), *Lincoln Battalion* (1939), *First Love* (1951). His "Elegy for Our Dead" was published in 1938. A volunteer in Spain, he fought with the International Brigades.

Langston Hughes (1902-1967), born in Missouri, traveled to Spain, where he preoccupied himself with the Negro soldiers among the Internationals. He wrote "Air Raid: Barcelona,"

"Madrid," "October 16th," "Post Card from Spain," as well as the collection *A New Song,* all published in 1938.

Genevieve Taggard (1894-1948), born in Washington, had three volumes with relevant poems: *Calling Western Union* (1936), *Collected Poems* (1938), and *Long View* (1942).

Louis MacNeice (1907-1963), born in Belfast, Ireland, went to Spain in 1936. Three volumes resulted: *Out of the Picture* (1937), *The Earth Compels* (1938), and *Autumn Journal* (1939). While MacNeice found inspiration in the human values at stake, his involvement with the Spanish people never went beyond a vague general sympathy. For example, he never supported the Republic in any political sense, probably because he was as aware as Spender of the hazards of mixing propaganda and poetry.

C. Day Lewis (1904-1972), a communist, was one of the leading British poets of the 1930s. The following are some of his Spanish war poems: "Noah and the Waters" (1936) and published in 1938: "Child of Misfortune," "Overtures to Death and Other Poems," "The Nabara," "Starting Point," "Bombers."

There were many other poets in English writing on the war, most of whom wrote single poems: John Malcolm Brinnin ("For a Young Poet dead in Spain"); Richard Church; Kenneth Fearing ("The Program"); Redmayne Fitzgerald; S. Funaroff ("To Federico García Lorca"); Brian Howard; Rolfe Humphries; John Lepper; Jack Lindsay; Edna St. Vincent Millay ("Say that we saw Spain die"); Geoffrey Parsons; Herbert Read ("Bombing Casualties" and "A Song for the Spanish Antichrists" from his volume *Thirty-Five Poems* (1940); Kenneth Rexroth ("Two Poems"); Edgell Rickword; Norman Rosten ("The March"); Vincent Sheean ("Puigcerdà"); Rex Warner; Sylvia Townsend Warner ("Waiting at Cerbere" and "Benicasim"); Tom Winringham ("Granien" and "The Splint"); and David Wolff ("The Defenses").

Among the German contributors, all writing in exile from Germany, Bertolt Brecht (1898-1956), whose original name was Eugen Berthold Friedrich Brecht, was the best known among them. Born in Ausburg, Bavaria (now in West Germany), he died in East Germany. He was a poet, playwright, and theatrical reformer, whose epic theater departed from the conventions of theatrical illusion and developed the drama as a social and ideological forum. His "epic" theater kept his audience at an objective distance from the dramatic artifice.

He abandoned medical studies for the theater. His military service in World War I made him a pacifist for the rest of his life. In the late 1920s his antipathy to middle-class society took the form of Marxism. His first major success, *Dreigroschenoper* (1928), gained him an international reputation.

After the rise of Hitler in Germany, Brecht lived in Denmark (1933-1939), Sweden, Finland, and the U.S. (1941-1947). Among his important mature plays are: *Leben des Galilei, Der gute Mensch von Sezuan, Mutter Courage und ihre Kinder,* and *Der Kaukasische Kreidekreis.* He returned to Europe in 1947 and, in his last years (from 1949 on), directed the Berliner Ensemble, a company of actors in East Berlin. More than forty plays and operas have established Brecht as one of our century's most provocative playwrights.

Themes of death, decay, and drowning reappear constantly in Brecht's poetry, especially in verses written in the 1920s, before his radical nihilism was replaced by Marxist ideology. Although he wrote a play that touches on the war, *Die Gewehre der Frau Carrar,* I could find only one poem written by Brecht on the Spanish Civil War, "Mein Bruder War ein Flieger," for which music was later composed by Paul Dessau:

Mein Bruder war ein Flieger
Eines Tags bekam er eine Kart
Er hat seine Kiste eingpackt
Und sudwarts ging die Fahrt.

Mein Bruder ist ein Eroberer
Unserm Volke fehlt's an Raum
Und Grund und Boden zu kriegen, ist
Bei uns ein alter Traum.

Der Raum, den mein Bruder eroberte
Liegt in Guadarramamassiv.
Er ist lang einen Meter achtzig
Und einen Meter fünfzig tief.[1]

(My brother was a pilot
One day he received his orders
He packed his bags
And made his journey southward.

My brother is a conqueror
Our people lack space
To conquer land is
For us an old dream

The space which my brother
  conquered
Lies in the Guadarrama mass of
  mountains
It is 8 feet long
And 6 feet deep.)

Brecht's figurative brother lies in a coffin in the Guadarrama mountain range, his plane having crashed during the Spanish Civil War. The insinuation that his brother was looking for more land to conquer, his homeland never having been enough for the Germans, is ironic and bitter in tone. This criticizes German expansionism in general and surely doesn't do justice to this dead pilot who volunteered and gave his life for the cause in Spain. This second point is intentionally made obliquely.

Erich Fried (b. 1921), born in Vienna, fled to England in 1938 after the German occupation of Austria and has lived in London since 1946. He wrote "Schulkinder," a generally antiwar poem which clearly includes the Spanish Civil War.

Louis Fürnberg wrote "Die Spanishe Hochzeit," which was published in 1948.

Rudolf Leonhard extolled the revolutionary struggle and its international aspects in his Spanish war poems; he showed how in the Spanish Civil War were pitched: "Deutsche gegen Deutsche vor Madrid in der Schlacht,/die Freiheit gegen die Niedertracht," and in so doing he anticipated a struggle in Germany in which Germans would be lined up on opposite sides. In a "Londoner Ballade," England's aloofness from the Spanish people's struggle is scorned; the British "gehen geruhig in ihrem sehr hübschen Garten/und wollen warten" until their realm also would be brutally violated.

Erich Weinert (1890-1953), a popular communist poet, wrote two poems, "Kinderspiel in Madrid" and "Internationale Brigade," that were published in *Romancero de los voluntarios de la libertad* (1937).

Among the French poets who focused attention on the war were: Louis Aragon (b. 1897), who began as a surrealist and became a spokesman for communism; Eugene Guillevic (b. 1907), who wrote *Requiem* in 1938; and Paul Claudel (1868-1955), whose mystical crisis led him into Catholicism and the Nationalist side.

There were a number of Russian poets. Evgenii Aronovitch Dolmatovski (b. 1915) wrote *Stikhi i pesni* (1952), which included "Pis'mo k Rafael Alberti."

Ilya Grigorievitch Ehrenburg (1891-1967) was a correspondent in Spain in 1936 and mostly wrote journalism. One of his poems, "Kino," touched on the war.

Semion Isaakovitch Kirsanov (b. 1906), born in Odessa, wrote *Vojna Tchume* (1936), *Tvojá Poema* (1937), and *Sočinenija v dvuch tómach* (1954). Among his poems was "Vy iz Madrid."

Born in Milan, Italy, Giuliano Carta (b. 1914) wrote *Madrid, Vega, Santa Margherita Ligure* (1938), which included "Madrid."

Note

1. Bertolt Brecht, *Gedichte 1934-1941* (Frankfurt: Suhrkamp Verlag, 1961), p. 31.

APPENDIX II

Translations into English
of Analyzed Poems

"La insignia" by León Felipe

THE INSIGNIA
Poetic Speech (Address) (1937)

This war poem was begun right after the fall of Málaga and
acquired this expression after the fall of Bilbao. So the way
it is here is the last variation (of the text), the most
structured, that which the author prefers and subscribes to.
And it annuls all the other anterior editions that the press
has published. This is not said for editorial reasons or
interests. Here there is no Copyright. Five hundred copies
have been printed to throw in the air of Valencia and so that
the wind may multiply them.

—León Felipe

spoken already?
Spaniards spoken already?
responsible revolutionary spoken
responsible ones;
commissary spoken,
dinate commissaries;
ical parties spoken,
orations spoken,
es
icates;
kers and the peasants spoken;
hanics spoken;
r spoken
the café
tblacks.
he eternal demagogues spoken also.
ne spoken.
hat everyone has spoken.
missing?
some Spaniard that might not have pronounced his
. . .
answers? . . . (Silence).
only I am missing.
ause the poet has not yet spoken.

Who has said that now there are not poets in the world?
Who has said that now there are not prophets?

One day the kings and the people
to forget their fatal and dramatic destiny
and to be able to replace the sacrifice with cynicism and the
    pirouette
substituted the clown for the prophet.
But the prophet is no more than the native voice of a people,
the legitimate voice of its History,
the cry of the first soil that is raised in the confusion of the
    market, above the clamor of the dealers.
Nothing of prides:
neither divine hierarchies nor ecclesiastical genealogies.

The voice of the prophets—remember it—
it is that which has more flavor of clay.
Of clay,
of the clay that has made the tree—the orange tree and the
    pine—
of the clay that has formed
our body also.
I am not more than a voice—yours, that of everyone—
the most genuine,
the most general,
the most indigenous now,
the most ancient of this earth.
The voice of Spain that today is united in my throat as it
    could unite itself in any other.
My voice is no more than the wave of the land,
of our land,
that seizes me today like a favorable antenna.
Listen,
listen, revolutionary Spaniards,
listen on your knees.
Don't kneel down before anyone.
Kneel down before yourselves,
before your own voice,
before your own voice that you had almost forgotten.
On your knees. Listen.

Spaniards,
revolutionary Spaniards.
Spaniards of the legitimate Spain,
that carries in its hands the genuine message of the race to
    place it humbly in the harmonious pictures of the
    Universal History of tomorrow, and together with the
    generous effort of all the peoples of the world . . .
listen:
There they are—look at them—
there they are, you know them well.
They walk in all of Valencia,
they are in the rear guard of Madrid

and in the rear guard of Barcelona also.
They are in all the rear guards.
They are the Committees,
the small parties,
the factions,
the Syndicates,
the criminal guerrillas of the city rear guard
There you have them.
Embraced with their recent booty,
guarding it,
defending it,
with an avarice that the most degraded bourgeois never had.
Their booty!
Embracing their booty!
Because they have nothing more than booty.
Don't even call it attachment to property.
Booty is made a lawful privilege when it is sealed by an
    ultimate and heroic victory.

One goes from the domestic to the historic,
and from the historic to the epic.
This has always been the order that has guided the conduct
    of the Spaniard in History,
in the plaza
and even in their transactions,
that it has always been said therefore that the Spaniard never
    learns well the merchant trade.
But now
in this revolution,
the order has been reversed.
You have started with the epic,
you have passed through the historic
and now here,
in the rear guard of Valencia,
facing all the defeats
you have stopped yourselves in domesticity.
And here you are anchored.
Syndicalists,

Communists,
Anarchists,
Socialists,
Trotskyites,
Republicans of the Left . . .
Here you are anchored,
guarding the plunder
so that your brother might not take it away.
The historical curve of the aristocrat, since his popular and
    heroic origin, until his final present degeneration, covers
    in Spain more than three centuries.
That of the bourgeoisie, seventy years.
And yours, three weeks.
Where is man?
Where is the Spanish man?
Do not go to seek him on the other side.
The other side is the cursed land, the cursed Spain of Cain
    although the Pope might have blessed it.
If the Spaniard is in some place, it has to be here.
But, where, where? . . .
Because you have already stopped yourselves
and all you do every day is hoist new banners with the ripped
    shirts and dirty rags of the kitchen.
And if the fascists were to enter Valencia tomorrow, they
    would find everyone standing guard before the strong boxes.
This is not defeatism, as you say.
I know that my prophetic line is not broken,
that the men do not break it,
and that I have to arrive before God to give him an account
    of something that he put in my hands when the First
    Spanish substance was born.
That is inexorable logic.
The ones who conquer and have always conquered in
    immediate History are the people and the army that have
    had a point of convergence, although this point may be as
    weak and as absurd as an aluminum medal blessed by a
    bloodthirsty priest.
It is the insignia of the fascists.

This medal is the insignia of the fascists.
A medal stained with the blood of the Virgin.
Very little thing.
But, what do you have now that unites you more?

Revolutionary Spanish people,
you are alone!
Alone!
Without a man and without a symbol.
Without a mystical emblem where sacrifice and discipline
are crystallized.
Without a single symbol that captures in a solid and unique
block all your forces and all your dreams of redemption.
Your insignias,
your plural and sometimes enemy insignias, you buy them in
the market capriciously from the first (second hand) dealer
of the Plaza de Castelar,
of the Puerta del Sol
of the Ramblas de Barcelona.
You have exhausted already in a thousand egotistical and
heterodox combinations all the letters of the alphabet.
And you have put in a thousand different manners, on the
cap and on the sheepskin jacket
the red
and the black,
the sickle,
the hammer
and the star.
But you do not even have a star ALONE,
after having spit out and extinguished that of Bethlehem.

Spaniards,
Spaniards who live the most tragic moment of all our History,
You are alone!
Alone!
The world,
all the world is our enemy, and half of our blood—the rotted
and bastard blood of Cain—has turned against us also.

We have to light a star!
One alone, yes!
We have to raise a banner.
One alone, yes!
And we have to burn the ships.
From here one goes only to death or victory.
Everything makes me think to death.
Not because no one defends me
but because no one understands me.
No one in the world understands the word "justicia." Not
    even you.
And my mission was to imprint it on the forehead of man
and to hammer it after on the earth
like the flag of the final victory.
No one understands me.
And we will have to go to another planet
with these useless goods here,
with these Iberian and quixotic goods.
Let us go to our death!
However,
we have not yet lost here the last battle,
that which is always won thinking that there is no longer any
    exit but death
Let us go to death!
This is our motto.
To death!
This is our motto.
Let Valencia wake up and put on the shroud.

Shout!
all shout!
You, the town crier and the speaker
produce edicts,
light the corners with red letters
that announce this proclamation alone:
Let us go to our death!
You, the Commissars, the captains of Censureship,
sheath your swords

guard your red pen
and open to this shout the doors of the wind:
Let us go to our death!
Let all hear it. All.
Those who deal in silence
and those who deal in insignias.
Dealers of the Plaza de Castelar,
dealers of the Puerta del Sol,
dealers of the Ramblas de Barcelona,
destroy,
burn your goods.
There are no longer domestic insignias,
there are no longer insignias of brass.
Neither for the caps
nor for the sheepskin jackets.
There are no longer identification cards.
There are no longer legal letters
neither by the Committees
nor by the Syndicates.
Let them take away all identification cards!
Now there is only one emblem.
Now there is only one star,
one alone, ALONE and RED, yes,
but of blood and on the forehead,
let every Spanish revolutionary do it for himself
just today
right now
and with their own hands.
Prepare the knives,
sharpen the blades,
heat the irons to live red.
Go to the forges.
Let there be put on your forehead the stamp of justice.
Mothers, revolutionary mothers,
stamp this indelible shout of justice
on the forehead of your children.
There where you have always put your cleanest kisses.
(This is not a rhetorical image.

I am not the poet of rhetoric.
Now there is no rhetoric.
The revolution has burned
all the rhetorics.)

Let no one deceive you any more.
Let there be no false passports
neither of paper
nor of cardboard
nor of tin plate.
Let there be no more disguises
neither for the timid
nor for the frivolous
nor for the hypocrite
nor for the clown
nor for the actor.
Let there be no more disguises
neither for the spy who sits at your side in the café,
nor for the ambusher who does not leave his hole.
Let not those who wait for Franco with the last bottles of
    champagne in the wine cellar hide any more in a
    proletarian garment.
All those who do not wear tomorrow this Spanish
    revolutionary emblem, this shout of justice, bleeding on
    their forehead, belong to the Fifth Column.

No outlet now
to possible treacheries.
Let no one finally think
of ripping compromising documents
nor of burning boxes of official cards
nor of throwing the cap in the trench
in premeditated flights.
There are no longer flights.
In Spain now there are only two fixed and immovable
    positions.
For today and for tomorrow.
That of those who raise their hand to say cynically: I am a
    Spanish bastard,

and that of those who shut it with ire to ask justice under
    the implacable skies.
But now this play of hands finally is not enough.
More is necessary.
Stars are missing, yes, many stars
but of blood
because the rear guard has to give theirs also.

A star of red blood,
of red Spanish blood.
Let there no longer be someone who might say:
that star is of foreign blood.
And let it not be obligatory either.
Tomorrow let no one speak of impositions,
let no one say that a pistol was put in his chest.
It is a revolutionary tattoo, yes.
I am a revolutionary,
Spain is revolutionary,
Don Quijote is revolutionary.
We all are. All.
All who feel this taste of justice that there is in our blood
    and that makes for us bitterness and dust when the North
    wind blows.
It is a revolutionary tattoo,
but Spanish.
And heroic also.
And voluntary, besides.
It is a tattoo that we seek only to define our faith.
It is only a definition of faith.
There are two furious winds today that shake at the men of
    Spain,
two gusts of wind that push the men of Valencia.
The dramatic wind of the great destinies, that moves the
    heroes to victory or death,
and the gust of wind of incontrollable panics that carries dead
    and rotted flesh of shipwrecks to the beaches of cowardice
    and silence.
There are two winds, do you not hear it?

There are two winds, Spaniards of Valencia.
One goes to History.
The other goes to silence.
the one goes to the epic,
the other to shame.

Responsible ones:
the great responsible one and the small responsible ones:
Open the doors,
overthrow the barricades of the Pyrenees.
Give open road
to the yellow gust of wind of those who tremble.
Once more I shall see the flock of cowards flee toward scorn.
Once more I shall see cowardice in herd.
I shall see you again,
assaulting with bulging eyes, the buses of evacuation.
I shall see you again
robbing the seat
from children and mothers.
I shall see you again.
But you will be seeing yourselves always.
One day you will die outside of your country. In bed perhaps.
   In a bed of white sheets, with naked feet (not with shoes
   put on, as one now dies in Spain), with naked and anointed
   feet, maybe with sacred oils. Because you will die very
   simply, and securely with a crucifix and with an oration
   of repentance on your lips. You will be already almost with
   death, which always arrives. And you will remember—
   clearly you will remember—that this time you fled and
   ridiculed, usurping the seat of a child in an evacuation bus.
   It will be your last thought. And there, on the other side,
   when finally you are only a disembodied conscience, in
   time and space, and you plunge swiftly to the depth of
   Dantesque torments—because I believe in the inferno also
   —you will only see yourselves in this manner,
always, always, always,
robbing the seat from a child in an evacuation bus.
The punishment of the coward finally without peace and
   without salvation for all eternity.

It does not matter that you do not have a gun,
remain here with your faith.
Do not listen to those who say: the flight can be a political
  one.
There is no more politics in History than blood.
Blood that flows does not scare me,
blood that flows makes me happy.
There is a flower in the world that can only grow if it is
  irrigated with blood.
The blood of man
is made not only to move his heart
but to fill the rivers of the Earth,
the veins of the Earth
and to move the heart of the world.

Cowards: towards the Pyrenees, to exile!
Heroes: to the fronts, to death!

Responsible ones:
the great and small responsible ones:
organize the heroism,
unify the sacrifice.
A unique command, yes.
But for the final martyrdom.
Let us go to death!
Let all the world hear it.
Let the spies hear it.
What does it matter now that the spies hear it?
Let them hear it, the bastards.
What does it matter now that the bastards hear it?
What do all those voices there below matter now
if we begin to ride (on horseback) above the epic?
At these heights of History one no longer hears anything.
One goes towards death . . .
and below remains the world of the foxes,
and of those who make a pact with foxes.

Below you remain, England,
old greedy fox,

you halted the History of the West more than three centuries
   ago,
and enchained Don Quijote.
When your life finishes
and you come before the great History
where I wait for you,
what are you going to say?
What new cunning are you going to invent then to deceive
   God?
Fox!
Daughter of foxes!
Italy is more noble than you.
And Germany also.
In their plundering and in their crimes
there is an obscure Nietzschean breath of heroism in which
   merchants cannot breathe,
an impetuous and confused gesture of gambling everything
   on the last card, that practical men cannot understand.
If they were to open their doors to the winds of the world,
if they were to open them wide
and if Justice
and the heroic Democracy of man were to pass through them,
I would make a pact with the two to throw in your face of an
   old fox without dignity or love,
all the saliva and all the excrement of the world.
Old greedy fox:
you have hidden,
buried in the yard,
the miraculous key that opens the diamantine door of
   History . . .
You know nothing.
You understand nothing and you enter all the houses
to close the windows
and to blind the light of the stars!
And the men see you and leave you.
They leave you because they believe that the beams to
   Jupiter have already been exhausted.
But the stars do not sleep.

You know nothing.

You have heaped your plunder behind the door, and your children, now, cannot open it so that the first rays of the new dawn may enter.

Old greedy fox,

you are a great merchant.

You know very well how to keep

the accounts of the kitchen

and you think that I do not know how to count.

Yes I know how to count.

I have counted my dead.

I have counted them all,

I have counted them one by one.

I have counted them in Madrid,

I have counted them in Oviedo,

I have counted them in Málaga,

I have counted them in Guernica,

I have counted them in Bilbao . . .

I have counted them in all the trenches,

in the hospitals,

in the deposits of the cemeteries,

in the gutters of the highways,

in the rubbish of the bombarded houses.

Counting dead people this fall by the Paseo de El Prado, I believed one night that I was walking on mud, and there were human brains that for a long time were stuck to the soles of my shoes.

The 18th of November, only in one cellar of cadavers, I counted three hundred dead children . . .

I have counted them in the cars of the ambulances,

in the hotels,

in the street cars,

in the subway . . . ,

on livid mornings,

on black nights without illumination and without stars . . .

and in your conscience all of them . . .

And all of them I have charged to your account.

Now you see if I know how to count!

You are the old porter of the Western world,
since long ago you have the keys of all the ports of Europe,
and you can let enter and leave whomever you take a fancy to.
And now through cowardice,
through nothing more than cowardice,
because you wish to guard your pantry until the last day of
    History,
you have let intrude in my ancestral mansion
the foxes and the conspiring wolves of the world
so that they might be satiated in my blood
and might not ask at once for yours.
But finally they will ask for it,
finally the stars will ask for it . . .

And here again,
here
in these solitary altitudes
here
where one hears if I relax the millenary voice
of the winds,
of the water
and of the clay
that has been forming all of us men.
Here,
where the shrieked clamor of mercenary propaganda does not
    arrive.
Here,
where the asthma of diplomats has not breathing nor life.
Here,
where the comedians of the Society of Nations do not have a
    part.
Here, here,
in the presence of History,
in the presence of great History
(the other
the one which your worm-like pride teaches to school
    children
is only a record of lies

and an index of crimes and vanities).
Here, here,
under the light of the stars,
above the eternal and pristine earth of the world
and in the very presence of God.
Here, here. Here
I wish to say now my final word:

Spaniards
revolutionary Spaniards:
Man has died!
Quiet, quiet.
Break the loudspeakers
and the antennas,
tear up by the roots all the posters that announce your drama
   in the corners of the world.
Denunciations? Before whom?
Rip the White Book,
no longer turn your mouth with calls and laments toward the
   vacant.
Man has died!
And only the stars can form now the choir of our tragic
   destiny.
No longer shout your martyrdom.
Martyrdom is not proclaimed,
it is endured
and casts itself on the shoulders like a legacy and a pride.

The tragedy is mine,
mine,
let no one rob me of it.
Get out,
get out all of you.
All of you.
I here alone.
Alone
under the stars and the Gods.
Who are you?
What is your name?

From what womb do you come?
Outside . . . Outside . . . Foxes!
Here,
I alone. Alone,
with Justice killed by hanging.
Alone,
with the corpse of Justice between my hands.
Here,
I alone,
alone
with human conscience,
quiet,
stopped,
assassinated for always
in this hour of History
and in this land of Spain,
for all the foxes of the world.
For all,
for all.
Foxes!
Foxes!
Foxes!
The world is only a den of foxes
and Justice a flower that now does not grow in any latitude.

Spaniards,
revolutionary Spaniards.
Let us go to death!
Let the spies hear it.
What does it matter now that the spies hear it?
Let them hear it, the bastards.
What does it matter now that the bastards hear it?
At these heights of History
now nothing is heard.
One goes toward death
and below remains the unbreathable world of the foxes and
    of those who make a pact with foxes.
Let us go to death!

Let Valencia awaken
and put on the shroud! . . .

Epilogue

Listen still . . .
Beforehand, refresh my lips and my forehead . . . I am
    thirsty . . .
And I want to speak with words of love and hope.
Listen now:
Justice is worth more than an empire, although this empire
    were to include all the curve of the Sun.
And when Justice, fatally hurt, calls to all of us in desperate
    agony no one can say:
"I am still not prepared."
Justice is defended with a broken spear and with a paper
    visor.
This is written in my Bible,
in my History,
in my infantile and grotesque History
and as long as men do not learn it, the world will not be
    saved.

I am the first, livid and cardinal shout of the great sunrises
    of the West.
Yesterday upon my early risen blood the bourgeois world
    built in America all its factories and markets,
upon my dead ones of today the world of tomorrow will raise
    the First House of Man.
And I shall return,
I shall return because there are still spears and bitterness on
    Earth.
I shall return,
I shall return with my chest (figuratively: heart) and with the
    Dawn again.

"Vientos del pueblo me llevan" by Miguel Hernández

THE WINDS OF MY PEOPLE CARRY ME

1   The winds of my people carry me,
the winds of my people move me,
they scatter my heart,
and inflate my throat.

5   Oxen bow their forehead (figuratively:
     head)
impotently tame,
before punishments:
lions lift theirs
and at the same time punish
10   with their strident claw.

I am not from a people of oxen,
I am from a people that impede
the grazing of lions,
single flights of eagles,
15   and mountain ranges of bulls
with pride in their horn.
They never breed oxen
on the bleak highlands of Spain.

Who spoke of setting a yoke
20   on the neck of this race?
Who has ever put
yokes or braces on the hurricane,
or detained a thunderbolt
prisoner in a cage?

25   Asturians of bravery,
Basques of armored stone,
Valencians of happiness
and Castilians of soul,
worked over like the soil
30   and airy as wings;
Andalusians of lightning,

born amidst guitars
and forged in torrential
anvils of tears;
35   Estremadurans of rye
Galicians of rain and tranquillity,
Catalans of firmness,
Aragonese of caste,
Murcians of dynamite
40   fruitfully propagated,
men of Leon and Navarre, masters
of hunger, of sweat, and of the axe,
kings of mining
gentlemen of farming,
45   men who among roots,
like brave roots yourselves,
you go from life to death,
you go from nothing to nothing:
they wish to put yokes on you
50   people of bad grasslands,
yokes that you have to leave
broken across their backs.
Dawn is indicating
the twilight of the oxen.

55   Oxen die clad
in humility and the odor of stables:
the eagles, the lions
and the bulls of arrogance,
and behind them, the sky
60   neither disturbs itself nor ends.
The agony of the oxen
is of little countenance,
that of the virile animal
enlarges all of creation.

65   If I must die, let me die
with my head very high.
Dead and twenty times dead,
my mouth against the grass,

I shall have my teeth clenched
70   and my chin firm.

Singing I await death,
for there are nightingales that sing
above the rifles
and in the midst of battles.

"Recoged esta voz" by Miguel Hernández

HEAR THIS VOICE

1   Nations of the earth, countries of the sea,
         brothers
of the world and of nothing:
lost inhabitants—more distant
from sight than from the heart.

5   Here I have an impassioned voice,
here I have a life attacked and angered,
here I have a message, here I have a life.

Open I am, look, like a wound
Sunk I am, look, I am sunk
10   amidst my people and its ills.
Wounded I go, wounded and badly wounded,
bleeding through trenches and hospitals.

Men, worlds, nations,
pay attention, listen to my bleeding sound,
15   gather up my beats of affliction
in your spacious hearts,
because I clutch the soul when I sing.

Singing I defend myself
and I defend my people when
20   the barbarians of crime imprint
their hooves of powder and clatter on my
         people.

This is their work, this:
They pass, they destroy like whirlwinds,
and before their funereal choler
25   the horizons are arms, and the roads, death.

The lament that pours through valleys and
     balconies,
deluges the stones and works in the stones,
and there is no space for so much death,
and there is no wood for so many coffins.

30   Caravans of beaten-down bodies.
All is bandages, pains, and handkerchiefs:
all is stretchers on which the wounded
have broken their strength and their wings.

Blood, blood through the trees and the soil,
35   blood in the waters, blood on the walls,
and a fear that Spain will collapse
from the weight of the blood which soaks
     through her networks
right to the bread that is eaten.

Gather together this wind,
40   nations, men, worlds,
that proceeds from the mouths of disturbed
     breath
and from the hospitals of the dying.

Apply your ears
to my clamor of a violated people,
45   to the "ay!" of so many mothers, to the
     complaints
of so many a bright being whom grief has
     devoured.

The chests that pushed and hurt the
     mountains,
see them weakened without milk or beauty,

and see the white sweethearts and the black
   eyelashes
50   fallen and depressed in an obscure siesta.

Apply the passion of your entrails
to this people who die with an invincible
   gesture
scattered by the lips and the brow
beneath the implacable airplanes
55   that snatch terribly,
terribly, ignominiously, every day
sons from the hands of their mothers.

Cities of work and innocence,
youths that blossom from the oak,
60   trunks of bronze, bodies of power
lie down rushed into ruin.

A future of dust advances,
a fate advances
in which nothing will remain:
65   neither stone on stone nor bone on bone.

Spain is not Spain, it is an immense grave,
it is a vast cemetery red and bombarded:
the barbarians want it this way.

The earth will be a dense heart laid waste,
70   if you, nations, men, worlds,
with the whole of my people
and your people on their side,
do not break the ferocious fangs.

II

But it will not be: that a pawing sea
75   always triumphant, always decided,
made for the light, for the heroic deed,
stirs its head of unmanageable diamond,
pounds its shoed foot amidst the noise
of all the cadavers of Spain.

80   It is youth: gather up this wind.
        Its blood is the crystal that does not tarnish,
        its hat the laurel wreath and its breath the
            flint.
        Where the force of its teeth holds on fast
        buds a volcano of transparent swords,
85   and its beating shoulders,
        and its heels open up sudden blazes.

        It is composed of working men:
        of red blacksmiths, of snow-white masons,
        of plowboys with faces of harvesting.
90   They pass oceanically beneath
        a clamor of sirens and manufacturing tools
        and of gigantic arcs illuminated with arrows.

        Despite death, these men
        with metal and lightning equal to shields,
95   make cannons draw back
        Intimidated, trembling, mute.

        The powder cannot harm them and they
            make fire from powder
        sap, explosion, sudden greenness:
        with their power of impassioned youth
100   they precipitate the soul of the lavender
            plant,
        the creation of the mine,
        the fertile movement of the plow.

        They make of each ruin a pasture,
        of each pain a fruit of happiness,
105   of Spain a sky of beauty.
        See them make gigantic the midday
        and beautify everything with their young
            bravery.

        They deserve the foam of the thunder,
        they deserve life and the odor of the olive
            tree,

110   the Spaniards—extensive and serene
        who move their glance like a proud bird.

        Nations, men, worlds, this I write:
        the youth of Spain will leave the trenches
        on foot, invincible like the seed,
115   because it has a soul full of flags
        that never surrenders or kneels down.

        There go through the deserts of Castille
        the bodies that seem struggling colts,
        bulls of victorious conclusion,
120   telling in their blood of generous flowers
        that to die is the greatest thing that one does.

        They will remain, in time, victors,
        always covered by sun and majesty,
        the fighters of bones so brave
125   that if they are dead they are brave dead:
        the youth that will save Spain, although it
            had to
        fight with a gun of nards
        and a sword of wax.

"Pequeño responso a un héroe de la República" by César Vallejo

A BRIEF FUNERAL LITURGY FOR A HERO
OF THE REPUBLIC

1   A book remained at the edge of his dead waist,
        a book was sprouting from his dead corpse.
        They carried away the hero,
        and carnal and sad his mouth shared our
            breath;
5   all of us sweated, our navels a burden;
        the wandering moons were following us;
        the dead man from grief was sweating too.

And a book, in the battle of Toledo,
a book, behind a book, above a book, was
    sprouting from the corpse.

10   Poetry of the purple cheek bone, between
          saying
and keeping silent,
poetry in the moral message that might have
    accompanied
his heart.
The book remained and nothing more, for
    there are no
15   insects in the tomb,
and there remained at the edge of his sleeve
    the air soaking itself
and making itself vaporous, infinite.

We all sweated, our navels a burden,
the dead man also sweated from grief
20   and a book, I saw it feelingly,
a book, behind a book, above a book
sprouted from the corpse abruptly.

"Masa" by César Vallejo

MASSES

1   At the end of the battle,
and the combatant dead, a man came toward
    him
and said to him: "Do not die; I love you so
    much!"
But the cadaver, alas! went on dying.

5   Two approached him and repeated to him:
"Don't leave us! Courage! Return to life!"
But the corpse, alas! went on dying.

Twenty arrived, one hundred, one thousand,
    five hundred thousand,
shouting: "So much love, and not to be able
    to do anything against death!"
10 But the corpse, alas! went on dying.

Millions of individuals surrounded him,
with a common plea: "Remain brother!"
But the corpse, alas! went on dying.

Then all the men of the earth
15 surrounded him; the corpse looked at them
    sadly, deeply moved;
he sat up slowly,
he embraced the first man; he began to
    walk . . .

"España, aparta de mí este cáliz" by César Vallejo

SPAIN, REMOVE FROM ME THIS CHALICE

1   Children of the world,
if Spain falls—I say, it's merely conjectural—
if its forearm falls
from the sky down, that two terrestrial segments
5   would grip in a halter;
children, how aged are her concave temples!
how early in the (history of the) sun what I was
    telling you!
how soon in your chest (figuratively, heart) the
    ancient sound!
how old the "2" in your copybook!

10 Children of the world, it is
mother Spain with her womb on her shoulders;
it is our teacher with her rulers,
it is mother and teacher,
cross and wood, because it gave you height,

15   dizziness and division and sum, children;
      she is doing her duty, while men tend to legal
          matters!

      If she falls—I say, it's just a way of speaking—if
          Spain
      falls, from the earth down,
      children, how you are going to stop growing!
20   how the year is going to punish the month!
      how your teeth are going to remain at 10,
      in outline the diphthong, the medal in tears!
      How the lambskin is going to continue
      tied by the foot to the great inkwell!
25   How you are going to lower the grades of the
          alphabet
      until the letter in which pain was born!

      Children,
      sons of fighters, among so many,
      lower your voice, for Spain
30   is now dividing its energy among the
      animal kingdom, little flowers, comets, and men.
      Lower your voice, for it is
      with its rigor, which is great, without knowing
      what to do, and in its hand is
35   the speaking skull and it speaks and speaks
      the skull, that of braids,
      the skull, that of life!
      Lower your voice, I tell you
      lower your voice, the canto of syllables, the
          weeping
40   of the material and the murmur less than the
          pyramids, and even
      that of the temples (anatomical) that walk with
          two stones!
      Lower your breath, and if
      its forearm comes down,
      if the rulers make noise, if it is night,
45   if the sky fits in two earthly limbos,

if there is noise in the sound of doors,
if I am late,
if you don't see anyone, if your pencils
without point scare you, if mother
50   Spain falls—I say, it's merely supposing—
go forth children of the world; go to find her! . . .

"Explico algunas cosas" by Pablo Neruda

I EXPLAIN SOME THINGS

1   You will ask: And where are the lilacs?
And the metaphysics covered with poppies?
And the rain which often was pounding
his words filling them
5   with gullies and birds?

I am going to tell you all that happens to me.

I was living in a suburb
of Madrid, with bells,
with clocks, with trees,
10   From there could be seen
the dry face of Castille
like an ocean of leather.

    My house was called
the house of the flowers, because everywhere
15   geraniums were exploding: it was
a beautiful house
with dogs and little children.
    Raúl, do you remember?
Do you remember, Rafael?
20   Federico, do you remember
under the ground,
do you remember my house with balconies where
the light of June was drowning flowers in your
    mouth?

Brother, brother!

25   All
was big voices, the salt of the merchandise,
agglomerations of vibrating bread,
markets of my suburb of Arguelles with its statue
like a pale inkwell among the hake:
30   oil was arriving to the spoons,
a profound throb
of feet and hands was filling the street,
meters, liters, the active essence
of life,
35   heaped fish,
texture of roofs with cold sun in which
the deflection tires itself
delirious fine ivory of the potatoes,
tomatoes repeated until the sea.
40   And one morning all was burning
and one morning the bonfires
sprang from the earth
devouring the living,
and since then fire,
45   gunpowder since then,
and since then blood.

Bandits with airplanes and with Moors,
bandits with rings and duchesses,
bandits with black, blessing friars
50   were coming via the sky to kill children
and in the streets the blood of the children
was flowing plainly, like the blood of children.

Jackals that the jackal rejected,
stones that the dry thistle would eat spitting out,
55   vipers that vipers would hate!

Facing you I have seen the blood
of Spain uplift itself
to drown you in a single wave
of pride and of knives!

60   Generals
    traitors:
    look at my dead house,
    look at broken Spain:
    from each dead house sprouts burning metal
65   in place of flowers,
    from each ditch of Spain
    Spain emerges,
    from each dead child sprouts a gun with eyes,
    from each crime bullets are born
70   that will discover one day the place
    of your hearts.

    Will you ask why his poetry
    does not speak to us of the soil, of the leaves,
    of the great volcanoes of his native country?

75   Come see the blood in the streets,
    come see
    the blood in the streets,
    come see the blood
    in the streets!

"Llegada a Madrid de la Brigada Internacional" by Pablo Neruda

ARRIVAL IN MADRID OF THE INTERNATIONAL BRIGADE

1   One morning in a cold month,
    in a dying month, stained with mud and smoke,
    a month without knees, a sad month of siege and
        misery,
    when through the wet window panes of my house
        African jackals were heard
5   to howl with the rifles and their teeth full of blood,
        then
    when we were having no more hope than a dream
        of gunpowder, when we were already believing

that the world was full of only ravenous monsters
    and rages
then, crushing the white frost of the cold month in
    Madrid in the fog
of the dawn
10   I have seen with these eyes that I have, with this
    heart that looks,
I have seen arrive the clear, the dominating soldiers
of the thin and hard and mature and ardent brigade
    of stone.
It was the afflicted time in which women
were sustaining an absence like a terrible coal,
15   and Spanish death, more acid and sharp than other
    deaths
filled the fields until then honored by wheat.
In the streets the broken blood of man was joining
the water that leaves the destroyed heart of the
    houses:
the bones of undone children, the heartbreaking
20   mourning silence of mothers, the eyes
of the defenseless closed for always,
were like the sadness and the loss, were like a garden
    spit upon,
were faith and flower assassinated for always.

Comrades,
25   then,
I have seen you,
and my eyes are until now full of pride
because I saw you through the foggy morning arrive
    at the pure forehead of Castille
silent and firm
30   like bells before the dawn,
full of solemnity and blue eyes coming from far away
    and even farther,
coming from your corners, from your lost countries,
    from your dreams
full of burned sweetness and of guns

to defend the Spanish city in which entrapped
   freedom
35   could fall and die eaten by beasts.
Brothers, from now on may
your purity and your force, your solemn history
be known by the child and by the man, by the
   woman and by the old man,
may it come to all the beings without hope, that
   might go down to the mines corroded by the
   sulfuric air,
40   may it rise to the inhuman staircases of the slave,
may all the stars, all the wheat of Castille and of the
   world
write your name and your rough fight
and your strong and terrestrial victory like a red oak
   tree.
Because you have made to be born again with your
   sacrifice
45   the lost faith, the absent soul, the confidence in the
   land,
and by your abundance, by your nobleness, by your
   dead,
as through a valley of hard rocks of blood
passes an immense river with doves of steel and hope.

"Almería" by Pablo Neruda

ALMERÍA

1   A dish for the Bishop, a dish that is chewed and
   bitter,
a dish made of iron-ends, ashes, tears,
a dish submerged with sobs and fallen walls,
a black dish, a dish of blood of Almería.

5   A dish for the banker, a dish with cheeks
of children of the happy South, a dish of
explosions, crazed waters and ruins and terror,

a dish of smashed axles and trampled heads,
a black dish, a dish of blood of Almería.

10   Each morning, each turbid morning of your lives
      you will have it smoking and burning on your table:
      you will push it away with your delicate hands
      in order not to see it, in order not to digest it so
          many times:
      you will remove it a little between the bread and
          the grapes,
15   to this plate of silent blood
      that will be there each morning, every
      morning.

      A dish for the Colonel and the wife of the Colonel,
      at a party in the barracks, at every party
20   above the oaths and the spit, with the light of wine
          of the morning
      so that you might see it trembling and cold over
          the world.

      Yes, a dish for all of you, rich from here and there,
      ambassadors, ministers, atrocious table companions,
      ladies of comfortable tea and sofa seat:
25   a dish wasted, overflowing, dirty with poor blood,
      for every morning, for every week, for ever and ever,
      a dish of blood of Almería, before you, always.

"Barcelona" by Johannes R. Becher

BARCELONA

1   Our city built high by the sea,
      And the sea has imbued her with blue light,
      And the sea looks dreamily at her,
      For there, where she stands, was once the sea—

5   City of columns and forums.
      Look, it glows like muscles and corals,

And lowered bells resound from nearby,
Saint Anna, Saint Monica . . .

Sounds of friends and a song full of lament
10   Were carried by you to us from afar.
Barcelona! Oh, your name has
Enchanted us. The city has become a part of us.

They contained you like a holy treasure.
Your squares found their place in us
15   And in my heart your streets
Crossed each other and enlivened me.

We—we along with you were outraged,
And the whole world heard you,
As you spoke with the voice of the people—your
20   Voice made my voice strong and firm.

Also for me the sky stood horribly open,
And I saw how you sank mortally wounded,
And I ignited a fire in myself
Against those cowardly monsters . . .

25   Barcelona, Ruins. Bloody puddles.
Henchmen in the Red Basque caps.
Foreign mercenary is a murderous fellow.
Franco's flag on the citadel.

Bad advice speaks within me treacherously:
30   "Be quiet and stop the questioning!"
No, I'm going to ask about the truth,
And I myself must speak the truth to myself.

How did it happen? How is it possible that—
I'm asking, I'm asking incessantly,
35   And I'm not afraid of this truth:
Stakes, torture, death court (court that sentences
    to death).

That which the authorities never succeeded in
    doing,
Was accomplished by treachery, by treachery,

And I ask in London and Paris,
40   Who is it who allowed the fortresses to fall? . . .

Barcelona. City rich in sacrifices.
City which also bled for me.
Our graves however are opening.
Barcelona—that's you and I—

45   And the sea looks dreamily at you,
For there where you stand was once the sea,
And the sea has imbued you with blue light.
Our city built high above the sea!

"General Mola: Aus dem spanischen Bürgerkrieg" by Johannes R. Becher

GENERAL MOLA
from the Spanish Civil War

1   When he sat there, without looking up,
Signing one judgment after another:
Nothing human sat there—an emaciated horror,
On which only his jacket still remained human.

5   As if it could weep or laugh,
So human was the jacket made of fine cloth,
By a human hand, as if it were an attempt,
To make the picture of a human being from a
        jacket . . .

When one day an unknown airplane
10   Crashed in the mountain range and burned up,
From nothing was his origin discernible:

Until a piece of a jacket was found,
From which one could recognize him, the
        General—
The only thing that was still human about him.

"Fliehende Mutter" by Johannes R. Becher

FLEEING MOTHER

1 "I don't really know if I'm welcome
   In your land . . . I have been banished from
       so far away . . .
   In this bundle? . . . Weapons? . . . in it
   Is something dear to me, Sir . . . I lost
       everything else . . .

5 Here's how it happened . . . The village had
       been empty for a long time,
   The men gone to war . . . only children,
       women . . .
   Then came a thundering, Sir, from the direction
       of the Ebro . . .
   We ran out on the field to look around . . .

   Not a morsel of bread. Nothing—for many
       days . . .
10 And then, then they came . . . so quickly from
       above . . .
   And one of them, who swooped down low . . .
   No cries . . . I picked up my child—

   And suddenly the road was no longer there.
   It was a chasm. It was ice. A boulder
15 Offered me support . . . They came back
       again . . .
   The boulder protected me. Also the boulder
       wept . . .

   I don't know, am I anywhere? . . .
   May I bed him down in your earth? . . .
   Forgive me, Sir . . . I was overwhelmed . . .
20 The dead . . . the dead must be rescued . . ."

"Novembre 1936" by Paul Eluard

NOVEMBER 1936

1   Look at the builders of ruins at work
They are rich, patient, orderly, black and stupid
But they do their best to be the only ones on
      earth
They are at the extreme edge of being men and
      are full of trash
5   They construct on the bare ground palaces
      without brains.

One gets used to everything
Except to these leaden birds
Except to the hatred of that which is shining
Except to yielding space to them.

10   Talk of the sky the sky empties itself
The autumn matters little to us
Our masters stamped their feet
We have forgotten autumn
And we will forget our masters.

15   City as if at the base of the ocean made of only
      one saved drop of water
From only one diamond cultivated in plain day
Madrid city accustomed to those who suffered
From this terrible good which denied being an
      example
Of those who suffered
20   From the indispensable misery to the glare of
      this good.

That the mouth rises towards its truth
Blows a rare smile like a broken chain
Which man delivered from his absurd past

Raises before his brother a similar face
25   And gives reality to vagabond wings.

"La Victoire de Guernica" by Paul Eluard

THE VICTORY OF GUERNICA

1

1   Beautiful world of hovels
Of mine and of fields

2

Faces good in the fire faces in the cold
In the denials of night of insults of blows

3

5   Faces good for everything
Here is the void which stares at you
Your death will serve as an example

4

Death a heart overturned

5

They make you pay for bread
10   For sky for earth water sleep
And the misery
Of your life

6

They said to desire good intelligence
They rationed the strong judged the fools
15   Gave charity split a halfpenny in two
They greeted the cadavers
They overburdened themselves with politeness

7

They persevere they exaggerate they are not of
        our world

8
The women the children have the same treasure
20   Of green leaves of spring and of pure milk
And of endurance
In their pure eyes

9
The women the children have the same treasure
In their eyes
25   The men defend as they can

10
The women the children have the same red roses
In their eyes
Each one shows its blood

11
Fear and the courage to live and to die
30   Death so difficult and so easy

12
Men for whom this treasure was sung
Men for whom this treasure was spoiled

13
Real men for whom despair
Feeds the devouring fire of hope
35   Let us open the last bud of the future together

14
Pariahs death earth and hideousness
Of our enemies have
The monotonous color of our night
We shall overcome.

"En Espagne" by Paul Eluard

IN SPAIN

1   If there is in Spain one tree stained with blood
It is the tree of liberty

If there is in Spain one talkative mouth
It talks of liberty

5   If there is in Spain one glass of pure wine
It is the people who will drink it.

"Espagne" by Paul Eluard

SPAIN

1   The most beautiful eyes in the world
Began to sing
That they want to see further
Than the walls of prisons
5   Further than their eyelids
Made black and blue by grief

The bars of the cage
Sing of liberty
An air that escapes
10   Over human roads
Under a furious sun
A huge sun of tempest

Life lost regained
Night and day of life
15   Exiles prisoners
You feed in the shade
A fire that brings dawn
Freshness dew

Victory

20   And the pleasure of victory.

"Ispantsi otstupili za Pirenyiei" by Níkolay Semyónovich
Tíkhonov

THE SPANIARDS HAVE RETREATED
BEYOND THE PYRENEES

1   As if the ink were full of incantations
       I am not able to touch the pen,
       In a thick strange forest
       A woodpecker hammered only about the war.

5   Women only are seen by me
       On the rocky winter road,
       Only infants fallen in the snow,
       Only scorched leaves of the thicket.

       And about the thicket full of ashy hair,
10   So pierced through with powder,
       About the people begging for water
       At night behind the barbed wire,—

       Whatever you say of such a life
       All is inadequate,—
15   All has already been said by the child's hand
       Sticking out from the snow on the cliff.

"Govorit fashist" by Níkolay Semyónovich Tíkhonov

THE FASCIST SPEAKS:

1   This they say: the Fascist power
       Ignores human rights
       That we look on things too simply
       That we love only the graveyard stillness.

5   Now let me explain to you why:
       The people are children, we are their Führer

The child, so that he grows into a titan
You nourish him from infancy with the drum.

Dazzle them nightly with torches of parades,
10　　Encourage their taste for martial speech.
Enough of books—instead let the bonfire gleam
Round the bonfire hold a dance
Such as our ancestors performed in bearskins,
And strike up a song at the end
15　　So that you threaten the whole world of people
And are called upon to dominate them.

But since your people do not till the end
Obey the will of our Führer-father
And want to live, work, rejoice
20　　And do not want to be proud of their ancestors
And you cannot make them obey
Arm yourselves with a good axe.

And now, when according to the power of growth
Throughout the country there is the greatness of
　　　　the graveyards,
25　　And the war supplies are provided,
There is a command: work and keep silent!—
Then, so that disorder does not break out,
You, take care of the education of the spirit:

Return women to the kitchen and feather bed,
30　　Let them be the joy of the soldiers hereafter,
Strengthen the roar of batteries of newspapers:
The Marxist and the Jew are to blame for all evils
And they are at times one and the same—
Let our thunder destroy them quickly!
35　　We were oppressed by miserable neighbors,
We need victory in war!

Repeat this to all: feeling injured by fate,
Henceforth let us set ourselves to banditry!
So that the whole country howls behind you:
40　　"War! War! Long live war!"
Long live war always and everywhere,

And the flaming bosoms of cities,
And women's wails, and the din of weapons,
The boom of victories and the grumble of the
    conquered,
45   Peace and work is the Marxist grimace,
All races are dust, there is only our race!

When all is in ashes, on the ashes our banner,
Let the enemies' skulls be bowls for us
Let us inhale from them the aroma of wine,—
50   To the dregs: then long live war!

"Govorit antifashist" by Níkolay Semyónovich Tíkhonov

THE ANTI-FASCIST SPEAKS:

1   That over me stood day and night
The dangling shadow of the jailer,
That the free motion of each thought
Immediately came under suspicion,
5   That the Fascist bonfire destroyed in a flash
The pages of my beloved books,
That instead of simple human words
I heard the endless roar of the Führers,
That all my life under the wild howl of songs
10   I strode with a shovel in the labor camp,
That giving value to a contemptible life,
I went as sentry to imprisoned peoples
And took part in piratic raids,
That I glorified the assassins in servile odes,
15   That I stood like a corpse silent and, like a
    corpse,
Rotted alive among factory pipes
Emitting smoke only for the glory of war
Spattered with the blood of my friends,
So that I might forget reason exists in the world,
20   I squinting at the world with hateful eye.

No! The world will remain unshaken!
It remembers all that was suffered by it
Fires, executions, disasters, battles,
Ages of shame, of servitude, of degradation,
25   Wherever the new Rome should whistle with
               its whip,
We shall not surrender anything to it!

Neither our wheatfields, rustling with a sea of
       bread,
Nor our mountains, thrusting their peaks to
       heaven,
Nor our rivers, streaming in tranquillity,
30   Nor our songs of heart and soul,
Nor our songs of love or of friendship or of
       worries
Nor the works begun by the people
Nor our cities where the streets rumble merrily,
Nor those fields where villages blossom;
35   And the nightingale should not die,
He will roar out our glory,
And the hawks above the humps of the hills
Let them soar like simple hawks,
And not the little path of spring roses,
40   Nor the highly foaming seas
Nor the bonfire that whirls off reddish smoke
In the autumn forest—we shall not surrender
       them.
We shall not surrender the smiles of our daring
       ones,
Nor the sails on our white boats,
45   Nor the air that we breathe,
Nor brightness of day, nor darkness of warm
       night,
The last boughs of rosy apple trees,
The rays of dawn on a sleeping glade,
Nor the pride of being ourselves
50   Nor the rights of a conquered destiny.

Fascism will find only ruin ahead—
We will never surrender anything!

Let a northern or a southern Rome arise—
We will have a fatal conversation in battle!

"Terra di Spagna . . ." by Giorgio Braccialarghe

LAND OF SPAIN

1   Land of Spain when night falls. Roars
through the olive groves and over the burned
    land
the new voice of one who is no longer afraid
the imminent shame of war.

5   For those to whom another destiny will come
the voice sings, and we who listen to it
find in it the command:
There is no resurrection without death.

Land of Spain when night falls. You
10   with the sublime language of heroes
this command you transmitted to us
and to those adventurers who will come after us.

You died, oh comrades, but death
illuminated life. We will live
15   because life illuminates the death
of those who choose the ultimate sacrifice.

"Notti di Spagna" by Giorgio Braccialarghe

NIGHTS OF SPAIN

1   There is so much white in the sky
that it seems that a bride

has forgotten her veil
attached to a rose.

5   And the floating veil in the country
like a filter full of enchantment
permits the brightness of the moon
to pass
through the roaring of the wind.

10   Nights of Spain,
the toads singing
along the long ditches
in the meadows.

There is a drowsy murmur
15   as if beautiful women
were listening to the secrets
of their lovers.

Nights of Spain,
capes of peace thrown
20   over tortured days
returns of calm
indefinite whispers
quiet murmurs.

The immobile sentry in the shadow
25   seems like a lost statue
on the paths of a park.

Nights of Spain
in the winding trenches
innocent confidences
30   one speaks of his fiancée
one speaks of the last advance.

And in the brief silences
that punctuate the phrases
distant voices
35   of comrades gone away
murmur strange words.

Meanwhile, in the starry night
resounds a gunshot.

"Ai fratelli lontani . . ." by Giorgio Braccialarghe:

TO DISTANT BROTHERS . . .

1   Tonight I wish to sing for you
without rhyme or meter.
Poor palpitant words
as when after having cried very much
5   one searches for one who is gone forever.
And speaks to him. And knows not what he says
nor what he would say.
I wish to speak to you, Oh distant brothers
as when you were nearby
10   and seemed titans.
Titans in war, young boys in peace.
I can't believe that anyone lies down
pale, on a white bed
with his youthful appearance
15   who does not wish to die.
I can't believe that
the day of resurrection may not come
for our battalion.
The third: the strongest!
20   First in attack and first in victory.
Wrote the most beautiful pages of history
between one song and another.
Gallant colony of gallant heroes.
Fewer than a thousand,
25   a thousand souls in each one.
Onward, onward, onward.
Enduring fatigue and hunger
sleep and thirst but onward
like so many giants
30   who nourish themselves on ideals

and who ask no more than wings
for the triumphant flight
towards the final goal.
Fewer than a thousand,
35   but how much, how much faith!
On the tortured hills of Jarama
in the woods of Alcarria
nothing but a hymn of glory
written with your blood
40   immortalized by your sacrifice.
—Madrid, meanwhile
endured the gloomy song
of the enemy cannons.
And up there in Viscaglia
45   the eternal scoundrel
was destroying everything.—
What does it matter? On the beds
of the field hospitals
grew a rose
50   of blood, grew a smile
on your faces of young heroes
You had faith in us.
In us who remaining at the battlefront
occupied, fiercely, your posts
55   oh disappeared of yesterday
oh destined to live tomorrow.
Tomorrow, when from the liberated camps
of restored offices
shall rise solemnly in chorus
60   the hymn of peace and work.

"Fratelli dell'Internazionale" by Giorgio Braccialarghe

BROTHERS OF THE INTERNATIONAL

1

The first six months of war have passed: onward, brothers
of the International.

2

The victory is not yet attained: onward, brothers of the
International.

3

Inch by inch and on our side the sacrifice which is
beautiful, and with the memory of our fallen ones in
our heart: onward, brothers of the International.

4

You are the sowers of tomorrow. Already the dawn has
shown itself in the sky, red from the revolution, already
the land of Spain knows about your sowing: onward,
brothers of the International.

5

Today's struggle brings the promise of peace tomorrow,
the sowing of yesterday, the fruits of the future:
onward, brothers of the International.

6

Among all your songs is missing that of a liberated Spain.
You would be the epic poets of it, you would create it
with your deeds, day by day, hour by hour: onward,
brothers of the International.

7

I know you one by one, but if I knew only one of you,
I would know all of you. By the heritage of faith,
discipline, and willpower that makes you all equal, by
the simplicity that endows each of your splendid
actions.

8

After six months I recognize you one by one. You are
still the same, still you carry within you the constant
desire for victory that kissed the white forehead of our
fallen ones.

9

Onward, brothers of the International. To other battles,
other triumphs; united; by receptive Spain, to her
bleeding bosom, the destinies of the world: invincible.

10

Onward, brothers of the International. With you justice, against you the rage of false powers.

11

Each one of you who falls is a drop of oil in the votive lamp of Liberty. Every enemy whom you bring down is a violated net from among the chain that has Humanity tied.

12

Onward, brothers of the International. Onward, onward, onward. For the tomorrow of Spain. For the future of all the world. Onward!

BIBLIOGRAPHY

Poetry:

Alberti, Rafael, ed. *Romancero de la guerra española*. Buenos Aires: Patronato Hispano Argentino de Cultura, 1944.

Auden, W. H. *Collected Poetry*. New York: Random House, 1945.

————. *Spain*. London: Faber & Faber, 1938.

Becher, Johannes R. *Ausgewählte Dichtung aus der Zeit der Verbannung, 1933-1945*. Berlin: Aufbau-Verlag, 1945.

————. *Gedichte 1936-1941*. Berlin: Aufbau-Verlag, 1966.

Caillet Bois, Julio, ed. *Antología de la poesía hispanoamericana*. Madrid: Aguilar, 1958.

Campbell, Roy. *Collected Poems*. London: The Bodley Head, 1957.

————. *Flowering Rifle. A Poem from the Battlefield of Spain*. London: Longmans, Green and Co., 1939.

Eluard, Paul. *Cours naturel*. Paris: Editions du Sagittaire, 1938.

————. *Poèmes politiques*. Paris: Gallimard, 1948.

Felipe, León. *Obras completas*. Buenos Aires: Editorial Losada, 1963.

Hernández, Miguel. *Imagen de tu huella, el silbo vulnerado, el rayo que no cesa, otros poemas, viento del pueblo.* Buenos Aires: Editorial Losada, S.A., 1963.

————. *Obras completas.* Buenos Aires: Editorial Losada, 1960.

————. *Poemas.* Barcelona: Plaza & Janes, S.A., Editores, 1964.

MacDiarmid, Hugh. *The Battle Continues.* Edinburgh: Castle Wynd Printers Limited, 1957.

————. *Stony Limits and Other Poems.* London: V. Gollancz, Ltd., 1934.

Neruda, Pablo. *Poesía política.* Santiago (Chile): Editora Austral, 1953.

Puccini, Dario. *Romancero della resistenza spagnola, 1936-1965,* 2. Rome: Editori Riuniti, 1965.

Romancero de los voluntarios de la libertad. Madrid: Ediciones de Comisariado de las Brigadas Internacionales, 1937.

Rukeyser, Muriel. "Mediterranean." New York: *New Masses,* XXIV, September 14, 1937.

————. *Theory of Flight.* New Haven: Yale University Press, 1935.

————. *A Turning Wind.* New York: The Viking Press, 1939.

Spender, Stephen. *Collected Poems, 1928-1953.* London: Faber and Faber, 1965.

Spender, Stephen, and John Lehmann, eds. *Poems for Spain.* London: The Hogarth Press, 1939.

Tíkhonov, Níkolay Semyónovich. *Izbránnye proizvédenija v dvuch tómach.* Moscow: State Publishing Co. of Literature of Art, 1955.

Vallejo, César. *España, aparta de mí este cáliz.* Mexico: Editorial Séneca, 1940.

————. *Poemas Humanos.* New York: Grove Press, 1968.

Prose:

Alonso, Amado. *Poesía y estilo de Pablo Neruda.* Buenos Aires: Editorial Sudamericana, 1966.

Alsterlund, B. "Biographical Sketch." New York: *Wilson Library Bulletin,* 15:110, October, 1940.

Ayala, Francisco. *Histrionismo y representación*. Buenos Aires: Editorial Sudamericana, 1944.

Barea, Arturo. *The Forging of a Rebel*. New York: Reynal & Hitchcock, 1946.

Beach, Joseph Warren. *The Making of the Auden Canon*. Minneapolis: University of Minnesota Press, 1957.

Benson, Frederick R. *Writers in Arms*. New York: New York University Press, 1967.

Blair, John. *The Poetic Art of W. H. Auden*. Princeton: Princeton University Press, 1965.

Bowra, Sir Cecil Maurice. *In General and Particular*. London: Weidenfeld and Nicolson, 1964.

————. Poetry & Politics. Cambridge (England): Cambridge University Press, 1966.

Brinnin, J. M. "Social Poet and the Problem of Communication." *Poetry*, no. 61 (January 1943), 554-75.

Buthlay, Kenneth. "Hugh MacDiarmid." *Writers and Critics Series*. Edinburgh, 1964.

Calvo Serer, Rafael. *La literatura universal sobre la guerra de España*. Madrid: Ateneo, 1962.

Cano Ballesta, Juan. *La poesía de Miguel Hernández*. Madrid: Gredos, 1971.

Collier's Encyclopedia. New York: Crowell-Collier Publishing Co., 1965.

Coyné, André. *César Vallejo*. Buenos Aires: Ediciones Nueva Visión, 1968.

del Río, Angel. *Historia de la literatura española*, Tomo II. New York: Holt, Rinehart and Winston, 1963.

Dizionario biografico degli italiani. Rome: Istituto della Enciclopedia Italiana, 1971.

Duval, K. D., and S. G. Smith, eds. *Hugh MacDiarmid: a Festschrift*. Edinburgh: Duval, 1962.

Eberhart, Richard, and Selden Rodman, eds. *War and the Poet*. New York: The Devin-Adair Co., 1945.

Encyclopaedia Britannica. Chicago: Encyclopaedia Britannica, Inc., 1967.

Ford, Hugh D. *A Poets' War: British Poets and the Spanish Civil War*. Philadelphia: University of Pennsylvania Press, 1965.

Fuller, John. *A Reader's Guide to W. H. Auden.* New York: Farrar, Straus & Giroux, 1970.

Greenberg, Herbert. *Quest for the Necessary: W. H. Auden and the Divided Consciousness.* Cambridge (Mass.): Harvard University Press, 1968.

Guerrero Zamora, Juan. *Miguel Hernández, poeta (1910-1942).* Madrid: Colección El Grifon, 1955.

Guttmann, Allen. *The Wound in the Heart.* New York: The Free Press of Glencoe, 1962.

Hemingway, Ernest. *For Whom the Bell Tolls.* New York: Scribner, 1940.

Jackson, Gabriel. *The Spanish Republic and the Civil War, 1931-1939.* Princeton: Princeton University Press, 1967.

MacDiarmid, Hugh. *Lucky Poet. A Self-Study.* London: Methuen & Co., Ltd., 1943.

Malraux, André. *Man's Hope.* New York: Random House, 1938.

Muste, John M. *Say That We Saw Spain Die.* Seattle: University of Washington Press, 1966.

Parkinson, T. "Some Recent Pacific Coast Poetry." *Pacific Spectator* 4, no. 3 (1950), 300-02.

Pujals, Esteban. *España y la guerra de 1936 en la poesía de Roy Campbell.* Madrid: Ateneo, 1959.

Replogle, Justin. *Auden's Poetry.* Seattle: University of Washington Press, 1969.

Rukeyser, Muriel. "Under Forty." *Contemporary Jewish Record.* Vol. VII, no. 1. February, 1944.

Scarfe, Francis. "W. H. Auden." *Contemporary British Poets.* Monaco: The Lyrebird Press, 1949.

Spears, Monroe K., ed. *Auden: A Collection of Critical Essays.*
———. *The Poetry of W. H. Auden: The Disenchanted Island.* New York: Oxford University Press, 1963.

Spender, Stephen. *The Still Centre.* London: Faber and Faber, Ltd., 1939.
———. "W. H. Auden and His Poetry." *Twentieth Century Views.* Englewood Cliffs (N.J.): Prentice-Hall, 1964.
———. *World Within World. The Autobiography of Stephen Spender.* London: Hamilton, 1951.

Thomas, Hugh. *The Spanish Civil War.* New York: Eyre, 1961.

Valbuena Prat, Angel. *Historia de la literatura española.* Tomo
II. Barcelona: Editorial Gustavo Gili, S.A., 1946.

Weintraub, Stanley. *The Last Great Cause.* New York: Weybright
and Talley, 1968.

Wright, David. "Roy Campbell." *Writers and Their Work.* No.
137. London: Longmans, Green & Co., 1961.